THE INVITING RELATIONSHIP
an expanded perspective for professional counseling

William W. Purkey

Department of Counselor Education
University of North Carolina, Greensboro

John J. Schmidt

School Counseling Section
State Department of Public Instruction
Raleigh, North Carolina

Prentice-Hall, Inc.
Englewood Cliffs, New Jersey 07632

Library of Congress Cataloging-in-Publication Data

Purkey, William Watson.
  The inviting relationship.

  Bibliography.
  Includes index.
  1. Counseling. I. Schmidt, John J.
II. Title.
BF637.C6P87 1987   158'.3   86-476
ISBN 0-13-505538-5

Editorial/production supervision
  and interior design: Virginia L. McCarthy
Cover design: Wanda Lubelska Design
Manufacturing buyer: Barbara Kelly Kittle

Printed in the United States of America

10 9 8 7 6 5 4 3 2 1

ISBN 0-13-505538-5 01

Prentice-Hall International (UK) Limited, *London*
Prentice-Hall of Australia Pty. Limited, *Sydney*
Prentice-Hall Canada Inc., *Toronto*
Prentice-Hall Hispanoamericana, S.A., *Mexico*
Prentice-Hall of India Private Limited, *New Delhi*
Prentice-Hall of Japan, Inc., *Tokyo*
Prentice-Hall of Southeast Asia Pte. Ltd., *Singapore*
Editora Prentice-Hall do Brasil, Ltda., *Rio de Janeiro*

With deepest affection to

Elizabeth Reynolds Purkey

and

Alvara and Harold "Bud" Schmidt

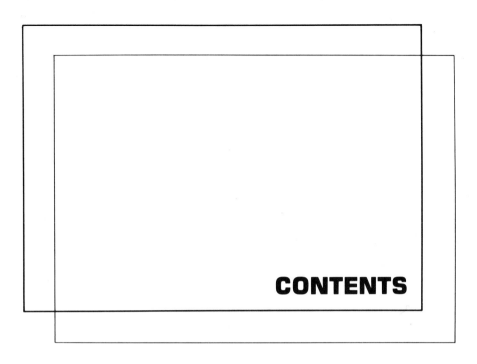

CONTENTS

5 THE FOUR CORNER PRESS   85

6 COMPATIBLE SYSTEMS OF COUNSELING   105

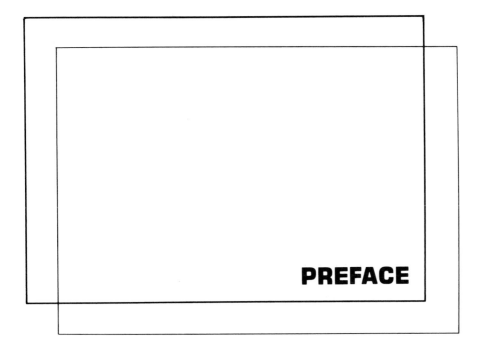

PREFACE

Since we are what we do, if we want to change what we are we must begin by changing what we do, must undertake a new mode of action.

A. Wheelis, *How People Change,*
1973, p. 101

This book is written for counselors in training, practicing counselors, and counselor-educators, as well as those related professional helpers who come in contact with clients in a wide variety of counseling, consulting, and allied human service roles. It is written especially for those counselors of psychodynamic, behavioral, and humanistic orientations who are seeking new paradigms of professional functioning that can be accepted and shared by most if not all counselors regardless of orientation.

We undertook this book because we believe today's counselors and other professional helpers are seeking ways to integrate what they know, who they are, what they do, where they work, and what they accomplish into a viable and practical model of professional functioning. We further believe that *The Inviting Relationship* provides an encompassing framework of philosophy, theory, and action that can serve as an integrative model for enhanced professional practice. To provide this framework, our book takes a "contextual approach" to counseling and human services as identified by Pentony (1981), Hobbs (1982), and others. The contextual approach maintains that changes are brought about by altering the human ecosystem of constantly interacting components of which the individual and his or her behavior are only parts. Thus, *The Inviting Relationship* provides an expanded perspective for professional counseling that ties together many seemingly unrelated aspects of the helping process and puts them together so that they make a new kind of sense. These seemingly unrelated aspects include the characteristics of helpers, the processes they employ, the environments they create and inhabit, and the outcomes they accomplish.

The Inviting Relationship consists of seven chapters. The first five chapters define the invitational model, introduce its major assumptions and components, identify its origins, and present the processes by which it can be applied. These chapters also provide theoretical foundations and empirical support for the inviting relationship, which is based on a particular model of professional functioning.

Chapter 6 presents the integrative quality of invitational counseling and describes its compatibility with four contemporary theories of counseling: Adlerian Counseling, Reality Therapy, Cognitive Behavior Modification, and Person-Centered Counseling. Chapter 7 is an overview of the emerging counseling profession: its historical development, its current direction, and its promises for the future. Significant signs of the future indicate that counselors will require broad-based models of service delivery systems such as the one presented by invitational counseling.

Annotated reading lists are included at the end of each chapter to encourage the reader to explore the foundations of invitational counseling in depth. In addition, appendixes provide a detailed collection of practical inviting counseling activities.

We believe that the small size and compact nature of *The Inviting Relationship* will appeal to counselors and other helpers in many professional areas, including school counseling, mental health service, pastoral counseling, marriage and family therapy, student development, rehabilitation service, and a host of related specialties. We further believe the reader will find this book to be personally and professionally rewarding—and that reading it will be an enjoyable experience.

As with most major projects, writing this book was greatly facilitated by the encouragement and careful critiques of many colleagues and students. We especially want to thank Sandy Damico, Don McBrien, John Novak, Daniel Shaw, William Stafford, and Nancy Tobias for their valuable comments and suggestions.

W.W.P.
J.J.S.

1

INTRODUCTION TO THE INVITING RELATIONSHIP

Here, you see, is the greatest, the most inglorious default, namely, to encounter the nothingness represented by one's lack of essence and to interpret this lack as a kind of deformity to be corrected or made up for by others. It is precisely the opposite of a deformity! The lack is an *invitation to be*—an invitation to be something worth being, an invitation to fill up the nothingness with an essence that is worthy of existing and undeserving of being lost.

Van Cleave Morris, *Existentialism in
Education: What It Means,* 1966, p. 28

Professional counseling consists of a broad range of activities and services provided by a wide variety of trained professionals. It is an emerging profession that includes services offered by counselors and related specialists in educational, industrial, medical, residential, recreational, correctional, pastoral, and countless other work settings.

As the counseling profession has emerged, practicing counselors, counselor-educators, and counseling students have continuously searched for viable theories and effective techniques that could be integrated into human service programs for a variety of populations. Counselors, psychotherapists, and others have developed many theories and approaches to counseling, as well as numerous definitions of the helping relationship. In 1976, for example, more than 130 counseling theories and therapies were identified (Parloff, 1976) and the number continues to grow. According to Ivey (1980), there appear to be almost as many psychotherapies as there are therapists!

The purpose of this book is not to offer yet another theory of counseling. Rather, the reason is to provide an expanded framework for professional practice that we have named "the inviting relationship" (at times to be referred to as "invitational counseling"). This framework has three goals: (1) to serve as an expanding structure for a variety of counseling theories and techniques, (2) to provide a logical blueprint for understanding and organizing the wealth of knowledge now being generated in the burgeoning field of counseling, and (3) to present a proactive guide for professional human service useful to a wide variety of professional helpers in countless professional settings. We believe that a clear need exists in the counseling profession for a dependable structure of understanding that can be used to select, bring together, and orchestrate seemingly unrelated theories and approaches to professional helping. We also believe that invitational counseling provides this structure.

WHAT IS THE INVITING RELATIONSHIP?

> Man wishes to be confirmed in his being by man, and wishes to have presence in the being of the other . . . secretly and bashfully he watches for a Yes which allows him to be and which can come only from one human person to another. It is from one to another that the heavenly bread of self-being is passed.
>
> Martin Buber, *The Knowledge of Man:*
> *Selected Essays,* 1965, p. 71

Many people believe that they already know all they need to know about inviting, but in fact it is an extremely complex matrix of human experiences that occurs at identifiable levels, involves a series of skills, requires a hierarchy of choices, and applies to particular areas and styles of human interaction. The therapeutic attitude, knowledge, and skills that are basic to the inviting relationship are similar to those found in other counseling models; but differences exist, which is the reason behind this book.

The inviting relationship is based on a model of professional helping first articulated by Purkey (1978) and Purkey and Novak (1984). This model is anchored in the belief that intentional choice has the potential to improve both the immediate human condition and the long-term growth and health of people. The essence of the inviting relationship is that counselors and related helpers should be *intentionally* optimistic, respectful, and trusting toward themselves and others, personally and professionally. The inviting relationship is as much a therapeutic attitude, an orientation in character, a "dispositional quality," as it is a methodology. As such, it can be applied to interactions with people in a wide variety of places involving many different policies and programs. It can be used effectively by counselors to relate with themselves and with others whom they encounter each day in personal and professional interactions. With this as a starting point, the inviting relationship is defined in the following manner:

> The inviting relationship is the incorporation of compatible theories, systems, and techniques of human service into a therapeutic "stance" for professional helping. This stance is based on four basic assumptions: (1) people are able, valuable, capable of self-direction, and should be treated accordingly, (2) helping is a cooperative alliance in which process is as important as product, (3) people possess relatively untapped potential in all areas of human development, and (4) this potential can best be realized by places, policies, and programs that are *intentionally* designed to invite development, and by people who *consistently* seek to realize this potential in themselves and others, personally and professionally.

The inviting relationship employs the important skills and techniques provided by a variety of counseling theories and therapies that seek to assist people with immediate concerns, and it seeks to go beyond remediation by helping people recognize their opportunities for achieving lives of rich significance. This "going beyond" immediate concerns to seek improved and enriched levels of functioning is a hallmark of the inviting relationship.

Fortunately, counseling theories and techniques abound that provide important components of the inviting relationship. These theories and techniques are incorporated into invitational counseling when they are effectively and ethically used by practicing counselors and other helping professionals. The inviting relationship uses compatible theories and techniques as building blocks to provide an *expanded structure* for *professional practice.*

An Expanded Structure

The inviting relationship offers an expanded structure within which compatible approaches for establishing helping relationships can be incorporated. This structure enables counselors to assess the compatibility of various approaches to counseling and to select those that provide the most caring and appropriate professional service. It recognizes the importance of the "core" conditions as outlined and researched by client-centered therapists (Carkhuff, 1969a, 1969b; Patterson, 1959, 1985a, 1985b; Rogers, 1957). It also incorporates techniques useful with specific disorders (Mahoney, 1977; Martin & Pollard, 1980; Meichenbaum, 1977; Rimm & Masters, 1974). Moreover, it embraces the insights and assumptions of perceptual psychology (Combs & Snygg, 1959; Combs, Richards, & Richards, 1976) and self-concept theory (Combs, Avila, & Purkey, 1978; Purkey, 1970; Purkey & Novak, 1984), and accepts the influence of the individual psychology of Alfred Adler (Ansbacher & Ansbacher, 1956; Dreikurs, 1967; Sweeney, 1981) and the personal construct theory of George Kelly (1963).

By providing an expanded structure for professional counseling, the inviting relationship offers a systematic way of thinking about personal existence and human potential that helpers may incorporate into their personal and professional lives. Other counseling systems offer some sort of structure, but most limit their beliefs and assumptions to particular theoretical frameworks and to specific remedial relationships. By contrast, invitational counseling takes a wide-lens view of helping people to scale the highest peaks of human potential.

While respecting the contributions of various theories and models to the counseling process, the inviting relationship also recognizes the philosophic and theoretical differences in these approaches. There are methods that are not congruent with invitational counseling and should not be considered as such. Any approach to counseling that employs fear, coercion, aggression, duplicity, seduction, embarrassment, ridicule, subversion, or physical punishment, *regardless of good intentions* or *successful outcomes,* should not be viewed as part of the inviting relationship.

A Professional Practice

As a professional practice, invitational counseling identifies ways whereby counselors and allied professionals may employ their approaches and skills in arenas far beyond the remediation of immediate problems. Counselors involved in inviting relationships seek to assist people in recognizing their potential to develop optimally: to become *more* self-reliant, *more* emotionally and physically healthy, *more* unique and creative, *more* able to set realistic goals, and *more* capable of achieving those goals. All of this takes place within the context of a larger invitation to maintain the present culture while participating in the progress of civilization. Most counseling theories adhere to these goals, but the majority are severely limited in terms of an expanded structure. They tend to focus on *one* interpretation, system, or method. By comparison, the inviting relationship provides an expanded view of professional practice and a defensible rationale for using few or many approaches and techniques depending on the counseling situation.

Counselors who create and maintain inviting relationships understand, accept, and reflect a special responsibility inherent in all their intra- and interactions, both personal and professional. They work to maintain a particular "stance" based on the belief that in its most beneficial form the counseling relationship is a cooperative, collaborative process—a therapeutic partnership. This spirit of shared responsibility manifests itself in "doing with," rather than "doing to" relationships as advocated by Purkey, Schmidt, and McBrien (1982), Russell (1984), and others. This "doing with" stance is at the very heart of invitational counseling.

In sum, the inviting relationship is based on all of Carkhuff's variables (Carkhuff, 1969a, 1969b; Carkhuff & Berenson, 1967), all of Rogers' belief in caring (Rogers, 1951, 1980), all of Adler's concept of social interest and responsibility (Ansbacher & Ansbacher, 1956; Dreikurs, 1967), and all the assumptions of the perceptual tradition and self-concept theory (Combs, Avila, & Purkey, 1978; Purkey, 1970). At times it also incorporates the views and methods of many other approaches to counseling. Primarily, however, the inviting relationship is based on the model developed by Purkey (1978), Purkey and Novak (1984), Purkey, Schmidt, and McBrien (1982), Russell, Purkey, and Siegel (1982), and others acknowledged throughout this book. An overview of the invitational model is presented in this opening chapter. Its various components will be detailed in future chapters.

THE INVITATIONAL MODEL

I now believe there is no biological, geographical, social, economic, or psychological determiner of man's condition that he cannot transcend if he is suitably invited or challenged to do so.

Sidney Jourard, *Disclosing Man to Himself*, 1968, p. 59

Philosophically, the invitational model is based on the belief that each individual has relatively untapped potential for intellectual, psychological, and physical development, and that this potential is best realized in a humane environment of people, places, policies, and programs that intentionally invite the process. The invitational model of professional helping is a description of what people, places, policies, and programs can and should *do* and *be* to benefit human existence and the quality of personal development. As such, it has implications for professional helpers in educational, industrial, managerial, medical, institutional, recreational, and a host of other settings.

The invitational model was first introduced by Purkey (1978) who described the model and its application in educational settings. This basic model has since been greatly enriched by the research and writing of Amos (1985), Amos, Purkey, and Tobias (1985), Lambeth (1980), Purkey and Novak (1984), Ripley (1985), Russell, Purkey, and Siegel (1982), Schmidt (1982), Stehle (1981), Stillion and Siegel (1985), Turner (1983), and many others. Figure 1-1 portrays the invitational model.

As can be seen in Figure 1-1, the invitational model begins with a particular stance that the helper assumes regarding oneself and others, personally and professionally. This stance is based on four elements: optimism, respect, trust, and intentionality. The particular stance the helper assumes leads to the level at which the helper is likely to function. But the invitational model goes beyond describing levels of functioning to explore the inviting process itself, which includes four factors involved in the method, four areas of interaction, four choices in human relations, and four styles of behavior. The dynamic ways in which these forces come together and interact eventually result in the helper being either a beneficial presence or a lethal presence in the lives of oneself and others, personally and professionally. Each of these forces will be considered in turn, beginning with the four elements of the invitational model.

Four Elements

The invitational model is still under construction, with definitions inexact and opportunities unexplored. Nevertheless, it can be put into operation, and empirical research is underway that promises to give it added credibility (Amos, 1985; Ripley, 1985; Smith, 1985). Meanwhile, four basic elements stated in the model provide it with substance, structure, and direction. When applied to the professional practice of counseling, these elements offer the practitioner a consistent "stance" that can be used to create and maintain inviting actions, programs, policies, and places. As Corey, Corey, and Callanan point out, "practicing counseling without an explicit theoretical rationale is somewhat like flying a plane without a map and without instruments" (1984, p. 102). The theoretical rationale offered here provides a particular therapeutic attitude, a "dispositional quality" in relationship to oneself and others, personally and professionally. These four elements are *optimism, respect, trust,* and *intentionality*.

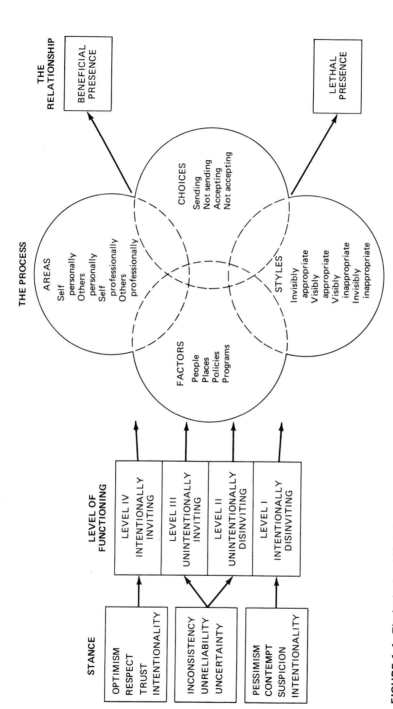

FIGURE 1-1 The Invitational Model

Optimism. The invitational model is based on a positive vision of human existence: that individuals are valuable, able, capable of self-direction, and should be treated accordingly. It operates on the assumption that the deepest urges of human nature are to be intimately involved in inviting relationships. It assumes that what people desire most is to be affirmed in their present worth while being summoned cordially to realize their potential. Goethe described the process with these words: "If we take people as they are, we make them worse. If we treat them as if they were what they ought to be, we help them to become what they are capable of becoming" (cited in Frankl, 1968, p. 8). When people exhibit behaviors that appear to contradict this assumption, it is thought to be because they have met with repeated negative experiences and have thus lost respect for themselves, trust in their abilities, and faith in their potential.

A corollary to the element of optimism is that no person, place, policy, or program can be absolutely neutral. Inviting and disinviting forces are unavoidable. In the invitational model everything counts. Whatever happens, and whatever ways it happens, adds to or takes from present existence and future potential. Every inviting or disinviting force, no matter how small or in what area has limitless potential to influence the positive or negative course of human events. By analogy, every human being is both a radio station and a recording studio—constantly creating and sending signals while simultaneously receiving and recording them as well, filing them away for replay at some later time. The importance of sending and receiving signals of optimism, respect, and trust regarding people and their potential is self-evident.

Respect. Nothing is more important in the invitational model than the people in the process, and so it embraces a special "being with" attitude with oneself and others. Central to this "being with" attitude is a respect for the rich complexity and unique value of each human being. This respect is manifested in such behaviors as civility, politeness, courtesy, and caring. Respect is also reflected in appropriateness, in appreciating the importance of knowing when to invite and when *not* to invite, when to accept, and when *not* to accept. The concept of appropriateness is an important part of the invitational model and will be considered in detail later in this chapter.

A further ingredient of respect is responsibility. From an invitational perspective, each individual is the world's greatest authority of his or her own existence, and each is ultimately responsible for oneself and one's actions. As Bugental (1965) stated: "The consultant is always in some measure external to the on-going business of the patient's life. No matter how much the patient may seek for the consultant to take over—indeed, no matter how much the therapist tries to guide or manage his patient's affairs—the existential reality is unchanged, the patient is the only responsible one in his own life. This does not obviate the very real, and often very heavy responsibility a psychotherapist bears in his own right. Certainly as we work with our patients we can try to do much to aid them in the exercise of their autonomy, but we need always to recognize and respect that autonomy" (Bugental, 1965,

p. 72). Establishing a position of equality, equity, and shared power is a major indicator of respect.

Trust.   The third element embedded in the invitational model is trust, based on the recognition of the interdependence of human beings. This interdependence is most likely to be enhanced when people give a high priority to human welfare, when they view places, policies, and programs as capable of contributing to or subtracting from this welfare, and where there is freedom and willingness to trust feelings and risk involvement. As Carl Rogers pointed out, counseling based on withholding one's self as a person and dealing with others as objects does not have a high probability of success. From the viewpoint of the invitational model, helping is a cooperative, collaborative activity.

Unfortunately, it often works out that people who are most likely to benefit from the inviting relationship are least likely to trust the process. On the one hand this is because their negative self-perceptions permit few positive experiences to filter into their self-systems. On the other hand it is because those who are normally inviting are often misled by this nonacceptance into thinking that these people do not want to be involved. The element of trust, therefore, is dependent on a dispositional quality that is manifested in an inviting *pattern* of action, as opposed to a single inviting act. This pattern (which is referred to at times as "stance") is the force which creates and maintains inviting relationships.

Although consistent patterns of inviting are important, it should be acknowledged that even the smallest inviting act, which at the moment may appear to be of little or no consequence, can have far-reaching consequences. A basic premise of the invitational model is that everything counts. Human potential, though not always apparent, is always there, waiting to be discovered and invited forth.

Intentionality.   By definition, an invitation is a purposive act intended to offer something beneficial for consideration. The invitational model not only emphasizes the importance of purpose and direction but it also stresses that an intentional pattern of behavior based on publicly affirmed ideals is the foundation for any therapeutic relationship.

From the viewpoint of the invitational model, human potential can best be realized by places, policies, and programs that are specifically designed to affirm human worth and encourage its development, and by people who are intentionally inviting with themselves and others, personally and professionally. Therefore, the more intentional a counselor is, the more accurate his or her judgments are likely to be. This is because the purposeful nature of the inviting relationship encourages consistency in direction.

The four elements of the invitational model—optimism, respect, trust, and intentionality—when blended together into a therapeutic attitude, provide the professional helper with a consistent stance that can be used to develop personally and professionally inviting actions, places, policies, and programs.

Four Levels of Functioning

The four levels of functioning proposed in the invitational model include both harmful and helpful behaviors. Most professionals function at each of the four levels from time to time, but it is the *typical* level of functioning that creates one's "stance" and eventually determines the degree of success or failure in each person's personal and professional life. Of course, whether a particular behavior is inviting or disinviting is a matter of perception, and what one person views as "inviting" may be seen as very "disinviting" by another. This paradox emphasizes the importance of counselors understanding the nature of perception and taking into account their own perceptions as well as those of their clients.

According to the invitational model, each person at any given moment is functioning at one of the following four levels. While everyone functions at all four levels from time to time, it is the *typical* level of functioning that determines one's stance.

Level I: Intentionally disinviting. The most toxic and lethal level of functioning involves those actions, places, policies, or programs that are deliberately designed to dissuade, discourage, defeat, demean, or destroy. Examples of *Level I* functioning might be a counselor who is deliberately insulting to a client, a hospital policy that is intentionally discriminatory, a prison program that is willfully designed to demean inmates, or an environment made purposefully unpleasant. Unfortunately, there are those few individuals who resemble Elmira Gulch in the 1939 film version of L.F. Baum's *Wizard of Oz,* and who take a special kind of pleasure out of hurting people or seeing them upset. From the viewpoint of the invitational model there is no justification for people, places, policies, or programs to be, or remain, at this bottom level.

Individuals whose stance is based primarily on pessimism, contempt, and suspicion, and whose level of functioning is intentionally disinviting, are fortunately few in number. Their deliberate signals to themselves and others that they are unworthy, incapable, and irresponsible may be understandable—and even forgivable—but never justifiable. Disinviting people, places, policies, and programs can never be justified, according to the invitational model, regardless of effectiveness or efficiency.

Level II: Unintentionally disinviting. People, and the places, policies, and programs they create that are characteristic of this second level repeatedly face such questions as "*Why* are we having so many personnel problems?"; "*Why* are people avoiding this place?"; "*Why* are they not following our policies?"; "*Why* are our programs not working?" Professionals who typically function at *Level II* are usually well-meaning people, but the behaviors they exhibit, the places they create, and the policies and programs they design are often viewed as uncaring, chauvinistic, condescending, patronizing, sexist, racist, dictatorial, or just plain thoughtless. Examples of such insensitivity appear again and again in accounts of being disinvited: "I feel insulted when the director always asks a female to take minutes at our meetings," reported one counselor, while another commented that she found her supervisor's habit of calling her "Sweetie" to be overly friendly. An older adult complained that her pastoral counselor always shouted in her presence, assuming incorrectly that she was hard of hearing. Although unintended, such behaviors can be very disinviting.

Unintentionally disinviting processes can also be found directed at oneself, as in cases where people have the unwitting habit of referring to themselves in negative terms. Individuals often speak of themselves in terms so demeaning ("I'm so stupid," "I'm such a klutz," "I can't sing," "I'm *just* a teacher") that if anyone else spoke to them in such disinviting terms they would feel insulted. They are unaware that they are functioning at the unintentionally disinviting level with themselves.

Level III: Unintentionally inviting. This third level of functioning may be pictured as the domain of the "natural born" professional. Individuals functioning at this level are generally well liked and reasonably effective. The behaviors they exhibit and the places, policies, and programs they create and maintain are often congruent with the spirit of the invitational model. However, because they have little or no understanding of the principles involved in the invitational model, they are unaware of why they are successful. There is a certain "sophisticated ignorance" associated with these individuals. They know *what* they are doing, but they do not know *why*. When they encounter problems, or when things stop working, they sometimes have a difficult time figuring out what is wrong or starting things up again. Even worse, they sometimes lack consistency in direction. They may be unreliable in their responsibilities and uncertain in their decisions. When faced with threatening situations or challenges, they may drop to *Level II,* or even *Level I* functioning. It is easy to be inviting when everything is going well and the sun is shining. A requirement of the invitational model is to create and maintain a consistently inviting stance—even in the rain—which brings us to *Level IV.*

Level IV: Intentionally inviting. In the invitational model, *everybody* and *everything* adds to, or subtracts from, the quality of personal existence and human potential. Ideally, the four factors of people, places, policies, and programs should be so intentionally inviting as to create a world where each person is cordially summoned to develop intellectually, physically, and psychologically. From this standpoint, *Level IV*—based on optimism, respect, trust, and intentionality—is the wellspring of professional functioning. The more intentional an act, the more it lends itself to understanding, consistency, and direction.

Recognition of the importance and acceptance of the responsibility to be intentionally inviting can be a tremendous asset for professionals. Those who view their role to be intentionally inviting not only strive to reach *Level IV* but once there they continue to master the areas, choices, and styles identified by the invitational model. These are embedded within four factors of personal and professional functioning.

Four Factors

In the invitational model, four factors—people, places, policies, and programs —are highly significant for their separate and combined influence on human existence and potential. The combination of these four factors with the soon-to-be-introduced areas, choices, and styles of personal and professional functioning provides a multidimensional perspective by which counselors and allied professionals can establish effective helping relationships. The invitational model depicts an almost limitless number of possible interactions among these various forces.

What people do is always enmeshed within and influenced by their existing places, policies, and programs. As Hobbs (1982) explained, human problems and promises do not reside within individuals but rather within individuals' ecosystems of which the individual is only one part. Therefore, in applying the invitational model it is important to take the matrix of people, places, policies, and programs into account. As Figure 1-2 illustrates, the challenges facing professional helpers and their clients can often be related to the process of combining the right pieces of the people, places, policies, and programs puzzle.

People. An appreciation of the *people* involved in the inviting relationship depends on an awareness of the contributions made by social, biological, and psychological forces toward the development of healthy individuals. Counselors who employ the invitational model require a sound knowledge of how people develop. This includes an understanding of human growth trends, psychological and emotional developmental processes, and principles of learning and behavior.

As professionals, counselors seek to be sensitive not only to the "here and now" existence of individuals but also to be sensitive to people's potential for controlling their own lives and developing their own capabilities. As stated earlier, the invitational model requires unconditional respect for people. This respect is manifested in the caring and appropriate behavior that people exhibit toward themselves

FIGURE 1-2   Four Factors of the Inviting Relationship

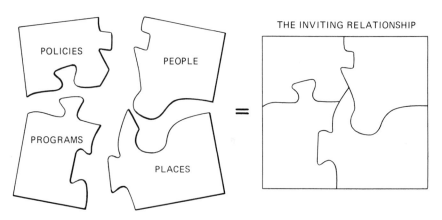

and others, in the quality of life reflected in the places they create and inhabit, and by the policies and programs they establish and support.

Decisions that have tremendous effect on people's lives are too often made by those in authority for reasons of efficiency, effectiveness, and conformity that have questionable relationship to the welfare of individuals. Moreover, these decisions are often designed for the convenience of a few at the inconvenience of many. For example, school regulations that allow only three minutes between classes (to reduce misbehavior) or five minutes for the buses to load (to convenience drivers) force students to run, push, and shove. The problem is magnified when some drivers gun their engines loudly, warning students that they have the choice of running or being left behind. The invitational model is based on proper regard for the value of systems, regulations, and policies, but people come first. It advocates altering, wherever possible, those places, policies, or programs that directly or indirectly inconvenience people or inhibit their development.

An example of the importance of people in the inviting process was observed by one of the authors while working as a consultant for a large hospital. An elderly male patient had been placed on a wheeled stretcher and moved into the hospital hallway. As he lay there, a burly hospital electrician, complete with leather belt and a hundred dangling tools, came striding down the corridor. When the electrician spotted the frail patient, he struck up a friendly conversation. After a few words, the electrician asked the patient if there was anything he could do for him. The man replied that he felt cold and would appreciate a blanket. The electrician walked over to the nurses' station, got a blanket, and tenderly covered the patient. At that moment the electrician was as much a professional helper as any person in the hospital. Places, policies, and programs are important, but it is the people in the process that create an inviting relationship.

Places. The invitational model also focuses on physical environments, the "places" that add to or subtract from respect and trust for people. Individuals cannot be disconnected from their circumstances, and counseling cannot take place without taking into account the surroundings. For example, consider the problem of "burnout," the process whereby professionals change in negative directions. As Pines and Aronson (1981) noted: "Burnout is not a function of bad people who are cold and uncaring. It is a function of bad situations in which once-idealistic people must operate. It is then that situations must be modified so that they promote, rather than destroy, human values" (Pines & Aronson, 1981, p. 61). A significant situation is the physical environment. Counselors who adopt the invitational model evaluate environmental factors to determine their influence on people and, where possible, to improve them. The invitational model requires a continuous assessment of the places where people live and work.

In most cases an assessment of environmental factors will identify variables that can be modified, adjusted, and improved upon. For example, visitor parking at universities, hospitals, and clinics is sometimes located several blocks away, whereas parking for faculty and staff adjoins the buildings. A more equitable assignment of parking space may improve the mood of those who visit institutions. Counselors who are alert to both negative and positive physical influences have an advantage in creating the inviting relationship.

A further example of how physical environments contribute to human welfare may be seen in residential group care facilities. A fresh coat of paint, new curtains, improved lighting, carpets, or rearrangement of furnishings can produce highly beneficial results. One secretary reported that when the tall counter and plate glass that divided her office was removed and replaced by an attractive receptionist's desk, she felt as if she had been let out of prison.

An often overlooked part of professional helping related to "places" is the need for privacy. A professor known to one of the authors once commented that a successful counselor needs "two big ears, one small mouth, and privacy." While the need for privacy is almost self-evident in the counseling relationship, it is sometimes overlooked because the physical environment has not been taken into proper account.

Improving the physical environment may not always lead to immediate benefits, but according to the invitational model it is important that the total setting be continuously assessed, alternatives explored, and necessary improvements made in the places where people live and work.

Policies.   People and places are in turn influenced by the regulations, codes, orders, mandates, plans, rules, and edicts created by those in charge. Sometimes policies are created that, while well-intentioned, place undue restrictions on individuals or groups. Examples might be a cafeteria policy requiring that an identical amount of food be served to each patron (whether he or she weighs 75 pounds or 275 pounds!), a nursing home that requires "lights out" at 9:00 P.M. regardless of the personal desires of the people who live there, or an elementary school principal who demands complete silence from children during their lunchtime. Such insensitive, uncaring, or inappropriate policies limit opportunities for people to contribute to their own well-being and to that of others.

On occasion, policies actually contribute to human difficulties. An illustration is the case of a nursing home resident who often exhibited difficult behaviors for the staff and other residents and was very cross, particularly when she first got up in the morning. A contributing factor was found to be the "bed check" policy, which required checks at various hours of the night. This would awaken the older adult and she was unable to return to a sound sleep. Altering the bed check policy and advising floor nurses to be extra quiet at night when they entered residents' rooms, coupled with providing ear plugs for this particular resident, resulted in restful nights and beneficial effects on her behavior. The policies people create add to or subtract from the quality of life and the overall effectiveness or ineffectiveness of professional helpers.

Counselors who understand how policies affect people, and who use this understanding to develop procedures that facilitate human functioning and development, are more likely to encounter success in their work. But policies are seldom made in isolation. They are made in relation to programs designed and administered by organizations and institutions.

Programs. Organizations routinely develop programs as part of their overall service. Special-education classes in schools, work release programs in prisons, social activities in retirement centers, food and nutritional services in nursing homes, infant care training in hospitals, and salary incentives in industry are all examples of programs designed to contribute to the goals and objectives of the respective institutions.

Counselors who use the invitational model are aware of the importance of programs, not only within their own institutions but also in the larger community. They strive to become knowledgeable about existing community programs that contribute both to their clients' welfare and to the welfare of larger groups. Moreover, these counselors are sensitive to the ways in which programs are created, implemented, and administered.

Sometimes well-intentioned programs harm individuals or groups because they focus on narrow goals and objectives and neglect a wider perspective of human needs and conditions. For example, programs that "label" and "group" participants can negatively affect the positive purposes for which these programs were originally created. Although some classifications are essential, there is a danger in programs that label and group human beings. As Hobbs (1975) warned: "Categories and labels are powerful instruments for social regulation and control, and they often are employed for obscure, covert or hurtful purposes: to degrade people, to deny them access to opportunity, to exclude 'undesirables' whose presence in society in some way offends, disturbs familiar customs, or demands extraordinary efforts" (Hobbs, 1975, p. 10). The invitational model requires that helpers closely monitor programs that add to or detract from the goals for which they were designed.

Counselors who adopt the invitational model consistently think in terms of the "Four P's": *p*eople, *p*laces, *p*olicies, and *p*rograms. They understand how the dynamics of the "Four P's" influence the welfare and development of people. They accept Hobbs' (1982) principle that emotional disturbance is a symptom not of individual pathology but of a malfunctioning human ecosystem. The following example underscores this principle.

A demonstration of the invitational model in action is an experience one of the authors had in consulting with an elementary school counselor and a teacher. The counselor had been working with a young student who had been referred by the teacher because of his inappropriate behaviors, particularly in the cafeteria. The counselor had worked with the boy individually and in groups, but little improvement was noted. While the counselor-client relationship seemed healthy and certain classroom behaviors had improved, the boy's actions in the cafeteria continued to be deplorable. He was often loud and boisterous, throwing food at other students, running around the cafeteria, and getting into fights.

In reviewing the "people" aspect of this situation, the consultant, counselor, and teacher agreed that people have a right to eat lunch in a peaceful setting without being bothered by others. It was also agreed that the student would benefit from a calm and appropriate lunch period.

The consultant and counselor asked the teacher to describe what occurred in the cafeteria, the "place" where the students ate lunch. The teacher described how students went through the lunch line, selected their food, paid the cashier, and sat at designated tables to eat their lunches. All students ate in the cafeteria.

The teacher also described the "policy" and "program" procedures for ordering lunch in the cafeteria. As the cafeteria workers prepared the lunch trays, students passed through the line and made choices about the vegetables, main courses, and desserts they wanted. This procedure was particularly difficult for the child in question. He often hesitated in responding to the cafeteria staff's questions. They in turn became frustrated with his indecision. The cafeteria workers would wait a few seconds for his answers and then just give him one of the choices. The boy would get angry at them for making his decisions, just as the workers would get upset with his indecision and belligerence. When this happened, the teacher reported that the boy would take his tray to the lunchroom, sit at the table, pick at his food, and eventually get into trouble.

After examining the people, places, policies, and programs involved, the consultant, teacher, and counselor agreed on the following processes. A conference between the young student and the teacher was scheduled so that the teacher could express concern that sometimes the student was not enjoying his lunchtime. At this conference the teacher explained to the student that each person has the right to enjoy a relaxing lunch and that disruptive behaviors were not helpful to him or others. The teacher explained that students were welcome to eat in the cafeteria as long as they allowed other people to enjoy their lunch. If the student decided not to do this, then the teacher would find a quiet place in the school where he could enjoy his lunch alone.

The teacher also conveyed to the student her understanding of how difficult it is to make decisions on the spur of the moment, such as deciding what to eat while moving through the cafeteria line. Therefore, every morning the teacher would give the student a copy of the menu and ask him to circle the items he wanted for lunch. He was asked to give the circled menu to the cafeteria workers. They proceeded to fill "his order" based on the items he had circled. The cafeteria staff was also requested to greet the young boy pleasantly as well as all the others who moved through the serving line. Meanwhile, the counselor continued seeing the student in group counseling sessions to focus on self-concept development and decision-making skills.

Subsequent follow-up by the consultant indicated that the student had no further difficulty in the cafeteria. The success of the teacher, counselor, and student in handling the situation was related to their ability to employ a wide-angle invitational perspective. The counselor focused on the student initially, but better results were achieved when "places," "policies," and "programs" were also considered.

Most people believe that they already know what they need to know about inviting, but in fact it is an extremely complex matrix of human experiences that, beyond the levels and factors already introduced, involves a series of skills. These forces will be explained in detail in later chapters, but it will be helpful here to introduce four areas of functioning, four choices of interacting, and four styles of behavior pictured in Figure 1-1.

Four Areas of Functioning

In addition to identifying the core values of optimism, respect, trust, and intentionality, and describing four levels and four factors, the invitational model identifies four *areas* of functioning. These areas have been nicknamed "The Four Corner Press" and are pictured in Figure 1-3. The four areas are: (1) being personally inviting with oneself, (2) being personally inviting with others, (3) being professionally inviting with oneself, and (4) being professionally inviting with others. These four areas will be introduced here and expanded upon in future chapters.

Being personally inviting with oneself. There are special pressures and particular sorts of isolation brought about by being a professional helper. Continuous interaction with clients who are troubled, who are unsure of their trajectory, or who are seeking to enrich their lives can result in the counselor being placed under considerable stress. Therefore, it is essential that professionals be personally inviting with themselves: to conserve their own personal energy levels and to nurture themselves physically, emotionally, intellectually, and spiritually. Some examples of being personally inviting with oneself would include taking pleasure in stillness, keeping in shape physically, reserving time for oneself, and finding satisfaction from sources completely removed from one's professional life. When one seeks to be of service to others, it is important to have one's personal life in reasonably good order.

Being personally inviting with others. The second area addressed by the invitational model is the importance of relating with others at a deeply personal level. Helpers are first human and only after that professional. It is important for

FIGURE 1-3 The "Four Corner Press"

BEING PERSONALLY INVITING WITH ONESELF	BEING PERSONALLY INVITING WITH OTHERS
BEING PROFESSIONALLY INVITING WITH ONESELF	BEING PROFESSIONALLY INVITING WITH OTHERS

counselors to cultivate personal friendships and cherish emotional intimacy. A dear friend, Betty Siegel, expressed it well: "All the professional success in the universe will not make up for lack of success with those you love and who love you." Professionals who employ the invitational model work to nurture their "life support systems"–family, friends, mentors, colleagues, and lovers who make living and helping worthwhile.

Being professionally inviting with oneself. Professionals who consistently invite themselves to grow professionally are in a favorable position to be a beneficial presence in the lives of clients. By contrast, counselors who allow themselves to stagnate in their particular field run the risk of becoming professionally obsolete. The invitational model requires that professionals be actively and continuously engaged in upgrading their skills, knowledge, and understandings.

In practical terms, being professionally inviting with oneself means participating in professional programs, seeking additional certification, spending time reading journals, joining and contributing to professional associations, and researching and writing for professional publication. Those who neglect to invite themselves professionally will probably become antiquated in a few years; and the sad part is that they may be unaware of their growing obsolescence.

Being professionally inviting with others. Being professionally inviting with others is best accomplished by building on the strengths of the previous three areas or "corners." In a sense, the first three corners are necessary but not sufficient preconditions for functioning optimally in the fourth corner. Once the first three are functioning smoothly they serve as a foundation for the fourth. Much of this book deals with being professionally inviting with others, but for now, the fourth corner requires that professionals envision the inviting relationship as a therapeutic alliance based on optimism, respect, trust, and intentionality.

The four corners of the "four-corner press" make explicit what is often implicit or overlooked in professional practice: *becoming a professional requires optimal development in being inviting with oneself and others, personally and professionally.* When the four corners are in harmony, the professional may reach a point beautifully described by Anne Morrow Lindbergh in her book *Gift from the Sea:*

> I want first of all–in fact, as an end to these other desires–to be at peace with myself. I want a singleness of eye, a purity of intention, a central core to my life that will enable me to carry out these obligations and activities as well as I can. I want, in fact–to borrow from the language of the saints–to live in grace as much of the time as possible. I am not using this term in a strictly theological sense. By grace I mean an inner harmony (Lindbergh, 1955, p. 23).

When the professional is being inviting in all four areas, the potential to "live in grace" is there, to reach a level of personal and professional functioning where the outward and inward person are as one. To live a harmonious life, personally and professionally, requires consistent success in making caring and appropriate choices in human interaction.

Choices of Interacting

The constant interactions of the four factors and four areas of the invitational model described earlier lead to a third component consisting of four choices: (1) sending, (2) not sending, (3) accepting, and (4) not accepting. Every human relationship is influenced by the decisions encompassed by these four choices. The first two choices are in the domain of the person who chooses to send or not to send.

Sending. According to the invitational model, a message, signal, or action is not an invitation until it is intentionally delivered. As James Russell Lowell, an early American writer noted, "Every man feels instinctively that all the beautiful sentiments in the world weigh less than a single lovely action." Intentionality is demonstrated by purposeful action.

Invitational counseling is an action-oriented approach to professional helping. Simply thinking about doing good things with people is not sufficient. To respect is to act respectfully, to trust is to act trustfully, to care is to act caringly, and to love is to act lovingly. Counseling is a special kind of respecting, trusting, caring, and loving. The inviting relationship is manifested when good intentions are acted upon.

Not sending. Because the inviting relationship requires adequate planning and accurate timing, there are occasions when it is best *not* to send a message or to take an action. Sometimes well-meaning professionals do not accomplish their intended goals because of a lack of planning or poor timing. In these instances it would probably have been better not to invite. Counselors who are sensitive to the developmental abilities and needs of their clients recognize that, sometimes, *not* sending an invitation can be the most inviting thing a helper can do.

A graduate student in counseling at the University of North Carolina at Greensboro provided an example of the value of "not sending" with the following story: "This past weekend my wife was talking to my son and me about something she wanted done. I was in a hurry to get outside to finish raking leaves and went out of the room without my wife knowing I had left, and she continued to talk. Steven, our five-year-old son, finally said, 'Mommy, stop talking. Nobody is listening.'" Counselors who employ the invitational model work to avoid inviting "when nobody is listening" or at other inappropriate times.

Accepting. The remaining two choices of the four in the invitational model are made by the receiver of invitations. The first of these remaining two choices is *accepting.* In this choice the receiver acknowledges the receipt of an invitation and agrees to a particular relationship. In a special way, accepting an invitation is a way of sending one in return. By accepting invitations people demonstrate their willingness to form relationships. Acceptance affirms both the sender and receiver. It indicates to the sender that the invitation was appropriate and caring; to the receiver it indicates that he or she is willing and able to accept. When an invitation is inappropriate or uncaring, or the receiver does not feel able or willing to accept, invitations are less likely to be accepted.

Not accepting. By not accepting invitations, people are indicating that the timing, content, appropriateness, personal taste, or other factors are influencing their decision to decline the opportunity. When invitations are not accepted, it is helpful for the sender to consider the components of the invitational model to see if it can assist in creating a more acceptable invitation. This is particularly important for counselors who find their clients resistant to change. Negotiations and a "doing with" stance will probably present the clients with more acceptable options.

Combined with the other three choices—"sending," "not sending," and "accepting"—the choice of "not accepting" interacts with all the levels, factors, areas, and styles identified in the invitational model. As such, the four choices are considered not as isolated behaviors but as part of an integrated system of personal and professional functioning. Each of the four choices requires equal attention and value in the inviting relationship. Sometimes the most inviting thing a counselor can do is *not* invite, *not* accept, and the same is true of clients who sometimes must learn that saying "no" to others is a way of saying "yes" to themselves. Those who have a difficult time with not sending or not accepting can often benefit from assertiveness training. In sum, accepting personal responsibility for the four choices is fundamental to the invitational model and is echoed throughout this book. We are now ready to examine the least-explored element of the invitational model, namely, the four styles of functioning.

Four Styles

Of all the dynamic forces found in the inviting relationship, those least examined and understood are the four styles of functioning: (1) invisibly inappropriate, (2) visibly inappropriate, (3) visibly appropriate, and (4) invisibly appropriate. The invitational model identifies these four styles and demonstrates their impact on the inviting relationship.

Invisibly inappropriate. What is the difference between a "gaze" and a "stare," a "touch" and a "feel," a "smile" and a "smirk"? Although such differences are hard to describe, experienced counselors are keenly aware of them. They sense that something in the counseling relationship is not right, although they would be hard-put to explain what that "something" is. Clients, too, report that at times they feel uncomfortable in human relationships although the reasons escape them. According to the invitational model the reasons can probably be discovered by considering the various components of the model, beginning with the stance of optimism, respect, trust, and intentionality. From the beginning of the relationship, something may not be right with the stance. Sometimes everything on the surface seems appropriate, but there are feelings of inconsistency, unreliability, and uncertainty. When counselors and clients become aware that something is out of kilter, it is helpful to face these feelings as directly as possible. By doing so, invisibly inappropriate forces become visible, making them much easier to confront and resolve.

Visibly inappropriate. Who has not encountered actions, places, policies, and programs that are *visibly* inappropriate? These disinviting forces are so obvious that they readily call attention to themselves. Fortunately, because they are so self-evident, they are usually the easiest to change. Examples of visibly inappropriate forces are the counselor who delights in telling racist or sexist jokes; the out-patient clinic sign that reads: "TAKE A NUMBER AND BE SEATED!"; the written school policy that encourages corporal punishment; the area supervisor who consistently refers to male subordinates as "hunks" or females as "broads"; the personnel officer whose behaviors are blatantly discriminatory. All of these represent visibly inappropriate styles of functioning. An accurate recognition of these styles for what they are often sets the stage for a more appropriate and caring style of functioning.

Visibly appropriate. This third style of functioning is the most common in the human service professions. The counselor who employs this third style is technically correct in style and function. Strategies and objectives are precise, paraphrasing is done with skill, wait-time is used with perfection, and body language is centered, balanced, and encouraging. Clients, too, often behave in a visibly appropriate style, responding in expected ways, disclosing in an appropriate manner, expressing their feelings fluently, working toward identified goals. In situations where the counselor and client communicate in visibly appropriate ways, most observers would agree that they have established an inviting relationship. But as good as this is, the invitational model proposes an even more advanced style of functioning: invisibly appropriate.

Invisibly appropriate. When a counselor functions consistently in a visibly appropriate style, the effort and the skill involved gradually become less obvious. They become almost automatic and do not call attention to themselves. With time and effort, the counselor reaches the invisibly appropriate style of functioning, where actions take on an almost effortless appearance. Only another highly skilled and experienced counselor can fully recognize and appreciate the talents of this highly skilled professional helper.

George Burns, the great comedian, expressed the process of functioning in an invisibly appropriate style this way: "I improved so much I finally got so good that nobody knew I was there" (Burns, 1976, p. 58). This would seem to be a goal for counselors: To help with such grace and style that the process itself becomes invisible, and the client leaves the counseling session with a growing sense of self-control, self-confidence, and self-responsibility.

Functioning in an invisibly appropriate style is analogous to learning to drive a standard-shift automobile. The beginning driver is clumsily shifting, grinding gears, and popping the clutch while the car jerks and stalls. After considerable driving experience, and with intentional effort, that same driver shifts gears with such skill that the vehicle accelerates from low to high speed with barely a whisper. The better the performance the more invisible the effort becomes. This seems to be true in almost any line of human endeavor, but it is particularly true of professional helping.

The invisibly appropriate style of functioning requires elaboration, for it relates to the concepts of authenticity, genuineness, and being "without front," so important to counselors. Therefore, it will be explored in future chapters, along with an in-depth consideration of the other three styles of functioning.

SUMMARY

> By declaring that man is a responsible creature and must actualize the potential meaning of his life, I wish to stress that the true meaning of life is to be found in the world rather than within man or his own *psyche,* as though it were a closed system.
>
> Viktor E. Frankl, *Man's Search
> for Meaning,* 1963, p. 175

This opening chapter introduced the inviting relationship, which is based on an expanded perspective for professional counseling, and suggested its relationship to other counseling theories and practices. At heart, invitational counseling is an approach to professional helping anchored on four assumptions: (1) that people are able, valuable, capable of self-direction, and should be treated accordingly, (2) that counseling should be a cooperative process where process is as important as product, (3) that people possess relatively untapped potential in all areas of human development, and (4) this potential can best be realized by places, policies, and programs that are *intentionally* designed to invite development and by people who *consistently* seek to realize this potential in themselves and others, personally and professionally.

The inviting relationship is based on the invitational model. The model stresses the importance of creating and maintaining a particular "stance" based on optimism, respect, trust, and intentionality. This stance leads to an intentionally inviting level of functioning. To create and maintain an intentionally inviting level of functioning, four factors, four areas, four choices, and four styles of interpersonal relationships embedded in the invitational model were explained. Each of these 16 elements was introduced and briefly explained in this chapter, and they will be analyzed in detail in future chapters.

The inviting relationship seeks to incorporate compatible counseling theories and techniques into an expanded perspective of professional counseling. By combining the remediation of existing concerns with an optimistic vision of human potential, invitational counseling seeks to assist clients in realizing their value, abilities, and self-directing powers in all areas of human endeavor. Invitational counseling involves the whole person and the total environment. Its goal is to serve people, all of whom are seen as possessing the ability to understand their situations, to recognize their potential, and to be an active force in their own development.

OPPORTUNITIES FOR FURTHER READING

Reading a book is kind of a conversation.

Mortimer J. Adler and Charles
Van Doren, *How to Read a Book,*
1972, p. 235

No person or theory blooms full-blown without the aid of everyone and everything that precedes it. Invitational counseling is no exception. The annotated list of books that follows this and all other chapters is illustrative of the many scholars who have profoundly influenced the authors of this book.

BLOOM, B.S. (1976). *Human characteristics and school learning.* New York: McGraw-Hill. Benjamin Bloom presented some startling evidence of the endless perfectability of the human being when presented with an optimally inviting environment.

COMBS, A.W., AVILA, D.L., & PURKEY, W.W. (1978). *Helping relationships: Basic concepts for the helping professions,* 2nd ed. Boston: Allyn & Bacon. This book introduces an approach to professional helping based on how people view themselves, others, and the world, and it focuses on the dynamic interactions that exist among these perceptions.

COMBS, A.W., SOPER, D.W., GOODING, C.T., BENTON, J.A., DICKMAN, J.F., & USHER, R.H. (1969). *Florida studies in the helping professions. Social Science Monograph No. 37.* Gainesville, Fla.: University of Florida Press. Combs and his associates reported the differences they found between successful and less-than-successful helpers in a number of professional fields. They presented evidence that the biggest difference between "good" and "poor" helpers is in their perceptual orientations.

DEWEY, J. (1933). *How we think.* Lexington, Mass.: Heath. This classic text deals with the problems people have and how they face them. Dewey pointed out that everything the professional helper does, as well as the manner in which he or she does it, invites others to respond in one way or another.

HUNT, J.Mc. (1961). *Intelligence and experience.* New York: Ronald Press. Hunt maintained, on the basis of detailed research, that intelligence is not fixed and that development is not predetermined. This book offers both rigor and enthusiasm to support the notion that human potential, though not always apparent, is always there, waiting to be discovered and invited forth.

JOURARD, S.M. (1971b). *The transparent self: Self-disclosure and well-being.* Princeton, N.J.: Van Nostrand. Jourard proposed in this deeply perceptive book that there are no barriers to human potential that cannot be transcended if people are properly invited to realize this potential.

PETERS, T.J., & WATERMAN, R.H. (1981). *In search of excellence: Lessons from America's best-run companies.* New York: Harper & Row. Peters and Waterman focused on eight basic characteristics that distinguish highly successful companies. These characteristics involve a number of factors identified by the invitational model, including optimism, trust, respect, and intentionality.

PURKEY, W.W., & NOVAK, J. (1984). *Inviting school success,* 2nd ed. Belmont, Calif.: Wadsworth. Purkey and Novak presented a perceptually based, self-concept approach to professional helping which focuses on inviting and disinviting signal systems that exist in and around schools and that result in success or failure in the classroom.

ROGERS, C.R. (1980). *A way of being.* Boston: Houghton Mifflin. This collection of writings and speeches by Carl Rogers provides an insightful glimpse into Rogers' own professional development and his vision for the future of professional helping in a complex world.

2

FOUNDATIONS OF THE INVITING RELATIONSHIP

It seems clear that relationships which are helpful have different characteristics from relationships which are unhelpful. These differential characteristics have to do primarily with the attitudes of the helping person on the one hand and with the perception of the relationship by the "helpee" on the other.

Carl R. Rogers, *On Becoming a Person,*
1961, p. 49

Counseling theories and organizational models categorize only part of a continuing list of philosophical, psychological, theological, and sociological areas that provide a framework for the practice of professional counseling. Practicing counselors

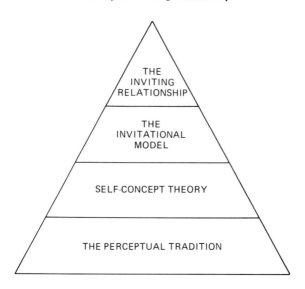

FIGURE 2-1   Foundations of the Inviting Relationship

choose approaches based on their agreement with, and acceptance of, these various theories and models. All approaches to professional counseling have roots in basic assumptions that speculate about what humans are like and how they develop physically, socially, psychologically, and spiritually.

Invitational counseling springs from the mainstreams of three theoretical perspectives: the perceptual tradition, self-concept theory, and the invitational model introduced in Chapter 1. Figure 2-1 illustrates the relationship formed by these three perspectives as they serve as successive foundations in the construction of the inviting relationship. The invitational model was introduced in Chapter 1. This chapter presents an overview of the other two foundations: the perceptual tradition and self-concept theory.

THE PERCEPTUAL TRADITION

> Human behavior is always a product of how people see themselves and the situations in which they are involved. Although this fact seems obvious, the failure of people everywhere to comprehend it is responsible for much of human misunderstanding, maladjustment, conflict, and loneliness. Our perceptions of ourselves and the world are so real to us that we seldom pause to doubt them. Since persons behave in terms of their personal perceptions, effective helping must start with the helper's understanding of the nature and dynamics of perceiving.
>
> A.W. Combs, D.L. Avila, and W.W.
> Purkey, *Helping Relationships,* 2nd ed.,
> 1978, p. 15

The perceptual tradition in professional functioning consists of all those systems of thought in which humans are viewed as they normally see themselves. The term *perceptual* refers not only to the senses but also to meanings—the personal significance of an event for the person experiencing it. These meanings extend far beyond sensory receptors to include such personal experiences as feelings, desires, aspirations, and the ways people view themselves, others, and the world.

The starting point of the perceptual tradition is that each person is a conscious agent: He or she experiences, interprets, constructs, decides, acts, and is ultimately responsible for those actions. Behavior is seen as a product of the ways people see themselves and the situations in which they find themselves. This view is in contrast to other theoretical viewpoints that depict behavior as basically a complex bundle of stimuli and responses or the product of a host of unconscious urges. In the perceptual tradition, primary importance is given to each person's perceived world, rather than to "objective" reality or "unconscious" forces.

Origins of the Perceptual Tradition

The perceptual tradition, which looks at the world as it is experienced by the perceiving person, could probably be traced back to the dawn of history. It is likely that our human ancestors, huddled around a fire in some forgotten cave, pulled their animal skins close around their shoulders and shared their thoughts about their fears, desires, and the ways they felt about themselves, others, and the world around them. Much later, with the advent of written history, people began to give disciplined thought to their own perceptions. Writers would describe this perceptual awareness in terms of "spirit," "psyche," "persona," "ego," "consciousness," "soul," or "self"—all acknowledging that there is an inner consciousness of personal existence.

A turning point in people's thinking about their nonphysical existence came in 1644, when Rene Descartes published *Principles of Philosophy.* In this masterpiece, Descartes proposed that doubt was a principal tool of disciplined inquiry, yet he could not doubt that he doubted! He reasoned that if he doubted, he was thinking, and therefore he must exist. Other philosophers of the period, among them Benedict Spinoza and Gottfried Leibniz, added their thoughts to the mysteries of perceived experience.

At the turn of the present century, when North American psychology began to take its place among the other academic disciplines, there arose a great deal of interest in perception. During this time there were two major American schools of psychology: *structuralism* and *functionalism.* Both schools spent a large amount of time exploring and explaining how people perceive themselves, others, and the world. These early schools of psychology were "laid low" in the early 1920s by the behavioral revolution headed by John B. Watson and his colleagues who argued that the internal worlds of people were too subjective for scientific study.

Although behaviorism dominated North American psychology for about the first half of the present century, from the 1920s to the 1970s, a number of psychologists, psychotherapists, and counselors persisted in the belief that each person consciously experiences events, interprets those experiences, gives them personal meaning, and acts accordingly. This view did not deny the influence of external factors or unconscious processes, but it attempted to place them within the context of human perception. These psychologists, psychotherapists, and counselors did a great deal to keep the perceptual tradition alive.

Among the pioneer perceptually oriented psychologists were George Kelly and his concept of personal constructs (1955, 1963), Gordon Allport and his theory of personality development (1937, 1943, 1955, 1961), and Kurt Goldstein and his work with self-actualization (1939, 1963). Additional support for the perceptual approach came from Germany, where *Gestalt* psychologists provided data from carefully controlled studies that indicated the active, selective nature of the perception process. As Diggory (1966) noted, the fact that these early psychologists were able to argue substantive matters of learning theory and motivation with the behaviorists helped to give perceptual psychologists, psychotherapists, and counselors credibility in the eyes of hostile critics.

Although most of the early researchers and writers on perception were psychologists, psychotherapists, and counselors, contributions to the perceptual approach were made by theologians, educators, philosophers, anthropologists, sociologists, and other scholars from many related fields. The philosophical theologians Paul Tillich and Martin Heidegger added greatly to present conceptions of individuality and personal responsibility, while anthropologists Ivan Malinowski, Ruth Benedict, Margaret Mead, and others forwarded the concepts of human resiliency, adaptability, and potentiality. Well-known sociologists, such as Talcott Parsons and Wilbur Brookover, also contributed heavily to the framework of the perceptual tradition by demonstrating the importance of the social environment on individual perception.

One of the most influential contributors to the perceptual tradition was George Herbert Mead. His classic work *Mind, Self, and Society* (1934) described the development of a person's perceptual world and explained how it becomes differentiated through interactions with significant others. He argued that personality, rather than being anchored in biological variables, environmental pressures, or unconscious forces, was highly active, constantly aware, and heavily influenced by social-psychological factors. Mead and countless other researchers and writers made major contributions to the creation of the perceptual tradition.

Over the years many writers and researchers who were interested in perception banded together and developed their own unique theories and approaches to understanding human experience. These theories and approaches became identified by such names as "phenomenology," "existentialism," "personology," "humanism," "holism," "perceptualism," and "transactionalism." Although differing in name, these various theories sought to understand human existence by focusing on the perceiving person and the ways he or she experiences oneself, others, and the world.

The focus of this book does not permit a proper recognition of the scholars from many disciplines who have contributed major concepts and systems to the perceptual tradition. However, among the many worthy contributors there is one man whose ideas can be singled out as representative of the perceptual approach to understanding humans and their behavior. This person is Arthur W. Combs, and his contribution has come to be called "perceptual psychology."

Perceptual Psychology

I believe the humanist movement in psychology is but a single expression in that discipline of the same deep stirrings in human thought going on everywhere else. Each humanist is attempting to bring some aspect of the basic concept into clearer figure, to give it organization and direction, to discover with greater clarity and sharpness its meaning for the science of behavior. We have called ourselves by different names: Personalists, Transactionalists, Phenomenologists, Self psychologists and Perceptualists, to name but a few. Like the blind man approaching the elephant, we have acquired a multitude of part answers. There is a need now for a unifying system which will provide: (A) a frame of reference capable of encompassing and giving meaning to these diverse contributions, and (B) a theoretical structure for research and innovation. The theme of this paper is to suggest that perceptual psychology can provide a start toward that end.

> Arthur W. Combs, "Why the Humanistic
> Movement Needs a Perceptual
> Psychology," *Journal of the Association
> for the Study of Perception,* 1974,
> *9,* p. 2

One of the most eloquent voices in objecting to what he perceived as the passive tenets of behaviorism and the unconscious forces of Freudianism was that of Arthur W. Combs. The continued insistence of Combs and his colleagues (David Aspy, Donald Avila, Sidney Jourard, Earl Kelley, Ann and Fred Richards, Betty Siegel, Donald Snygg, Daniel Soper, Richard Usher, and Hannalore Wass, among others) on giving major importance to the ways in which people see themselves, others, and the world was a significant contribution to contemporary psychology and counseling and served as a rallying point for many "splinter" theories in the area of perception.

According to Rollo May (1961), the book *Individual Behavior: A Perceptual Approach to Behavior* by Snygg and Combs (1949; 2nd ed., Combs & Snygg, 1959), was the first to state the position of the "American" school of phenomenology (the study of human consciousness). In this book and others, Combs and associates (1962, 1965, 1969, 1974, 1976, 1978, 1984) proposed that perception is the primary component in human behavior. They maintained that the basic drive of each individual is the maintenance, protection, and enhancement of the perceived self: one's own personal existence as viewed by oneself.

As explained by Combs, Avila and Purkey (1978), the perceptual tradition seeks to understand human behavior through the "eye of the beholder," that is, from the perspective of the person's own personal and unique experiences. Their position was that all behavior is dependent upon the individual's personal frame of reference and is a function of the perceptions that exist for the person at the moment of behaving.

Basic Assumptions

There are some basic "earmarks" of the perceptual tradition. These are reflected in the following fourteen assumptions:

1. There may be a preexistent reality, but an individual can only know that part which comprises his or her perceptual world, the world of awareness.
2. Perceptions at any given moment exist at countless levels of awareness, from the vaguest to the sharpest.
3. Because people are limited in what they can perceive, they are highly selective in what they *choose* to perceive.
4. All experiences are phenomenal in character: The fact that two individuals share the same physical environment does not mean that they will have the same experiences.
5. What individuals choose to perceive is determined by past experiences as mediated by present purposes, perceptions, and expectations.
6. Individuals tend to perceive only that which is relevant to their purposes and make their choices accordingly.
7. Choices are determined by perceptions, not facts. How a person behaves is a function of his or her perceptual field at the moment of acting.
8. No perception can ever be fully shared or totally communicated because it is embedded in the life of the individual.
9. "Phenomenal absolutism" means that people tend to assume that other observers perceive as they do. If others perceive differently, it is often thought to be because others are mistaken or because they lie.
10. The perceptual field, including the perceived self, is internally organized and personally meaningful. When this organization and meaning are threatened, emotional problems are likely to result.
11. Communication depends on the process of acquiring greater mutual understanding of one another's phenomenal fields.
12. People not only perceive the world of the present but they also reflect on past experiences and imagine future ones to guide their behavior.
13. Beliefs can and do create their own social reality. People respond with feelings not to "reality" but to their perceptions of reality.
14. Reality can exist for an individual only when he or she is conscious of it and has some relationship with it.

Judging by the 14 assumptions, it seems clear that the perceptual tradition is centered on the basic premise that all behavior is a function of the individual's perceptual field. A person's behavior may make little sense when observed from the "external" views of other people, but this same behavior makes great sense when understood from the vantage point of the "internal" view of the experiencing person.

The approach of Arthur Combs, Sidney Jourard, Earl Kelley, Abraham Maslow, Rollo May, Carl Rogers, Donald Snygg, and others representing the perceptual tradition is in contrast to both the psychoanalytic tradition, which views behavior as determined by unconscious historical events buried in the personality, and the strict behavioral tradition, which stresses the importance of learning based only on environmental stimuli and responses.

Thanks to the recent contributions of perceptually oriented scholars such as Aspy's perceptual characteristics of effective helpers (1972), Chamberlin's "preflections" of the future (1981), Meichenbaum's perceived self-efficacy studies (1974, 1977), and Powers' integration of perception with systems theory (1973), the perceptual tradition continues to develop and be applied to the study of helping relationships. It has also served as the essential building block for self-concept theory.

SELF-CONCEPT THEORY

> Important to modern man is not only the knowledge of the universe and some kind of civilized peaceful, ordered and materially adequate living—essential as these are to his maintenance and well-being. But more centrally and more personally, it is man himself that is of basic concern. He must finally live with himself. He is blessed or condemned by the fact that he must be his own agent and his own implement not only in the process of knowing and civilizing, but also in the process of living.
>
> Charles A. Curran, *Counseling and*
> *Psychotherapy: The Pursuit of Values,*
> 1968, p. 32

Of all the perceptions we experience in the course of living, none has more profound significance than the perceptions we hold regarding our own personal existence—our view of who we are and how we fit into the world. "The world has many centers," wrote Thomas Mann, "one for each created being." It is this center of created being that has come to be called *self-concept.*

In the center of every person's existence there seems to be a special recording studio that records every inviting or disinviting signal that arrives over various sensory pathways. These recordings are filed in such a way that they can be taken out by the experiencing person and played back again and again. As long as the recordings are messages affirming personal value, ability, and responsibility and containing hope, respect, and trust, the individual is strengthened in these perceptions and is likely to behave accordingly. When the recordings are messages announcing personal worthlessness, inability, and irresponsibility and containing pessimism, contempt, and suspicion, to that degree the person loses faith in oneself and one's abilities. Few, if any, can withstand the continued contempt of fellow human beings.

At present, comprehensive statements about the characteristics and origins of self-concept remain in the realm of theory. But an analysis of the various explanations of self and a review of related research provide valuable insights into how people see themselves.

Reviews of research on self-concept have been provided (Purkey, 1970; Hamachek, 1978; Wylie, 1979), and so an extended review of the literature is unnecessary. However, the following analysis of self-concept expands upon previous research and writing by Purkey (1970), Combs, Avila, and Purkey (1978), and Purkey and Novak (1984).

Qualities of the Self

Self-concept may be defined as the totality of a complex and dynamic system of learned beliefs that an individual holds to be true about his or her personal existence and that gives consistency to his or her personality. Embedded in this definition are five important characteristics regarding the self: it is (1) organized, (2) dynamic, (3) consistent, (4) modifiable, and (5) learned. These characteristics can be illustrated by a simple drawing, even though there are weaknesses in using a drawing to represent the multifaceted, multilayered, highly abstract, and hierarchical constellation of active ideas called self-concept. Yet analogies are helpful in expressing complex ideas. Therefore, the reader is directed to Figure 2-2 in which the five characteristics of self-concept are presented.

Self-concept is organized. Most self-concept theorists, such as Combs (1982), Combs, Richards, and Richards (1976), Jourard (1964), Purkey (1970), Rogers (1947, 1951, 1967), and Wylie (1979), agree that the self has a generally stable quality that is characterized by orderliness and harmony. To picture this internal symmetry please consider Figure 2-2 and imagine that the large spiral represents the organized unity of the self, which can be thought of as the "global self." The global self is orchestrated and balanced within itself, but it also contains smaller units. These units can be thought of as "subselves" and are pictured as small "me" spirals. These subselves represent the self-as-object, the various "me's" that are the objects of self-perception. Each of the small me-spirals within the global system is organized and balanced within itself, yet each is influenced by, and in turn influences, the global self.

The smaller me-spirals represent specific beliefs that a person holds to be true about his or her personal existence. These beliefs can be roughly divided into *attributes* (that is, strong, tall, loyal, short, fat, bright, young, friendly, trustworthy, sexy, and so forth) and *categories* (student, husband, mother, Christian, tennis player, American, veteran, Jew, lover, and so on). Perceived attributes and categories usually join together (for example, "good student," "loyal American," "sexy lover") and are positioned by the perceiving person in a hierarchical order within the global self. This order is critical for it gives meaning and stability to the entire self-system.

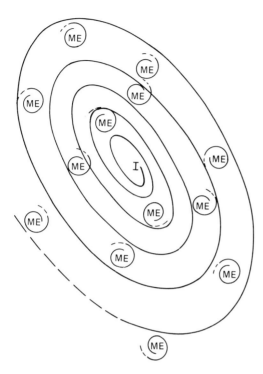

FIGURE 2-2 Self-Concept Analogy

Each person maintains countless subself me's regarding oneself, but not all are equally significant. Some are highly important and are located close to the center of the global self. This center is marked with an "I" in Figure 2-2 to indicate immediate personal awareness. It is this "I" that Fromm (1956) so beautifully referred to as "life being aware of itself" (Fromm, p. 8). Humans are aware of themselves, others, the world around them, as well as their past histories, and future potentials. It is this self awareness that gives consistency to the human personality.

Other subself me's are less central and therefore located toward the outside of the global self. Subselves closest to the "I" have the most influence on daily functioning; the individual "hears" those subselves the loudest for they are closest to the center of the self. By the same token, those subselves farthest away from the "I" have the weakest voices and thus have diminished influence on behavior.

The open areas between the lines of the global spiral in Figure 2-2 represent the "space" each person requires to evaluate oneself fairly and grow properly. Some people can become so crowded internally with often contradictory me's that they experience a sort of sensory overload, continuously adding subself me's without letting go of any.

George Sweazy, a graduate student of one of the authors, suggested an imaginative way of understanding the difference between the central "I" and the me's that surround it. The "I" can be imagined as a source of light. Light travels in all directions through the universe, but it is only visible when it strikes something. By analogy, the "I" of personal existence becomes visible only when it reflects off the various me's. The "I" cannot see itself directly, no more than the human eye can see itself. It is through the mirrored reflections of countless me's that the "I" can know itself.

As early as 1961, C.M. Lowe postulated that some parts of the self-system are peripheral and are therefore relatively unstable, while other parts are more central to the self (close to the "I") and are highly resistant to change. For example, who has not heard the comment, "Oh, I couldn't do that; that's just not me"? Anyone who has attempted to give up a cherished belief about oneself, or accept one that does not seem to "fit," can understand how difficult a task it is to change one's perceptions of personal existence.

In her classic studies of individuals in distress, Horney (1939) reported that individuals tend to cling to their pretensions as a drowning person clings to a straw. Closely held beliefs about oneself are difficult to change, while lightly held beliefs change easily. This concept has important implications for the inviting relationship, as explained in future chapters.

A second organizational feature of the self is that each subself (represented by a small me-spiral) has its own generally negative or positive value, or "charge." For example, being a homosexual might be very close to the center of the self, but this could be valued negatively by the experiencing individual. He or she might think, "Being a homosexual is the most significant thing about me, and I am constantly aware of it. But it is not good to be a homosexual." Thus, each subself carries its own plus or minus charge that contributes to the global self, positively or negatively.

A third organizational quality of the self is that perceived success and failure tend to generalize throughout the entire self-system. In his extensive research, Diggory (1966) concluded that when one dimension of the perceived self is important and highly valued by a person, a failure in that dimension lowers his or her self-evaluation in other seemingly unrelated abilities. Conversely, success in a highly valued activity tends to raise self-evaluations in other apparently unconnected abilities. This spread-of-effect phenomenon has been documented by Blailiffe (1978), Ludwig and Maehr (1967), and others.

To illustrate the spread-of-effect phenomenon, please return to Figure 2-2 and imagine each subself (small me-spirals) to be a tiny bell. When one bell sounds, all others chime in, echoing to some degree the positive or negative note sounded. This process can be illustrated by the perceptions of a professional athlete. If a professional football player considers himself to be an excellent athlete, and being an outstanding player is close to the "I" and highly valued, then consistent success on the football field raises self-regard in other, apparently unrelated, areas, such as outside business ventures or public-speaking activities. However, one caveat is necessary: A high achiever in any endeavor may become most unhappy with success if the achievement is not valued in the eyes of significant others. Individuals require positive regard from others as well as from themselves. Only those with a most atypical personality could, over time, retain a positive self-concept in the face of consistently disinviting external forces.

One final organizational feature of self-concept is that each person's self is marvelously unique. Like fingerprints, voice quality, or dental charts, no two people hold identical sets of beliefs about themselves. It is this uniqueness that makes for an infinite variety of human personalities. This uniqueness also helps explain problems in communication. Because no two people ever perceive exactly the same way, it is often difficult for them to agree about what it is they experience. For example, a counselor will need special sensitivity to understand the perceptual world of the Western Apache, where questions display "an unnatural curiosity," handshaking "violates a person's territory," and talking about trouble "increases its chances of occurrence" (Basso, 1979). Because there may be sharp perceptual differences between counselors and those they seek to help, mastery of *attending skills,* to be introduced in Chapter 5, is essential.

Self-concept is dynamic. Combs and associates (1959, 1962, 1978) have postulated that the maintenance, protection, and enhancement of the perceived self (one's own personal existence as viewed by oneself) are the basic motivations behind all human behavior. For example, a corporate executive might be neglecting her official duties (the "executive me" that she does not see as an important part of herself) while spending many hours on the golf course improving her already superior skills and polishing her valued self-as-golfer image. People tend to behave in ways that are most central to the self and closest to the "I." The self-concept is a road map for living.

To understand the dynamic nature of the self, picture the global spiral as a sort of personal gyrocompass: a continuously active system of subjective beliefs that dependably point to the "true north" of a person's perceived existence. This guidance system not only shapes the ways each person sees oneself, others, and the world, but it also serves to direct actions and enables each individual to take a consistent "stance" in life. Rather than viewing self-concept as the *cause* of behavior, self-concept is better understood as the gyrocompass of the human personality, providing consistency in personality and direction for behavior.

As explained by Spears and Deese (1973), self-concept is not the cause of a person's behavior, as some professionals assume. In the case of misbehavior, for example, the self-concept does not *cause* the problem. A better explanation is that the disruptive person has learned to see himself or herself as a troublemaker, that this self-image is closer to the center of the global self, and therefore the person is behaving accordingly. In a similar explanation of self, Shavelson, Hubner, and Stanton (1976) referred to self-concept as a "moderator variable" that serves as the reference point, or anchoring perception, for behavior.

Additional evidence regarding the dynamic nature of the self has been provided by Zimmerman and Allebrand (1965). They demonstrated that poor readers in school lack a sense of personal worth and adequacy to the point where they actively avoid achievement. For poor readers, to study hard and still fail provides unbearable proof of personal inadequacy. To avoid such proof and to suffer less pain, many students deliberately choose not to try. Their defense against failure is to accept themselves as failures. From their point of view it is better not to try than to try and be embarrassed or humiliated. By not trying, they maintain control. Glock (1972) stated the situation succinctly: "A negative self-image is its own best defender" (Glock, 1972, p. 406). To understand why this is so, it is important to recognize that, from the person's perceptual vantage point, any amount of anxiety involved in a particular action, no matter how painful, seems preferable to other available avenues of behavior. Counseling can be a tremendous help in such cases by assisting students in reevaluating and reorganizing their perceptions.

Self-concept is consistent. A noteworthy feature of self-concept is that it requires internal consistency. To maintain this consistency of personality each person acts in accordance with the ways he or she has learned to view oneself in an almost compulsive manner. From a lifetime of studying his or her own actions and those of others, each person acquires expectations about what things fit and what behaviors are appropriate in the person's perceived world. All subselves that exist within the global self-system are expected by the perceiver to be consistent with all others, no matter how inconsistent they may be from an external viewpoint. When these expectations are not fulfilled, "cognitive dissonance" results, which is the uncomfortable state of incompatible perceptions. This discomfort, according to Festinger (1962), is most apparent when one behaves in a way that is not in keeping with one's self-image.

If a new experience is consistent with experiences already incorporated into the self-system, the individual easily accepts and assimilates it. But if the new experience is in opposition with those already incorporated, the person will actively reject it. As Jersild (1952) described the process: "A person accepts and incorporates that which is congenial to the self-systems already established, but he seeks to reject and avoid experiences or meanings of the experiences which are uncongenial" (Jersild, 1952, p. 14). People seek support for their perceived self-identity, and they avoid evidence that threatens it. According to self-concept theory, there can be little happiness if the things a person believes to be true about oneself are in opposition to the things one does.

In understanding the consistency of self, it is important to consider how things appear from an *internal* point of view. Cases of anorexia illustrate this phenomenon. People who have anorexia see themselves as fat in spite of the fact that they are dangerously underweight. To reduce their "fatness" they avoid food, sometimes to the point of starvation. Individual behavior has a certain internal "logic" no matter how illogical, counter-productive, and self-defeating a particular behavior may appear to be from an *external* viewpoint. Counselors who can understand, accept (not agree), and reflect these internally logical perceptions to clients are in a good position to help clients reconsider them.

Sometimes the global self is comprised of contradictory subselves. Yet these various me's can coexist happily and may never encounter or challenge one another as long as the experiencing individual does not perceive the contradictions. For example, a father may neglect his own children while working actively with a youth group. It is only when the person faces some identity crisis, or becomes aware of the contradictions among self-perceptions, that resolution of the dissonance is required. If the dissonance is not resolved, the individual will suffer emotional distress. Again, in such cases counseling can be of great benefit.

Behaviors that are incompatible with the self-concept are likely to result in psychological discomfort and anxiety. For example, at a recent human sexuality conference, a university infirmary physician noted the reluctance of some coeds to use oral contraceptives although they were having sexual relations. When these coeds were questioned as to why they did not practice contraception, they responded with the reasoning that if they used contraception they would obviously be planning to engage in sexual activity, which they considered "bad" and could not accept. By not taking pills or using other contraceptive measures when they had sexual intercourse, they maintained the belief that they were "swept off their feet" in a moment of passion. "Spontaneous" sexual activity was far more acceptable to their self-image than the "premeditated" sort. Thus, people behave according to their perceptions even if the behavior seems to others to be odd or even self-defeating. Everything a person experiences is filtered through, and mediated by, whatever self-concept is already present in the self-system. This screening and mediating process insures internal consistency within the human personality and external consistency in individual behavior.

The tendency toward consistency appears to be an essential feature of the human personality. It provides the person with internal balance, a sense of direction, feelings of stability, and a certain consistency in behaviors. If individuals adopted new beliefs about themselves easily, or if their behaviors were unpredictable, the human personality would lack integrity. Under such conditions society would be difficult to imagine.

Counselors who understand the tendency toward self-consistency do not expect quick changes in themselves or others. People cannot be picked up and quickly shaped into something more suitable or desirable. It took a long time for individuals to get where they are now, and it will take time for them to change. Whether a person's self-concept is healthy or unhealthy, productive or counterproductive, it resists change.

One additional example might be useful here. Doctors and nurses often find it difficult to get patients who are diagnosed as diabetic to care for themselves properly. Such patients find it difficult to accept their new "diabetic me" and the accompanying use of insulin and dietary requirements. It takes time to assimilate this new "me" into the self-system. It is interesting to note that the English language allows a diabetic to reveal his or her self-concept by saying "I *am* diabetic." Certain conditions and diseases are not allowed this freedom. One never hears, "I *am* cancerous." Instead, a forced distancing process takes place: "I *have* cancer."

The consistency phenomenon may also be seen in schools. Students who have learned to see themselves as stupid will experience considerable anxiety over their own successful performance (Aronson & Carlsmith, 1962; Curtis, Zanna, & Campbell, 1975; Haan, 1963; Mettee, 1971). Moreover, students who have learned to expect failure may even sabotage their own efforts when they meet unexpected success. As Jersild (1952) noted, individuals are active in maintaining their self-postures "even if by misfortune the picture is a false and unhealthy one" (Jersild, 1962, p. 14).

One provocative insight relating to self-consistency is that being correct in one's assumptions about oneself has reward value, even if the assumption is negative. A student may take a certain pleasure in thinking, "See, just as I thought! I knew nobody in this damn school cares whether I live or die!" Being right, even about negative feelings toward oneself, can be satisfying.

Even though self-concept tends toward consistency, significant changes in the self are possible. Each person is involved in an endless quest for positive self-esteem and the favorable esteem of significant others. Over time and under certain conditions one's self-image can undergo significant alterations. The optimistic news for counselors is that self-concept is modifiable.

Self-concept is modifiable.   In each reasonably healthy person new perceptions filter into the self-concept throughout life while old ones fade away. This continuous flow creates flexibility in the human character and allows for infinite modifiability of the perceived self. The reason for the assimilation of new ideas and the expulsion of old ones is the quest to maintain, protect, and enhance the perceived self. This process involves an endless search for positive self-regard and favorable regard from others.

As noted earlier, the self-concept is not just the sum total of perceptions; it is also the ability to be conscious of these perceptions and to view them as favorably as possible. People tend to think as well of themselves and their prospects as circumstances permit, even if their thought processes are out of kilter with the external world.

The basic assumption that each person is constantly seeking to maintain, protect, and enhance his or her psychological self is a tremendous "given" for the counselor, for it means that the self is predisposed toward modification and development. Rather than seeking ways to "motivate" clients, the inviting relationship is based on the assumption that people are *always* motivated. People may not do what others wish them to do, but this does not mean that they are unmotivated. Counselors who accept this assumption can shift their energies away from a "doing to" process of trying to motivate people and toward a "doing with" process of helping people to modify their self-perceptions and choose the direction this already present motivation will take.

It is helpful to consider motivation from a self-concept point of view. According to Combs and Snygg (1959), Avila and Purkey (1966), Purkey (1970), and others, there is only one kind of human motivation—an internal and continuous incentive that every individual has at all times, in all places, during any activity.

Understanding human motivation from this perspective is a tremendous advantage for counselors, for it assumes that motivation is a basic force that comes from within the human being. Counselors who accept this view can use their talents in seeking a "doing with" rather than a "doing to" relationship with clients by assisting them in altering their self-perceptions. A "doing with" relationship encourages a cooperative spirit of mutual learning, which introduces another quality of the self: It is learned.

Self-concept is learned.   There are three general ways in which people change their self-perceptions, either for good or ill. The first way is through an extremely traumatic or ecstatic event. All of us have witnessed how the tragic loss of a loved one, or the joyous arrival of a baby, can have such impact that the very structure of a person's self-concept undergoes significant change (that is, "I am now a widow," "I am now a mother," "I am now retired"). The impact of such momentous events interrupts abruptly the internal balance of the self-concept and points it in a new direction.

A second way that people change their self-perceptions is through a professional helping relationship, such as spiritual guidance, medical treatment, or professional counseling. An abundance of empirical research has demonstrated that counseling and related therapeutic approaches can be beneficial in altering both self-regard and the regard of others. In addition, scientific and medical interventions continue to surpass our greatest expectations in overcoming handicaps and helping individuals to live long and healthy lives. Various forms of professional service, both separately and in conjunction with one another, can have powerful effects on self-concept.

But the third and greatest influence on self-concept takes place in repeated everyday experiences and events. Repeated experiences, either inviting or disinviting, witting or unwitting, can have a profound effect on the self. Children can be gradually but profoundly crippled by adults who were themselves psychologically crippled as children. In schools students who are repeatedly invited or disinvited gradually begin to see themselves as successes or failures. In business, workers who are consistently encouraged to participate in decision-making processes, or who are repeatedly excluded from such processes, will eventually see themselves as either valued participants or as mindless functionaries.

People become the ways they are treated, as W. Somerset Maugham explained in the *Razor's Edge*: "For men and women are not only themselves; they are also the region in which they were born, the city apartment or farm in which they learned to walk, the games they played as children, the old wives' tale they overheard, the food they ate, the schools they attended, the sports they followed, the poems they read, and the God they believed in." The confidence and enthusiasm brought on by honest successes, or the self-doubt and apathy brought on by successive failures, combine to shape each person's personality and influence every aspect of human functioning. This introduces a final characteristic of the self: It is a lifelong process.

The Self as a Lifelong Process

As far as is known, no one is born with a self-concept. It emerges experience by experience, thought by thought, perception by perception, filament by filament. Gradually, the self is acquired and modified through the constantly accumulating experiences of the developing person. This marvelous development has been described by numerous writers and researchers; the most graphic accounts are those of Cooley (1902), Mead (1934), Sullivan (1947), Jersild (1952), Block (1952), Farber (1962), Kelly (1963), Goldstein (1963), and Coopersmith (1967), among many others. What these authors make clear is that the construction of the self is a lifelong research project. The self is developed through accumulated experiences, accompanied by the constant interpretation of events in ways congruent with what is already present in the self-system.

As each person develops, his or her self-concept becomes increasingly complex and multifaceted. By experiencing the world through interactions with significant others, as well as through interactions with oneself, each person forges a self-concept, complete with many subselves, all organized into a consistent and dynamic system.

Of all contemporary theories and models of counseling, none depends more on self-concept theory than does the inviting relationship. Invitational counseling gives major importance to the counselor's and client's self and suggests ways to invite positive and realistic self-images in both parties. Because self-concept does not appear to be instinctive, but is learned through experience, it therefore possesses infinite capacity for growth and actualization. This capacity offers great optimism for the counselor who works to create the inviting relationship.

RATIONALE FOR INVITATIONAL COUNSELING

When choosing theories and models for professional functioning, practicing counselors seek a logical rationale for making a particular choice. Therefore, the following six-point rationale for invitational counseling is offered.

First, invitational counseling has potential for broad application. It cuts across traditional boundaries, counselor roles, therapeutic classifications, and professional practices. It encompasses almost all areas of human growth and development: psychological, social, and physical. In addition, it focuses not only on people but also on places, policies, and programs that influence people's lives. This wide-lens approach is not true of most counseling theories and approaches. Thus, it has the potential for application in a wide variety of situations throughout the helping professions.

Second, it is complementary. As an expanded model for professional practice, invitational counseling embraces and incorporates various approaches to the professional helping relationship. It provides a bridge between seemingly dissimilar viewpoints, such as "humanistic" and "behavioristic," "directive" and "nondirective," and "deterministic" and "free will" approaches.

A third quality of invitational counseling is that it is relatively easy to conceptualize and understand, to some extent even by young children. The fundamental ideas and concepts of the inviting relationship can be explained in terms relative to people's everyday experience and developmental levels. Its practical qualities allow the process to be operationalized at various developmental levels and to be entered into by people at almost all ages.

Fourth, invitational counseling is therapeutic in the highest ethical sense and is congruent with all major assumptions regarding the nature of healthy human development. It respects the autonomy and self-directing powers of the individual and advocates personal responsibility. Further, it strives for mutual cooperation, respect, and trust. Each participant in the inviting relationship is expected to establish "rules" under which his or her actions are governed. At the same time, each participant accepts the concept that others have the right and responsibility to establish their rules as well.

A fifth feature is that invitational counseling lends itself to both process and outcome research. The inviting relationship consists of stated theoretical foundations and systematic processes. These foundations and processes, when combined into a model of personal and professional functioning, are observable, measurable, and subject to empirical research and evaluation.

Sixth, and perhaps most important in establishing a rationale for invitational counseling, is that it is optimistic. Because it maintains that people are valuable, capable, and self-directing, invitational counseling presents an affirmative developmental model. It focuses on the positive and uplifting aspects of human existence and development.

Embedded in the six-point rationale for the inviting relationship is the implicit notion that the counselor is only one part of the client's life. No matter how much, and in how many ways, clients seek to have the counselor take charge, in the inviting relationship the client is the only one who is clearly responsible for his or her own life. Positive regard and respect for the client's right to self-determination are at the center of the inviting relationship, and these serve as the basic rationale for its existence.

SUMMARY

This chapter has presented the twin pillars supporting the invitational model and the inviting relationship: the perceptual tradition and self-concept theory. These two supporting systems have contributed significantly to the development of the invitational model and thus to the creation and application of the inviting relationship.

An understanding of the perceptual tradition is essential to the effective practice of invitational counseling. Therefore, a brief history of the perceptual tradition was presented along with some illustrations of the role of perception in everyday life.

Self-concept theory and its relationship to invitational counseling was also described in this chapter. The development of self-concept was outlined, along with its major organizational characteristics and the significant role it plays in the course of human development. In particular, the significant impact of repeated and incessant inviting or disinviting events on the developing self was explained.

Finally, a brief rationale for invitational counseling was provided. This consists of six points: Invitational counseling is (1) applicable, (2) complementary, (3) practical, (4) therapeutic, (5) verifiable, and (6) optimistic. The next chapter will present the ingredients of the inviting relationship and will consider in detail the four levels of invitational counseling introduced in Chapter 1.

OPPORTUNITIES FOR FURTHER READING

All writing is communication; creative writing is communication through revelation—it is the self escaping into the open. No writer long remains incognito.

William Strunk, Jr. and E.B. White,
The Elements of Style, 1959, p. 53

BUBER, M. (1958). *I and thou.* New York: Scribner's. The first English edition of this classic book appeared in 1937. In his poetic and somewhat mystical style of writing, Buber explored the phenomenon of human existence.

COOPERSMITH, S. (1967). *The antecedents of self-esteem.* San Francisco: W.H. Freeman & Company. In a series of carefully constructed studies, Coopersmith described the antecedents and consequences of self-esteem in children. He concluded that parental warmth, clearly defined limits, and respectful treatment were the primary forces in inviting positive self-regard in children.

AVILA, D., COMBS, A., & PURKEY, W. (1977). *The helping relationship sourcebook,* 2nd ed. Boston: Allyn & Bacon. This book of readings brings together a collection of original papers of broad relevance to professional helpers. Papers by Carl Rogers, Earl Kelley, Donald Snygg, David Aspy, and others explain and illuminate the perceptual tradition in professional helping.

COMBS, A., RICHARDS, A., & RICHARDS, F. (1976). *Perceptual psychology: A humanistic approach to the study of persons.* New York: Harper & Row. Originally published in 1949 under the title *Individual behavior: A new frame of reference for psychology,* by Donald Snygg and Arthur Combs, this book updates and expands the perceptual tradition in professional helping. It points out that perceptual psychology is more than an expression of the humanist movement; it is also a frame of reference for the solution of major problems facing humanity.

GOFFMAN, E. (1959). *The presentation of self in everyday life.* Garden City, N.Y.: Doubleday. This widely quoted book presents a sociological perspective of the ways individuals present themselves to others, the ways they seek to guide and control the impressions others have of them, and the things they do, and *not* do, while presenting their selves to others.

HAMACHEK, D.E. (1978). *Encounters with the self,* 2nd ed. New York: Holt, Rinehart & Winston. Hamachek focused on the very private self-picture that each person carries inside and which defines who one is and what one can and cannot do. Hamachek explained how this picture is developed, changed, and expressed in everyday behavior.

JOHNSON, D.W. (1981). *Reaching out: Interpersonal effectiveness and self-actualization,* 2nd ed. Englewood Cliffs, N.J.: Prentice-Hall. *Reaching Out* examines the process of accepting oneself and others and offers many ways to accomplish this accepting process. Johnson maintained that psychological health depends almost entirely on the quality of human relationships.

MASLOW, A.H. (1962). *Toward a psychology of being.* New York: D. Van Nostrand. This book is a continuation of Maslow's *Motivation and Personality* first published in 1954. Maslow expands on his thesis that all science needs to do to help in positive fulfillment of the human condition is to enlarge and deepen the conception of its nature so that it includes the "inner view" of human existence.

MAY, R. (1966). *Existential psychology.* New York: Random House. The existential philosophers whose works appear in this book of readings agree that reality must be seen in terms of human experiences that transcend rational thinking. As May explained, "there is no such thing as truth or reality for a living human being except as he participates in it, is conscious of it, has some relationship to it" (May, 1966, p. 17).

ROGERS, C.R. (1969). *Freedom to learn.* Columbus, Ohio: Chas. E. Merrill. The theme of this book is that students can be trusted to learn and to enjoy learning when a facilitative person sets up environments that encourage responsible participation in selecting and reaching goals.

3

INGREDIENTS OF THE INVITING RELATIONSHIP

Of all the exciting developments that have taken place, there is none more basic than the realization that a counselor can gain the whole world and lose his or her own soul . . . to me the most striking personal discovery of the past decade has been that people respond to my degree of caring more than to my degree of knowing.

> C. Gilbert Wrenn, *The World of the*
> *Contemporary Counselor,* 1973,
> pp. 248-249

The first two chapters of this book presented the invitational model and the twin pillars of the inviting relationship: the perceptual tradition and self-concept theory. This chapter introduces the ingredients of invitational counseling and explores in detail the four levels of professional functioning introduced in Chapter 1.

As with building a house, designing a boat, or baking a cake, the first consideration, after a blueprint, design, or recipe is decided on, is the quality of the ingredients and materials to be used. So it is with invitational counseling. Once the philosophy and theoretical foundations have been explicitly stated and understood, the next step is to consider the ingredients: the counselor's characteristics and the nature of professional functioning.

This chapter analyzes three ingredients related to the professional counselor and his or her functioning. The first analysis focuses on the system of beliefs that the counselor holds regarding oneself, others, and counseling. The second analysis considers the degree of intentionality the counselor and client use to forge a therapeutic alliance. The third analysis explores the concept of responsibility, which is central to respect and trust. Each will be considered in turn, followed by its integration into the four levels of professional functioning.

BELIEFS ABOUT SELF, OTHERS, AND COUNSELING

An idea whose time has come: the gradually formed and tested hypothesis that the individual has within himself vast resources for self-understanding, for altering his self-concept, his attitudes, and his self-directed behavior—and that these resources can be tapped if only a definable climate of facilitative psychological attitudes can be provided.

> Carl Rogers, "In Retrospect—Forty-six
> Years," *American Psychologist,* 1974,
> *29,* p. 115

The inviting relationship is founded in the perceptual tradition, self-concept theory, and the invitational model. This foundation can be seen in invitational counseling's axiom that for practicing counselors to develop and maintain helping relationships, it is essential that they nurture their ability to take an "internal" frame of reference: to view persons as they see themselves, others, and the world. Focusing on unresolved unconscious conflicts or on contingencies of reinforcement may remove problems, but from an invitational viewpoint there is an even greater potential in the counselor-client relationship: to develop fully. To achieve this potential, counselors require sensitivity to their own perceptions and those of their clients, and they need to understand how these perceptions interact with three existential questions embedded within the counseling relationship.

Client Perceptions

Invitational counseling assumes that people choose their actions—the ways they elect to function—and that these choices are made on the basis of the beliefs they maintain and the images they hold about themselves, others, and the world. These decision-making processes allow for consistency in thought and action and make individual personalities possible. They also explain individual differences in perception that occur constantly in the course of daily interactions.

An example of individual differences in perception may be observed when a couple attends a movie. Upon leaving the theater one praises the film, exclaiming, "It was the best I've ever seen!" The other person responds incredulously, "I thought it would never end!" Contrasting perceptions occurred even though they sat next to each other in the same theater for two hours, viewing the same film, even eating out of the same box of popcorn!

A similar indication of the relative uniqueness of perceptions is often witnessed by family counselors. The mother states that her rules are too lenient, while her teenage daughter complains, "Mom never lets me do anything!" Parents and children are sometimes at odds because of their individual perceptions of the same external events. They may agree on some aspects of what took place but differ dramatically in the meanings they attribute to them. Thus the uniqueness of personal perceptions permits an endless variety of interpretations of the same event.

From birth, individuals assimilate countless perceived objects, situations, interactions, and relationships into their perceptual fields. Based on this assimilated content, they then choose actions that seem most appropriate to their perceived fields. Moreover, people monitor, to various degrees, their own behavior and its impact on themselves, others, and the world. Information obtained through these processes is filtered through their perceptual system, which either confirms the perceptions in the perceptual fields or requires an alteration.

For example, a man who perceives himself as a capable company employee and good family provider may seek additional responsibilities at the office and at home. His consistently enthusiastic performance results in his continued success at the office and at home. These achievements produce praise from both employer

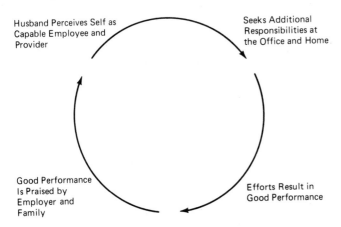

Husband Perceives Self as Capable Employee and Provider

Seeks Additional Responsibilities at the Office and Home

Good Performance Is Praised by Employer and Family

Efforts Result in Good Performance

FIGURE 3-1 Cyclical Relationship of Self-Perceptions

and family, who, respectively, tell him what a capable employee and provider he is. These messages validate and encourage his self-enhancing actions. The cyclical relationship, as demonstrated in Figure 3-1, continues to spiral in beneficial directions.

Through countless and continuous interactions, people develop both negative and positive perceptions about themselves, others, and the world. While a majority of these perceptions will undergo change over time, some fundamental ones remain relatively stable. It is these core perceptions that guide decisions and serve as a "frame of reference for judgment" (Combs and others, 1976, p. 109). These core perceptions serve as psychological road maps for living and are the heart of one's self-concept.

In the inviting relationship the counselor realizes that a client's perceptions are central to that person's total being. This realization permits the counselor to understand and accept the concerns that clients have with the views of others that contradict their own perceptions. The counselor who does not understand or accept the client's perceptual concerns, no matter how "wrong" these perceptions may be from the "external" viewpoint (in this case, the counselor's point of view), initiates an adversarial posture that is likely to weaken or destroy the inviting relationship.

Understanding, accepting, and accurately reflecting the client's perceptions serve to create a bond with which the client and counselor can explore feelings and examine ways of experiencing oneself, others, and the world. This pattern of understanding, accepting, and reflecting is a different process from agreement. A counselor can understand, accept, and reflect a client's perception that she or he is a worthless person without *agreeing* to that perception. The time for confrontation regarding differential perceptions may come, but it should be preceded by the client's understanding that he or she has been heard, understood, and that his or her feelings have been accepted and accurately reflected. This is part of the counselor's "stance" introduced in Chapter 1.

Counseling an alcoholic client provides an example of the understanding, accepting, and reflecting process. If a counselor refuses to understand, accept, and reflect the client's perception that she or he is *not* an alcoholic ("I'm just a social drinker"), but rather insists on forcing the alcoholic label on the client, it is likely to inhibit a productive counselor–client alliance. On the other hand, if the counselor understands, accepts, and reflects the client's perception of oneself as a social drinker, involvement at this level can productively assess current drinking habits, behaviors, and any resulting problems perceived by the client. Again, acceptance does not mean agreement. The counselor may decide at some appropriate point to confront the client about the contradictions between what he or she perceives to be true about the use of alcohol and how he or she uses alcohol and behaves when drinking. When done appropriately, confrontation is a most inviting way to interact with a client. The skill of confrontation from an invitational perspective will be presented in Chapter 5.

The centerpiece in understanding, accepting, and reflecting client perceptions is *acceptance*. No matter what interviewing approach is used, whether it is the life-style questionnaire of Adlerian counseling (Dinkmeyer & Dinkmeyer, 1977), script analysis of Transactional Analysis (Steiner, 1974), paraphrasing and reflection of client-centered therapy (Rogers, 1961), or one of many other therapeutic processes, the essential element is a genuine acceptance of client perceptions, to accept without protest the client's expressed feelings. In developing the ability to accept the perceptions of clients, an essential ingredient is the counselor's ability to understand, accept, and reflect his or her own perceptions *within oneself.*

Counselor Perceptions

Countless variables have been related to counseling outcomes, including counselor traits (Felker, 1973; Vargas & Borkowski, 1983), counselor behaviors (Dell, 1973), environmental factors (Chaikin, Derlega, & Miller, 1976; Haase & DiMatta, 1976), and counseling skills (Ivey & Authier, 1978). However, a pervasive variable that appears repeatedly in the professional literature is the counselor's own perceptual world. Counselors require an understanding of their own perceptions to understand the perceptions of clients.

Research by Combs and Soper (1963), Zarski, Sweeney, and Barcikowski (1977), and others have related counselor perceptions to the effectiveness of counseling relationships. Moreover, Carkhuff (1969a, b) stressed the importance of perceptual qualities in maintaining successful helping relationships. This supports the pioneering work of Carl Rogers who, as early as 1958, noted, "It seems clear that relationships which are helpful have different characteristics from relationships which are unhelpful. These different characteristics have to do primarily with the attitudes of the helping person on the one hand, and with the perception of the relationship by the 'helpee' on the other" (Rogers, 1958, p. 6). More recent work by Kegan (1982), Meichenbaum (1977), and others continues to provide support for the early conclusions drawn by Rogers regarding the importance of counselor perceptions in the helping relationship.

A primary goal of counseling is to assist individuals in understanding themselves, others, and the world so that they may enhance their present existence and future development. Counselors who understand, accept, and reflect accurately their own feelings *within themselves* are in a favorable position to encourage such processes in others. Conversely, counselors who have difficulty with their own self-explorations, or who harbor feelings they are unable to understand, accept, or reflect within themselves severely limit their value as helpers. A counselor's ability and willingness to self-examine, self-accept, and self-reflect are necessary for successful functioning, both personally and professionally. When combined with understanding, accepting, and reflecting the perceptions of others, the counselor creates and maintains an appreciation of how perceptions affect individual behavior.

Three Existential Questions

Perceptual issues in human behavior are connected to three basic questions regarding personal existence. These questions heavily influence the counseling process, for the answers they generate largely determine the outcome of the inviting relationship. At some point, the following three questions are asked by people as they move through the various stages of their lives.

The first question is, "What do I hold to be true about myself?" This is a fundamental self-concept question, for the answers may reveal the inner nature of a person's perceived being. The beliefs a person holds to be true about his or her personal existence serve as a sort of guidance system in formulating the direction of his or her behavior. In a sense, this perceptual guidance system indicates the true north, south, east, and west of a person's personality and the direction he or she should follow in life. Behaving in ways that are consistent with the perceived self contains a certain reward value and a special satisfaction whatever the final destination. A major difference in these perceptual guidance systems is that people who hold realistic and positive beliefs about themselves and their abilities are more likely to encounter success, while those who harbor unrealistic and negative beliefs are more likely to meet failure.

The second question affecting the counseling relationship is, "What do I believe others think about me?" This is a question of validation, for the answers it generates provide reasons for people to either justify their self-images or to re-examine them. When people believe others see them as able, valuable, and responsible, they tend to behave in ways that validate those beliefs. When people believe others see them as unable, worthless, and irresponsible, their behavior is likely to reflect this opinion as well. People tend to live up—*or down*—to the expectations of others, no matter in what direction these expectations may point.

The third question affecting the helping relationship is, "How would I like others to think of me?" Herein lies a fundamental conflict, for our self-perceptions and the perceptions we think others have of us are often in opposition to how we would *like* to be seen by others. Resolution of conflicts, coupled with realization of the opportunities among one's self-perceptions, one's perceptions of how others see oneself, and how one would like to be seen by others, is at the heart of invitational counseling.

Although the three questions have importance for the client, they are equally important for the counselor. The counselor's understanding that these questions are being internally processed by both client and counselor contributes to the success of the inviting relationship.

The counselor's ability to be in tune with his or her own perceptions as well as those of the client increases his or her sensitivity toward oneself and others. This sensitivity enables the counselor to maintain a consistent direction within the helping relationship, which has been referred to as "counselor intentionality" (Ivey, 1983; Ivey & Simek-Downing, 1980; Schmidt, 1984b). Intentionality plays a paramount role in invitational counseling.

INTENTIONALITY

> If intentionality is a significant process in perception, as I believe it is, more is the misfortune that the dimension has been left out of consideration in psychological studies.
>
> Rollo May, *Love and Will,* 1969, p. 237

Most students of perceptual characteristics of professional helpers have concluded that effective counselors possess positive self-perceptions, value personal freedom, and tend to perceive others as valuable, capable, and responsible. In a pioneering study, Combs and Soper (1963) reported that "good" counselors differed from "poor" counselors on several important aspects of perceptual organization. Good counselors were more likely to be concerned with people rather than with things, and they perceived their purposes as freeing and facilitating, as opposed to controlling and manipulating. This was later supported by additional findings of Combs and associates (1969) who reported that "good" helpers were characterized by their positive view of their clients and their capacity to help themselves. Good helpers also seemed to hold an essentially positive view of themselves.

A positive view of self appears to fuel an internal security, dignity, assurance, and confidence in the counselor. In *The Art of Loving,* Fromm pointed out that throughout much of human history, the helper most valued was the person who had the ability "to convey certain human attitudes" (Fromm, 1956, p. 117). Self-understanding and human desire, combined with a high level of training and professional skill, create counselor intentionality.

More recently, Zarski and others (1977) noted that a counselor's level of social interest, defined by Adlerian theory as the potential to cooperate and empathize with others, is positively correlated with client satisfaction with the counseling relationship as well as with client sociability and self-acceptance after receiving counseling. While not conclusive, the available research on perceptual characteristics of successful helpers indicates that effective counselors have a high degree of self-understanding, possess a reasonably accurate awareness of the world around them, and have a keen desire to utilize these qualities in creating successful counseling relationships. Thus the counselor's own self becomes an important resource in the practice of counseling.

The concept of intentionality in professional helping was first introduced by Rollo May in 1969. May viewed intentionality as a major client variable related to successful therapy. According to May, client perceptions are always colored by intentions. Intentionality is the basis for these intentions and provides the framework in which perceptions are organized and interpreted.

Only recently has the construct of intentionality been rediscovered as a counselor variable that may be vital to successful professional functioning (Ivey, 1983; Ivey & Simek-Downing, 1980; Purkey, 1978; Purkey & Novak, 1984; Schmidt, 1984b). Ivey and Simek-Downing (1980) noted: "The broad construct of intentionality underlies several descriptions of theoretical goals of counseling" and it relates to "counselors who are capable, can generate alternative helping behaviors in any given situation, have several alternative helping modes available to respond to the needs of the client at the moment, and the ability to utilize these responses to assist others to reach long-term goals" (Ivey & Simek-Downing, 1980, p. 8). A high degree of intentionality enables the counselor to create and maintain a caring purpose, a consistent direction, and a dependable posture for assisting clients.

Definition of Intentionality

May (1969) described *intentionality* as "the structure which gives meaning to experience" (May, 1969, p. 223). He traced its philosophical and epistemological roots from the early writings of St. Thomas Aquinas, Immanuel Kant, and Franz Bretano, and to the more recent works of Edmund Husserl and Martin Heidegger. May's analysis of intentionality as a derivative of the Latin words *intendere* and *tensum* illustrated the "stretching toward," "taking care of," and "purposeful" meanings the construct carries. He viewed intentionality as the ability of people to link their inner consciousness and perceptions with their intentions and overt behaviors. By this definition, intentionality "is not to be identified with intentions, but it is the dimension which underlies them; it is man's capacity to have intentions" (May, 1969, p. 224).

Intentionality, as May defined it, has implications for counselor qualities of caring and empathy as well as for the qualities of direction and purpose. A high degree of intentionality allows counselors to form intentions based on their perceptions of counseling and enables them to use intentions to move the counseling relationship through its various journeys and toward a successful conclusion.

Ivey (1969, 1983) has described intentionality as it applies to counseling. His observations combined the behavioral objectives of counseling with an understanding of the perceptual processes involved in effective helping. Ivey defined intentionality as "acting with a sense of capability and deciding from a range of alternative actions. The intentional individual has more than one action, thought, or behavior to choose from in responding to life situations" (Ivey, 1983, p. 3). Counselors who function with intentionality are able to respond to varying situations without becoming trapped in one response mode. By contrast, counselors who lack intentionality consistently use "only one skill, one definition of the problem, and one theory of interviewing, even when the theory isn't working" (Ivey, 1983, p. 4). Individuals who act with intentionality have a number of alternatives for their actions.

There are some differences between May's (1969) and Ivey's (1983) definitions of intentionality. For example, Ivey referred to the counselor's *lack* of intentionality. This implies that intentionality is an ability that is either present or absent. By contrast, May indicated that if a counselor does not see an appropriate alternative mode of counseling, it could be concluded that the counselor is *trapped* in an intentionality that makes it impossible for him or her to see any other alternatives.

A further difference between May's and Ivey's interpretations of intentionality is that Ivey placed more emphasis on conscious levels of awareness, while May maintained that the concept of intentionality "goes below levels of immediate awareness, and includes spontaneous, bodily elements and other dimensions which are usually called 'unconscious'" (May, 1969, p. 234). In any case, both Ivey and May have presented intentionality as an essential ingredient in the development of successful counselor-client relationships.

The invitational model also embraces the concept of intentionality. In the 1978 book by Purkey, and in a second edition in 1984 by Purkey and Novak, a significant difference was drawn from that of both Ivey (1983) and May (1969). In particular, Purkey and Novak differed in that they described intentionality as a bipolar concept and used the term *unintentional* to describe purposeless, accidental, or otherwise unintended behaviors. This bipolarity is a major way in which Purkey and Novak's definition differs from May's or Ivey's and will now be considered more closely.

Bipolarity. As presented in the invitational model, intentionality is a neutral, dispassionate concept. It can be positive or negative, constructive or destructive. Counselors who understand and employ the invitational model face a critical moral and ethical decision, for they are asked to embrace an intentionality that can be a significant force for psychotherapy or a powerful force for psychopathology. Intentionality spans a wide range of behaviors, and counselors can choose to be helpful or harmful. They can be a beneficial presence—or a lethal one—in the lives of their clients.

The positive or negative potential of intentionality can be an awesome concept when applied to professional counseling. Trained counselors have the knowledge and skills to be a profound influence for good or ill in the lives of human beings. The abuse of such knowledge and skills can have devastating effects. This is all the more reason for counselors to maintain a high level of ethical awareness and moral self-direction. However, even with the most careful attention to their own self-perceptions and purposes, there will be times when counselors are *unintentional* in their behavior.

Unintentionality.   As noted earlier, Ivey (1983) referred to a person's inability to choose from a number of behavioral alternatives as a lack of intentionality. May (1969) viewed this inability as a person being unconsciously trapped in an intentionality that prevents the exploration of other alternatives. By comparison, Purkey and Novak (1984) adopted the term *unintentional* to identify purposeless, accidental, or otherwise unintended behaviors. For them, behavior can be conceptualized as being on a bipolar continuum, running from intentionally disinviting, through unintentionally disinviting, unintentionally inviting, to intentionally inviting levels of functioning. Figure 3-2 illustrates this continuum, showing the bipolar characteristic of intentionality.

The upper portion of the bidirectional arrow indicates actions, policies, programs, and places designed to be inviting, while the lower portion illustrates those designed to be disinviting. The intentionality of each of the two ends of the continuum is illustrated by the clarity and precision of the arrow at both poles. By contrast, the middle area of Figure 3-2, illustrating unintentionality, is vague and ill-defined. Actions, policies, programs, and environments that are based on intentionality have clear purpose whatever the positive or negative direction.

A more detailed analysis of Figure 3-2 reveals that four areas of intentionality and unintentionality can be defined and illustrated using a correlational diagram. These areas are picture in Figure 3-3 as four quadrants.

The solid lines forming the outer boundaries of the upper right and lower left quadrants illustrate the clarity and precision of those areas. By contrast, the dotted lines of the other two quadrants illustrate their vagueness and uncertainty. The internal broken lines among the four quadrants in Figure 3-3 also suggest the continuum of relationships among actions, places, policies, and programs and emphasize the unsettled boundaries that exist among these quadrants. While the human condition prevents any one quadrant from becoming totally dominant, helping professionals strive to create actions, places, policies, and programs that function consistently in the intentionally inviting mode.

FIGURE 3-2 Bipolar Characteristic of Intentionality

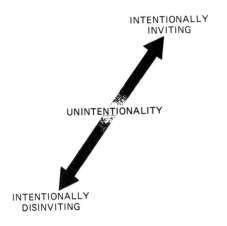

INTENTIONALLY
INVITING

UNINTENTIONALITY

INTENTIONALLY
DISINVITING

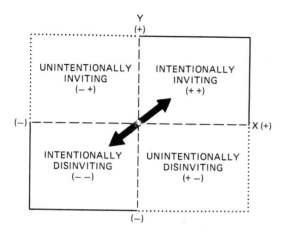

FIGURE 3–3   Four Quadrants of Intentionality

The exact ways in which *unintentionality,* defined by Purkey and Novak (1984) as being on a continuum, differs from Ivey's (1983) notion of a lack of particular intentionality, or from May's (1969) concept of being trapped in a particular intentionality, is unresolved. It is becoming increasingly apparent that intentionality and unintentionality need further exploration by theoreticians and researchers. What does seem clear at this point is that intentionality is the factor that enables people to have direction and purpose in their personal and professional lives.

Intentionality is of particular importance in invitational counseling, for it determines direction and purpose. These qualities are essential in charting and maintaining a course of personal and professional functioning.

Charting a Course

It is easy to recognize the significant roles that direction and purpose play in assisting people to lead successful lives. Who has not witnessed, in one's own life and that of others, the influence that direction and purpose have on the outcome of events? Those parts of a person's life that are "tended to" the most are those that usually turn out as planned. Even the language used to describe events contains aspects of direction and purpose: "I knew it would!," "If only I had done what I wanted to do," "I should have followed through," "Just as I planned!" These comments illustrate levels of intentionality that contribute to, or detract from, successful living. As Maslow observed, "Each act of consciousness *tends toward* something, it is a turning of the person toward something, and has within it, no matter how latent, some push toward a direction for action" (Maslow, 1962, p. 230). This statement underscores again the importance of direction and purpose.

Direction.   David Campbell (1974) described the importance of direction and purpose in his book *If You Don't Know Where You're Going, You'll Probably End Up Somewhere Else.* Invitational counseling embraces this theme, and adds two corollaries: (1) If you don't know where you've been, you probably don't know where you are, and (2) If you don't know where you are, you probably don't know where you're going. Counselors who function at a high level of intentionality are in a good position to help clients explore their perceptions and influence their futures.

People who seek assistance of counselors are often in search of direction concerning particular aspects of their lives. They seek assistance because they either need information to choose a direction, they are unsure of the course they have chosen, or they lack the skills to explore appropriate alternatives. Counselors who have direction in their own personal and professional lives are in a good position to assist others.

Purpose. People sometimes appear to have specific direction in their lives but they seem to lack an overall purpose. For example, a minister who directs his or her life toward pastoral leadership and church building may one day discover the need for a more personal and professional purpose in his or her life. While the minister's direction has produced desired results, it lacks an overall purpose for becoming fully functioning, both personally and professionally. The professional who only knows *what* is no match for the one who knows *why*. Knowing what to do reflects direction; knowing why reflects purpose.

People who know very well what they are doing, but who do not know why, can be assisted by professional counseling. Counselors who function with intentionality seek clear direction in what they are doing, but they also seek purpose by determining if their relationships are either successful or unsuccessful. Because they seek this understanding, they are more likely to arrive at a point where they are able to describe both what they are doing and why they are doing it. They are able to assess accurately their relationships and dependably provide assistance to their clients. They are also likely to have an appreciation of the responsibility they carry with regard to themselves, their clients, and the helping profession. This responsibility is a major ingredient of invitational counseling.

RESPONSIBILITY

I feel a sense of historical urgency, as well as an increased awareness of the responsibility of the psychologist. This is a responsibility to the human race, and it should give the psychologist a sense of mission and a weight of duty beyond those of other scientists.

A.H. Maslow, "A Philosophy of
Psychology: The Need for a Mature
Science of Human Nature," *Main
Currents in Modern Thought,* 1957,
13, pp. 27-32

Professional helpers who serve people should be keenly aware of the significant roles they play in the lives of those they seek to benefit. Their helping roles are based on what Kurt Goldstein (1963) referred to as "the experience of real unity" with other human beings. This experience of unity is best developed through personal and professional responsibility, which is the foundation for trust.

Responsibility is an awareness and acceptance of the personal control individuals have over the directions they take and the behaviors they choose, coupled with a resistance against blaming or crediting others for their own decisions. In terms of the inviting relationship, responsibility is placed on each professional for his or her personal and professional actions. This responsibility can be analyzed under the categories of using appropriate skill, forging a therapeutic alliance, and maintaining respect for self, others, and the helping profession.

Using Appropriate Skill

The demands placed on practicing counselors in North American society are steadily increasing. Under this growing pressure counselors are often placed in positions where they are expected to come up with magic answers, to "motivate" people, to "modify" behaviors, to "build" self-concept, to "enhance" self-esteem. For example, a parent was overheard saying, "I'm never going back to that mental health counselor. I've been taking my child to the clinic for weeks, and she hasn't changed a bit!" In such circumstances it is tempting for practicing counselors to look for "quick fix" short cuts, or attempt to work beyond their level of competence. But responsibility means using skills that are not only appropriate for the counselor and his or her training but also appropriate for the client and his or her situation. Responsibility requires that counselors accurately evaluate the strategies and techniques they choose, consistently monitor their own behaviors, and continuously seek ways to form a beneficial alliance with their clients.

Forming a Beneficial Alliance

A second component of counselor responsibility is establishing a beneficial alliance. This alliance is based on the quality of "being with," which involves a dimension of joint decision making and shared growth in the inviting relationship. Moreover, this alliance incorporates the element of mutual trust. The client places his or her faith in the counselor's professional skill, while the counselor maintains a realistic optimism for the client's ability to direct his or her own life, to clarify purposes, to make beneficial changes, and to develop optimally. Counselors who operate from a "being with" stance recognize that they have equal responsibility with their clients for making the counseling relationship successful. They also understand that the inviting relationship can be as beneficial for counselors as it is for clients.

Maintaining Respect

Counselor responsibility is indissolubly linked with maintaining respect. From an invitational perspective, counselors cannot be responsible without consistently demonstrating respect for themselves, their clients, and the counseling profession.

Demonstrating respect for themselves requires an accurate appreciation of their skill levels and limits as professional counselors. Counselors who maintain this appreciation are confident in their abilities while recognizing their limitations. This respect for oneself is also demonstrated by the ways the counselor is personally inviting with oneself, as outlined in Chapter 5.

Demonstrating respect for clients requires both a genuine acceptance of where they are in their development and a realistic appraisal of their future potential. This acceptance and appraisal includes the optimistic belief that people at all levels of life are influenced by everything that happens to them, and that they can improve their lives if given the necessary time and assistance.

Finally, demonstrating respect for the profession is exhibited by the ways in which counselors speak and behave toward their colleagues and the support they give to their profession. It would be difficult to imagine a counselor operating at the higher levels of invitational counseling without the qualities of respect for oneself, others, and the counseling profession. Respect is best measured by action—to respect is to *act* respectfully. Actions, in turn, are measured by the levels of functioning introduced in Chapter 1. These levels of functioning will now be considered in greater detail.

FOUR LEVELS OF PROFESSIONAL FUNCTIONING

> Now, one person can invite another to change his being in many ways. I can invite you to change the meanings you attach to things and events, to recognize your world. I can invite you to change from the inauthentic way to the authentic way.
>
> Sidney M. Jourard, *The Transparent Self*, 1971b, p. 99

Earlier in this book four levels of functioning were introduced: (1) intentionally disinviting, (2) unintentionally disinviting, (3) unintentionally inviting, and (4) intentionally inviting. These four levels will now be expanded upon and tied directly to the inviting relationship.

As with all models of human functioning, no one level of functioning is absolute. The four levels are on a continuum. People, as well as the places, policies, and programs they create, flow from one level to another. Communication processes exist at each of the four levels, and all counselors function at various levels from time to time. However, it is the typical level of functioning a professional helper exhibits that determines the sort of helper he or she is.

Because of the very nature of communication, no professional can ever be fully aware of what is being transmitted. In addition to what is communicated with verbal language and the language of behavior—the silent language—humans also communicate with the environments they create and maintain and the programs and policies they design and support. The least desirable and most destructive of these communicative processes is to function at the intentionally disinviting level.

Level I: Intentionally Disinviting

Counselors who function at the intentionally disinviting level deliberately create and maintain actions, programs, policies, and places that are designed to inform themselves and others that they are incapable, worthless, and irresponsible. Unfortunately, there are individuals whose dominant mode of functioning is to berate, belittle, and dehumanize themselves as well as others. Adding insult to injury, their intentionally disinviting behavior has direction and purpose. They seem to take a certain joy from functioning at the level of contempt, distrust, and pessimism. It may seem contradictory to say that a counselor, a "helping" professional, could willfully function at the intentionally disinviting level, but it occurs. Rarely perhaps, but it happens. Where it exists, it may be thought of as "lethal functioning."

Lethal functioning. There are at least two ways that lethal functioning occurs. The first happens when even the most skilled professional helper becomes angry and frustrated and makes a decision based on these feelings. One example is the psychotherapist who, in a moment of frustration, intentionally humiliates a client for missing an appointment. Another example is å school counselor who supports corporal punishment as "the only language some children understand." A third example is the process advocated by some professionals of locking juvenile offenders up in prison with hardened criminals for a day to "teach them a lesson." Intentionally disinviting methods such as these may be an indication of counselor anger, frustration, fatigue, or lack of knowledge, but regardless of the reason, the methods have no place in the inviting relationship. From the standpoint of invitational counseling, any behavior, policy, program, or environment that is designed to insult, hurt, humiliate, ridicule, embarrass, demean, or physically punish human beings should be judged unacceptable *regardless* of the intended benefits. Processes that are intended to initiate positive change must rise or fall on their own merits regardless of outcomes.

A second way that lethal functioning occurs is when counselors use their positions to behave unethically, immorally, or illegally. The counselor may present oneself as a "helper," but in fact is a "hurter." Examples of this type of lethal functioning are the family therapist with personal sexual problems who intentionally and consistently sides with a spouse of a particular sex in marital sessions, the prejudiced high school counselor who repeatedly discourages students of certain backgrounds from applying to college, or the counselor in private practice who entices clients to have sexual relations with him or her as part of the "therapy." Such lethal functioning is not only disinviting, but is also unethical and has no place in the inviting relationship. In the medical profession similar advice is given in the axiom *Primum, non nocere* (Above all, do no harm).

Toxic reacting. The negative impact of intentionally disinviting people, places, policies, and programs is not limited to those who receive such treatment. Such lethal forces also have the potential to inflict long-term pain on those who inflict such hurt on others. The following narrative, provided by a counseling student of one of the authors, reveals the "toxic reaction" process, whereby the person who intentionally disinvites others may end up being the victim of one's own cruelty:

> I have often reflected, with considerable pain, on something that occurred during my high school days. At that time I belonged to a forensic group which had the opportunity to attend a state tournament and stay overnight at a hotel. On this trip the supervising teacher brought along a high school girl who helped her at school with secretarial work to act as her secretary during the tournament.
>
> That night most of us gathered in one of the hotel rooms for talking and winding down from the day's activities. This girl came and knocked on the door, wanting to join our fun. But none of us would let the girl into the room. We got very quiet and pretended that no one was there. The girl may not have known what was happening, or if she did, she has probably forgotten. However, after 20 years, I still remember what happened, and it still makes me ashamed.

Inviting and disinviting acts may sometimes be soon forgotten by one party in the interaction—but not so quickly by the other.

Exactly why a few professional helpers elect to function at the intentionally disinviting level may never be known. But regardless of the reasons—whether because of perceived personal inadequacies, embedded prejudices, overriding jealousies, sexual hang-ups, negative self-images, or sadistic or seductive impulses—such people could themselves benefit from professional help. If counselors who employ toxic methods are unwilling or unable to change or seek help, then it is the responsibility of fellow professional helpers to caringly but firmly remove them from the profession. From the viewpoint of invitational counseling, no justification exists for intentionally disinviting actions, policies, programs, or places. They may happen, and they may be understandable—even forgivable—but never justifiable.

Being human, counselors may slip into disinviting modes on occasion. They are, after all, human beings first, and only after that professionals. However, the overwhelming majority of counselors, if they function in a disinviting way, do so unintentionally. "Unintentionally disinviting" is the second level of professional functioning.

Level II: Unintentionally Disinviting

Countless factors and variables influence the professional helper's daily activities. Interruptions from important work, pressures to complete tasks, demands from supervisors, physical ailments, noise level, disinviting clients and colleagues, even the temperature, weather, or time of day or month can influence both the degree of intentionality and level of functioning. At times these factors and variables can be such that counselors act or react in ways that are perceived by others as disinviting, even though this was not intended by the counselor. As examples, continuing to work at one's desk while someone stands there waiting to be recognized, drinking coffee during an interview without offering the client a cup, giving a finger-crunching handshake, telling off-color, tasteless jokes, or arranging office chairs with a "throne" for the counselor are but a few unintentionally disinviting actions. Sometimes such behaviors are caused by a simple lack of politeness and good manners. For this reason, civility and common courtesy are given high priority in the inviting relationship. Good manners are not only nice to have, they are also essential to invitational counseling.

On some occasions signals and messages are sent by counselors that in and of themselves would be viewed by most fair-minded observers as inviting. However, because individual perceptions play such an important filtering and interpreting role, the particular person who receives these signals may view them as disinviting. When people, places, policies, and programs are viewed by others as disinviting, it may indicate careless or inappropriate functioning on the part of the counselor.

Careless functioning.   Frequently, professionals are observed who appear to be blissfully unaware of what their clients would like in terms of direction and support. For example, many people who call or visit community college counseling centers to inquire about equivalency high school diplomas never follow up on their initial contact. One reason may be that their initial contact was with a careless counselor. A counselor who functions carelessly might say: "Go over to the Registrar's Office in Building 403 and pick up forms 193-A and 7-B-4. Complete the forms and proceed to the Business Office in Building 306, Room B-3, for processing." For insecure and hesitant students, such directions are overwhelming. These directives appear to be living proof that the community college is no place for them.

A more caring approach would be for the counselor to have all the necessary forms on hand and assist the visitor in completing the application. This could include escorting the visitor to the next office and following up on the process with a telephone call to the person a few days later. Thoughtful acts, while quickly forgotten by the counselor, may have long-lasting positive effects on the recipient.

Experienced counselors understand that by spending time with people who are simply "looking for information," "seeing what's available," or "just stopping by" allows relationships to form in which deeper, more pressing interests are revealed. To pass up such opportunities by sending individuals to the "next window, please" is uncaring. It is also inappropriate.

Inappropriate functioning.   The most well-meaning and high-minded counselors can be deeply caring but through their lack of experience or errors in judgment they behave in ways that are inappropriate to the situation. The result can be very disinviting. Over-friendliness (smiling continuously), over-familiarity (patting, hugging, kissing), and even over-counseling ("What I hear you saying is," "What are your feelings right now?") are sometimes characteristic of inappropriate functioning.

Beyond caring, counselors should ask themselves: "Is this the most *appropriate* thing to do at this moment?" Sitting on the hospital bed to hold the hand of a client who has just had surgery may be a very caring act, but the jarring pain it inflicts is most inappropriate. In the same vein, discussing a client's concerns with a colleague during a cocktail party is similarly inappropriate and can lead to disinviting results.

An illustration of inappropriate functioning happened to one of the authors when he was asked to keynote a convention of counselors. Following the keynote address all participants headed for small-group workshops. The keynoter approached the registration booth to inquire where he might get a cup of coffee. The registrar interrupted his query with an abrupt question: "What group are you with?" The speaker explained that he was without a group, to which the registrar responded, "You will have to wait; coffee is served at 10:30." At that moment a janitor walked by and said to the speaker, "There is a coffee machine on the second floor. I'm going that way. I'll show you where it is." The janitor was functioning in both a caring and appropriate manner.

Careless or inappropriate functioning indicates that the helper either lacks the time, has a problem, is insensitive, is unskilled, or simply does not care. Counselors who typically function in an unintentionally disinviting mode can benefit from additional training by learning or relearning counseling skills or by receiving counseling for themselves. Perhaps such professionals are more object-oriented than people-oriented, or low self-monitoring rather than high, or have difficulty focusing on the concerns of others. In any event, from the perspective of invitational counseling, they should be encouraged to pursue avenues that will improve their professionalism—or seek other career opportunities.

On occasion, counselors who function at a disinviting level may see positive results from their efforts. This is not too surprising. People are helped by all manner of things and improve in all sorts of ways. As the fictional detective Charlie Chan noted: "Strange events permit themselves the luxury of occurring!" However, when positive results occur frequently, it is a good indication that the counselor is functioning at an inviting level.

Level III: Unintentionally Inviting

Many counselors who function at the unintentionally inviting level have the personal qualities that contribute to successful counseling. Sometimes these professionals are referred to as "natural born" counselors. They are usually optimistic, respectful, and trusting. Yet the one element they lack is intentionality. They are helpful to clients and they exhibit the concern and caring that clients require, but because they lack intentionality they are inconsistent in their work. This lack of intentionality and its resulting inconsistency jeopardize the creation and maintenance of the inviting relationship. The result is that the counselor's credibility is vulnerable, for it depends far too often on serendipitous counseling.

Serendipitous counseling. Because counselors who function predominantly at the unintentionally inviting level have personal qualities and professional training that are conducive to successful relationships, they are generally considered capable counselors. They know *what* they are doing, but they do not know *why.* However, their lack of understanding of why they are successful forms a barrier between themselves and their potential for further improvement. It also places clients at risk, since the counselor's approach is a "trial and error" operation. The counseling relationship these counselors establish is not a product of intentionality, but rather a matter of serendipity or, more bluntly stated, luck.

An example of the unintentionally inviting counselor can be seen in the one who intuitively is able to establish excellent rapport with a client in the initial stages of the counseling process, but who is unable to move with the client through the exploration phase to an action phase of making decisions regarding future behaviors. The counselor is seen as empathetic by the client, but after several sessions both the client and counselor appear to be spinning their wheels, covering old territory, and increasing their frustration over the lack of progress. In instances such as this, clients sometimes stop coming for counseling, not because they are upset or dislike the counselor, but because they are no longer receiving any benefit from the relationship. When this happens, the counselor who is unintentionally inviting may recognize the lack of success but does not know why this is so. He or she may end up blaming the client for not "following through" with the commitment for counseling.

Seeking intentionality. By analogy, counselors who function at the unintentionally inviting level are like amateurs who enjoy looking for Indian arrowheads. They know *what* to look for, and while they may discover a valuable artifact, their luck is no match for the professional archaeologist who knows *where, when, how,* and *why* to look for Indian relics. The professional archaeologist of counseling is the one who knows where, when, how, and why to be intentionally inviting with oneself and others, personally and professionally.

Counselors who owe their success to serendipity will become far more effective when they recognize that they are equally responsible for using their talents in creating and maintaining a productive and purposeful direction in the counseling relationship. It is this responsibility and direction that enable counselors to be consistent in their actions and move them toward an intentionally inviting level of functioning.

Level IV: Intentionally Inviting

A combination of direction, purpose, and skill allows counselors to achieve intentionality in their relationships. This intentionality in turn gives counselors the opportunity to reach the highest levels of professional helping. It is through intentionality that counselors are able to choose appropriate and caring strategies and behave accordingly. They are also better able to avoid the inconsistency, unreliaability, and uncertainty that result from unintentional processes.

In rough waters the counselor who is functioning at the intentionally inviting level is consistent in direction and is able to persevere on course. Intentionality also allows counselors to evaluate the direction of the counseling relationship, to monitor feedback, and to make changes as needed.

Orchestrating actions, places, policies, and programs in an intentionally caring and appropriate direction is the art of invitational counseling. Some counselors become so skilled that they are "maestros" of the profession. They practice their skills with such talented ease that the transitions between phases in their relationships with clients are indiscernible. Most counselors in training have watched tapes of the "impressario" counselor who performs a counseling demonstration while the audience is awed by the skills with which he or she develops the relationship and brings it to a close. It is admirable to have these skills, but the true test of the intentionally inviting counselor is his or her ability to make these skills a part of oneself in the transition to and from personal and professional relationships. As noted earlier, counseling skills are not hung on the rack at the end of the day. The intentionally inviting counselor seeks to maintain a dependable stance in all relationships. This dependability is an expression of the counselor's self and goes beyond proficiency.

Beyond proficiency. A counselor's ability to maintain a consistent stance is important in personal and professional functioning, for it moves the counselor beyond the realm of technical proficiency toward a quality of character based as much on who the counselor *is* as what he or she *knows.* There is a special style in those helpers who have reached this point. This style is reflected in their ability to distinguish between those factors that are *visibly* appropriate and those that are *invisibly* so.

Visibly appropriate factors. Of all the behaviors exhibited by counselors in the inviting relationship, and of all the policies, programs, and places they create, those most noticeable are the ones that can be seen readily. In other words, they are visible to the untrained eye and are most apparent to observers. Organizing a peer helper program in a school, creating a cancer patient support program, being a "big brother" or "big sister" to some child, placing cheerful posters and living green plants in an out-patient waiting room, donating time to a retirement center, or creating a wellness program in a factory are all examples of visibly appropriate factors at work. They are genuine and generous uses of energies that reflect a dependably inviting stance. Their visibility is beneficial to the recipients of the actions, to the individual counselor's self-esteem, and to the public image of counseling. But there is even a greater style in invitational counseling, and that is to function in an *invisibly* appropriate fashion. With this style of professional functioning the counselor, in a sense, remains "invisible" and is able to keep the focus and attention on the client.

Invisibly appropriate factors. A relatively unique feature of invitational counseling is its emphasis on invisibly appropriate actions, places, policies, and programs. These are beneficial forces that do not call attention to themselves. Few people witness them, and only the trained eye of another professional can detect them, but they can have a tremendous impact in the lives of human beings. A doctoral student at the University of North Carolina at Greensboro described the process as "artlessly" inviting . . . done with such skill and grace that the art itself is invisible to all but the trained observer.

The inviting relationship does not depend on an unbridled display of one's immediate emotions. Just as skillful social behavior does not consist of rampant disclosure or unsparing authenticity, to maintain an inviting stance may at times require the curtailment of certain emotions and the display of feelings more appropriate to the immediate situation. In invitational counseling, authenticity is always modified by the verb "therapeutic." The goal of invitational counseling is to be *therapeutically* authentic. The counselor's desire to be authentic should be monitored by its relationship to the welfare of the client. To the degree that a counselor can hear, *accept,* and reflect the feelings of clients, regardless of how repugnant, abhorrent, unrealistic, or unacceptable these client disclosures may be, to that degree the counselor is practicing invitational counseling.

A moving example of professionals functioning in an invisibly appropriate fashion was provided by a speaker at an invitational education conference: "When I was in junior high school it was the dream of every young girl to become a member of the 'Dancing Boots,' a precision team of 100 high school girls. I had even taken dance lessons so I would be sure to make the squad. But in the ninth grade I was in an accident that damaged my left knee. I could still dance and kick and do almost anything . . . except hop to the left. Whenever I hopped to the left I lost my balance and fell. Because of this, I decided not to try out for the Dancing Boots. But at the strong encouragement of my school counselor I changed my mind and tried out. To my great relief, not one time during the tryouts did anyone have to hop to the left. I made the squad and throughout high school we led every parade, performed at every half-time, and did every routine imaginable, but not one time did we hop to the left. After graduation and many years later, I returned to the high school for a class reunion. In talking with a former teacher, I commented on the miracle of never having to hop to the left. It was only then that I learned that the director of the Dancing Boots had been informed by the counselor that I could not hop to the left, so he made sure that no one did." Such invisibly appropriate functioning is the *crème de la crème* of the inviting relationship.

Many beneficial things that are done to make living worthwhile go unnoticed. While most people enjoy recognition for the performance of good deeds, it is the willingness to go unnoticed that distinguishes a counselor who employs the invitational approach from other capable counselors. Making a phone call or writing a letter on someone's behalf without their requesting it, speaking favorably of someone when the voices of criticism are strong, donating anonymously to a charity, or quietly cleaning up a mess made by some careless colleague are just a few examples of invisibly appropriate behaviors. While visibly appropriate forces are valuable in professional helping, invisibly appropriate factors are especially helpful because they focus totally on the individual or group for whom the action was intended, or for whom the places, programs, and policies were created. It is often these "behind the scenes" factors that make the greatest differences in people's lives. At its highest level, invitational counseling is invisibly appropriate because the inviting stance has become a habit.

SUMMARY

This chapter has described the major characteristics of the inviting relationship, particularly as they apply to professional counseling. These characteristics include a keen awareness of the importance of perception and self-concept, the ability to understand, accept, and reflect client perceptions, and the willingness to self-disclose appropriately and caringly.

The concept of counselor intentionality was also defined and analyzed in this chapter. Its dimensions of direction and purpose were described and their interrelationships explored. Counselor responsibility and its components of appropriateness, respect, and mutual trust were also described in detail.

The qualities of successful counseling were related to the four basic levels of professional functioning contained within the inviting relationship. Added dimensions of invitational counseling explained in this chapter include the ability to distinguish between visibly and invisibly appropriate behaviors, between unbridled and therapeutic authenticity, and the ability to recognize the value of forces that function in invisibly appropriate ways for the welfare of clients.

OPPORTUNITIES FOR FURTHER READING

ALLPORT, G.W. (1955). *Becoming: Basic considerations for a psychology of personality.* New Haven, Conn.: Yale University Press. In this often-quoted book, Gordon Allport articulated a new perceptual direction for psychology at a time when, for all practical purposes, only behaviorism and psychoanalysis existed. It is a prophetic work in humanistic thought.

CAMPBELL, D. (1974). *If you don't know where you're going, you'll probably end up somewhere else.* Niles, Ill.: Argus Communications. This insightful book invites the reader to establish a direction and purpose in life by planning one's future, assessing one's strengths, weaknesses, career interests and goals, and enjoying life to the fullest.

COMBS, A.W., SOPER, D.W., GOODING, C.T., BENTON, J.A., DICKMAN, J.F., & USHER, R.H. (1969). *Florida studies in the helping professions.* University of Florida Monographs, Social Sciences, No. 37. Gainesville, Fla.: University of Florida Press. This monograph brings together a series of research reports on the perceptual organization of effective helpers. The interpretation of these studies provided by Combs is that "good" and "bad" helpers can be distinguished by their perceptual characteristics.

HALL, E.T. (1959). *The silent language.* New York: Doubleday. Hall's book was a pioneering study in the area of nonverbal communication. By using his sensitive powers of observation as a professional anthropologist, Hall pointed out differences in cultures that make for unintentionally inviting or disinviting behaviors.

JOHNSON, D.W. (1981). *Reaching out: Interpersonal effectiveness and self-actualization,* 2nd ed. Englewood Cliffs, N.J.: Prentice-Hall. This book combines theory and experience in developing effective interpersonal skills. In particular, Johnson focused on the skills needed to initiate and maintain friendships.

KEITH-LUCAS, A. (1972). *Giving and taking help.* Chapel Hill, N.C.: The University of North Carolina Press. In this book, Keith-Lucas presented the human qualities and characteristics that are necessary in both providing and accepting help.

MAY, R. (1969). *Love and will.* New York: W.W. Norton. Rollo May explored numerous aspects of human interactions and therapeutic relationships. His chapter on *intentionality* presents an insightful discussion of the concept and its importance to both the client and counselor in the professional helping relationship.

PIETROFESA, J.J., LEONARD, G.E., & VAN HOOSE, W. (1978). *The authentic counselor,* 2nd ed. Chicago: Rand McNally College Publishing Co. The authors of this book integrated a number of approaches in counseling into a synthesis of professional helping. Included in this text are descriptions of effective helpers and ways to achieve selected goals with specific clients.

ROGERS, C.R. (1961). *On becoming a person: A therapist's view of psychotherapy.* Boston: Houghton Mifflin. Rogers' purpose in this very influential book was to share with the reader his personal experiences as a psychologist and counselor in his search for personal growth and professional creativity.

4

THE INVITING PROCESS

Hospitality, therefore, means primarily the creation of a free space where the stranger can enter and become a friend instead of an enemy. Hospitality is not to change people, but to offer them space where change can take place. It is not to bring men and women over to our side, but to offer freedom not disturbed by dividing lines. . . . Hospitality is not a subtle invitation to adopt the life style of the host, but the gift of a chance for the guest to find his own.

Henri J.M. Nouwen, *Reaching Out:*
The Three Movements of Spiritual Life,
1975, p. 51

Do teachable skills or specific methods exist that can be employed to accomplish the goals of invitational counseling? Can the inviting relationship be divided into analyzable parts? Are identifiable choices embedded in the process? This chapter provides answers to these questions by identifying and examining a 3-stage, 12-step sequence in the inviting process. In addition, the four basic choices of "sending," "not sending," "accepting," and "not accepting" inherent in the inviting relationship and introduced in Chapter 1 will receive detailed attention. As these stages, steps, and choices are analyzed, it is important to think in terms of inviting *patterns* of beliefs, perceptions, and behaviors rather than single inviting acts. Just like the fluid swing of a master golfer who integrates athletic ability and learned techniques into a finely tuned rhythmic motion, the inviting process is made up of specific stages, steps, and choices that, when combined correctly, disappear into an invisibly appropriate practice of invitational counseling.

The inviting relationship does not happen by chance. First, it is the product of beliefs and behaviors working together governed by optimism, respect, trust, and intentionality. Second, it is an orientation of disciplined character. As Fromm stated, "I shall never be good at anything if I do not do it a disciplined way; anything I do only if 'I am in the mood' may be a nice or amusing hobby, but I shall never become a master of that art" (Fromm, 1956, p. 108). Invitational counseling requires disciplined effort as well as knowledge.

THE SEQUENCE

A number of counselors have proposed models that contain stages in the counseling process (Brammer, 1985; Egan, 1982; Gazda, Asbury, Balzer, Childers, & Walters, 1977; Ivey & Simek-Downing, 1980; Rogers, 1961). These models usually include an introduction/facilitation stage, an exploration/transition stage, and an action/follow-up stage. The inviting process is similar to these models in that it proposes a preparation stage, an initiating/responding stage, and a follow-up stage. Each of these three stages contains four steps.

Preparation Stage

The preparation stage of the inviting process consists of four steps: (1) having the desire, (2) expecting good things, (3) preparing the setting, and (4) reading the situation. It will be useful to consider these steps in turn.

Having the desire. It may seem obvious that counselors and other helping professionals must have the desire to help before they can be a beneficial presence in the lives of others, but sometimes the most obvious factors are overlooked. Glinda, the Good Witch of the North, pointed this out to Dorothy in the MGM film *The Wizard of Oz:* "Dear Dorothy, you've *always* had the power, you just didn't *want* hard enough." "Wanting hard enough" is an essential first step. Without a clear understanding that the intentional desire to help is fundamental to successful counseling, counselors may be unable to implement all other stages and steps of the inviting process.

While having the desire to help is essential, the counselor's desire should always be tempered with a proper regard for one's professional skills and resources. As noted earlier, invitational counseling stresses the importance of recognizing and honoring personal and professional boundaries. Having the desire is not enough if appropriate counseling skills are missing or personal and professional resources are lacking. It is essential that the desire to help is consistently filtered through the counselor's own energy level and time restraints as well as by the level of his or her professional expertise.

Expecting good things. A frequently appearing word in contemporary professional literature is *efficacy,* which is the belief that one can make a positive difference in human affairs. If counselors do not hold this perception, then why seek to help at all? Invitational counseling is based on an optimistic view of people and their relatively boundless potential. This spirit of positive expectations is central to invitational counseling, which holds that everything counts, and that every inviting act, no matter how small or in what area, has limitless potential.

Counselors sometimes overlook the positive things they accomplish because they may not become aware of them for weeks, months, or even years. In fact, some beneficial results may never be known. Because of this, counselors who practice invitational counseling work to maintain a special faith in themselves, their clients, and the efficacy of their relationships. This faith is not blind. They understand that seldom does one inviting act, or even one inviting counselor, make a monumental difference. It usually takes a great number of inviting acts and more than one inviting person to encourage optimal living. At the same time they keep a realistic faith that in life everything counts. Nothing is wasted. Even one inviting act, or one helper, can make a difference. Through positive expectations they continue to expect good things of themselves, their clients, and the inviting relationship.

Preparing the setting.   Although having the desire and expecting good things are essential to invitational counseling, it is equally important to make the actual process as attractive as possible. This requires considerable time and effort in preparing the setting. Having friends over for dinner provides an illustration.

Inviting friends into one's home for dinner is an enduring tradition. As such (in addition to having the desire and expecting good things), the invitation is usually accompanied by considerable preparation. Choosing the menu, setting the table, preparing the food, and straightening the house are all done to prepare an ambience in which the dinner party will be successful.

To increase the likelihood of success, hosts and hostesses will take time to consider their guests' likes and dislikes, schedule the dinner at the most convenient time, and plan activities that will make the evening enjoyable. Guests who understand that these efforts have been made on their behalf are likely to return the thoughtfulness by arriving on time, dressing appropriately for the occasion, and showing their appreciation during the evening.

As with dinner parties, other processes in life are most likely to be successful when time and effort are taken to prepare the setting. Counselors who take the time to prepare the setting have a head start in developing the inviting relationship. Preparing the setting includes scheduling sessions at times convenient to the client, collecting appropriate information or materials beforehand, and arranging a facilitative physical environment for the counseling session. Even physical factors such as lighting, temperature, the size, arrangement, and proximity of furniture, the nature of decorations, the degree of privacy, and sound levels have an important impact on the success or failure of the counseling process. (The Appendixes in this book offer some practical suggestions for preparing the counseling setting.)

Reading situations.   Reading situations, also called "sensitivity," "empathy," "interpersonal perceptivity," and "social intelligence" (Smith, 1966), is the ability to understand and predict what others are feeling and what they are likely to do. This ability to enter another person's perceptual world is essential to the inviting relationship for it helps to form a bridge between the sender's and receiver's perceptions. Because sharing perceptions is critical, it is important in the inviting relationship that the counselor use all the senses in reading situations.

Much of the research on interpersonal communication indicates that measurable differences exist among professionals and nonprofessionals in their sensitivity to various signal systems in the environment and in the clarity of their sending and receiving abilities through various verbal and nonverbal communication channels (Rosenthal, Archer, Koivumaki, DiMatteo, & Rogers, 1974). An example of reading situations was provided by a Moroccan waiter who approached one of the authors in a small cafe in Tangiers and asked for the order in English. When asked how he knew the author spoke English, the waiter replied: "North Americans smell differently." Because countless differences in perception exist, it is essential for counselors to sharpen their sensitivity to the content of messages sent, received, interpreted, and acted upon.

Reading situations requires specific skills that are presented in most counseling textbooks. These skills include attending, listening, clarifying, questioning, probing, structuring, summarizing, interpreting, compromising, and confronting, and they will be described in Chapter 5. Many contemporary counseling texts (Brammer, 1985; Egan, 1975; Ivey, 1983; and Pietrofesa, Hoffman, & Splete, 1984) pay particular attention to these communication skills. Without them, counselors would find it difficult to move toward the second stage of the inviting process: the initiating/responding stage.

Initiating/Responding Stage

While the preparation stage is essential in the inviting process, it is the decisions made during the initiating/responding stage that create the opportunities for self-maintenance and self-actualization. The initiating/responding stage requires that counselors (1) choose caringly, (2) act appropriately, (3) honor "the net," and (4) ensure reception.

Choosing caringly. To choose their actions caringly, counselors require "you and me" and "here and now" information about their clients. Any invitations extended must be appropriate to the client's perceptual world, particularly to his or her self-concept. Sending appropriate invitations is accomplished by listening, clarifying, reflecting, and other skills used in the beginning stages of the counseling relationship. By gathering immediate information, the counselor is in an excellent position to choose behaviors that encourage the client to explore past experiences in the light of present situations and future opportunities.

In choosing caringly, please keep in mind that invitations are most likely to be accepted and acted upon successfully when: (1) the invitation seems safe to accept, (2) there are repeated opportunities to accept, (3) good things have happened when invitations have been accepted in the past, (4) it is in keeping with the norms governing social behavior, (5) the invitation is clear and unambiguous, (6) the one invited believes that he or she is able and willing to live up to the expectations of the inviter, and (7) the invitation is not too demanding in intensity or duration. *The counselor can directly influence all seven of these factors.* Thus initial invitations should be simple, short-term, and not too demanding. For example, asking a client to describe his or her present work situation is a much more simple and short-range invitation to disclose than asking the person to present his or her family frustrations and aspirations. Gradually, as trust develops, invitations can be more complex, intimate, and long-range.

Acting appropriately. It is one thing to choose with care what one is going to do, and quite another thing to do it. Choosing caringly is important and requires skill and feeling, but the proof is in acting appropriately. Individuals often have the best of intentions but fail to act on them. For example, people will say: "Oh, we've been planning to have you over," or "I've been meaning to give you a call." These comments suggest invitations chosen caringly but never acted upon. Even the smallest inviting act counts for more than the greatest intention never realized. Invitational counseling is the product of beliefs and behaviors working together. To exist, the inviting relationship requires appropriate action.

Exploring opportunities, preparing plans, and following through with appropriate action offer the greatest likelihood of guiding the client–counselor relationship through the initial preparation stage. This guidance process is essential to invitational counseling as it is the democratic ideal. As early as 1960, Lippitt and White demonstrated that "guiding suggestions" are characteristic of a democratic relationship, that is, "What is most important to you . . . ?"–"Have you considered . . . ?"–"What else could you have done?"–"Did you try . . .?"–"What other choices do you have?" The major characteristic embedded in each of these guiding suggestions is a respect for the client's own self-directing powers, coupled with the counselor's cordial summons to take advantage of these powers. The purpose is to encourage clients to be responsible for their own destinies. From the invitational perspective, the best way to help people is to invite them to do what they can and should do to help themselves.

A theme that is echoed throughout this book is that invitational counseling requires a relationship that consistently strives to remedy current concerns while increasing the likelihood of optimal potential. This is most likely to happen in relationships in which realistic plans of action are made and acted upon responsibly. Goldberg (1977) suggested the establishment of "contracts" between counselors and their clients. These contracts clearly state what the understandings are between the counselor and client, what each will be doing, and what each can expect of the other in the therapeutic relationship. Such a contract system relates directly to the invitational counseling concept of honoring the "net."

Honoring the net.   The "net" is a hypothetical boundary between the counselor and client that marks an inviolable territory for each. While self-disclosure should occur in a trusting counseling relationship, the client remains in control of what he or she will or will not disclose. This is as it should be, for there is a certain etiquette involved in the inviting relationship. There are rules to be followed. The inviter determines the rules under which invitations are sent; but the invitee determines the rules of acceptance. In invitational counseling it is important to know where the boundaries are and to stay on one's own side of the net. There are things that clients may choose to do or not do, disclose or not disclose. In invitational counseling this is called *honoring the net.*

In recent years such phrases as "You're violating my space," "Get out of my face," or "Whose life is it, anyway?" have expressed the need to honor the net. No matter how helpful the counselor desires to be, in invitational counseling the net is always respected. But honoring the net, while necessary, is not sufficient. Therefore, the next step of the inviting process is ensuring that the invitation has been received.

Ensuring reception. Many times people send messages that are never received. Notes misfiled, verbal comments unheard, questions unanswered, phone messages misplaced, or a gesture unnoticed are everyday examples of messages sent but never received. Invitations are like letters—some get lost in the mail.

Because some messages are misdirected or misunderstood, it is vital that the sender ensure that the content of the message is received *and* acknowledged. This is clearly the sender's responsibility, but too often this responsibility is neglected. When an invitation is sent but not received, or received but misunderstood, the sender sometimes mistakenly assumes that the invitation has been accepted or rejected.

Breakdowns in communication can be avoided if the sender ensures that accurate reception has occurred. This assurance of reception is important in almost all human affairs. For example, it is given high priority in military services throughout the world. The receiver of a communication must repeat the message verbatim before it is considered sent: "Aye, aye, Captain—four degrees port rudder," acknowledges the message.

Acknowledgment is also an important part in maintaining good classroom discipline, as in the case where the teacher gently but firmly inquires, "Johnny, what did I ask you to do?" Unless the content of messages is received and acknowledged, it may remain meaningless. Even worse, it may add to confusion and misunderstanding. Therefore, feedback is essential to ensure reception.

In counseling, clients and counselors have been known to leave a session with the counselor thinking, "That went well; she will do that task successfully," while the client is thinking, "That was good. I'm glad the counselor is going to do that for me." Ensuring that the content of the invitation has been received, coupled with an acknowledgment of who is responsible for what, is a vital step in invitational counseling. When this step is not successfully completed, misunderstandings and hurt feelings often result. It is important that the counselor and client recognize and acknowledge the options that have been established in the initiating/responding stage of the inviting relationship.

Follow-up Stage

Invitational counseling is the process, in part, of receiving, decoding, and understanding obscure messages, recognizing and accepting the essential parts of what is being communicated, and reflecting these essential parts to the client. During the initiating/responding stage, counselors are magic mirrors of reflection. In the follow-up stage of the inviting relationship, counselors go beyond reflections to work through four steps: (1) interpreting responses, (2) negotiating positions, (3) evaluating the process, and (4) developing trust.

Interpreting responses. When invitations are sent and received, they become the property of the people receiving them. Individuals who receive these invitations have the options of accepting, not accepting, ignoring, modifying them with a counter proposal, or "tabling" them until another time. What is critical at this point is the sender's interpretation of the receiver's response.

If a client indicates acceptance of an invitation, is the entire invitation accepted or just parts of it? Does the receiver understand the responsibilities that are stated or implied in the invitation? When behavioral contracts are used in counseling, for example, it is essential that the client understand the obligations and consequences written and implied in the contract. Without this understanding, the contract can never be fairly accepted and acted upon successfully. Of course, when the client does accept an invitation, and begins to follow through, the counselor's encouragement is reinforcing.

If a client indicates rejection of an invitation, was it in fact a rejection, or was it nonacceptance? The two responses are quite different. If rejection did take place, was the entire invitation rejected, or just parts of it? Does it follow that future invitations will also be rejected? For example, a client's husband might be reluctant to participate in marriage counseling not because he dislikes the counselor, distrusts counseling, or wants the marriage to fail, but because he feels the process makes him appear weak or dependent. Rather than trying to pressure the husband into marriage counseling, the counselor might ask him to meet alone with the counselor to share feelings and concerns about the counseling process.

Counselors who employ invitational counseling call upon the skills required in the initiating/responding stage to interpret accurately the client's behavior. Attending, listening, questioning, and other communication skills are vital to the correct interpretation of a client's degree of acceptance or nonacceptance of the counseling process.

Negotiating. Counselors and their clients who seek to establish the inviting relationship but who encounter difficulties work to negotiate a way around these roadblocks. Too often, human relationships are damaged or even destroyed because people are either unwilling or unable to negotiate differences. Sadly, these differences often begin as minor problems, but they become inflated by vested personal or professional interests that prevent people from "putting in" as much as they are "taking out" of their relationships. This is directly connected to the nature of self-concept explained in Chapter 3. The self-serving quality of the self sometimes hinders a person's ability to reassess values, suspend judgments, accept perceptions, and negotiate differences. Counselors who find that some clients repeatedly have difficulty with the inviting relationship may want to help them work on their self-perceptions and assist them in strengthening their negotiating skills.

Most counselors seek to maintain direction and purpose in the counseling relationship, but there is little to be gained by holding doggedly to a plan that cannot or will not be accepted by a client. It is much more productive to find acceptable alternatives, even if these do not fulfill long-range goals. Counselors often discover that client acceptance and completion of an alternate plan frequently leads to the acceptance and completion of the original one.

A central part of the negotiating step is the ability to handle rejection. Invitational counseling has room built in for the rejection of invitations, no matter how well-meaning and high-minded these invitations may be, and the client's perfect right to decline is absolute. Counselor responsibility cannot be allowed to deteriorate into client exploitation.

But even when an invitation is rejected outright, it still does not mean that the counselor is rejected, that the invitation is worthless, or that all future invitations will be declined. Countless reasons exist why clients are unable or unwilling to accept even the most beneficial of opportunities. Perhaps the rejection is a means of eliciting an alternative invitation that requires a different commitment, or maybe the client is testing the counselor's sincerity (somewhat like declining an invitation to stay for dinner: If the host perseveres then the invitation is probably sincere). In the inviting relationship, the key to success is to continue the inviting process as long as there is mutual desire, and as long as hearts can endure.

Evaluating the outcomes. Formal or informal evaluation is unavoidable in any human endeavor. Dinner guests comment on menus, voters choose candidates, judges rule on evidence, teachers grade students, students evaluate teachers, managers get bonuses, parents monitor children, and audiences applaud performances. Proper evaluation of outcomes helps the counselor to gather valuable information for future inviting sequences.

Evaluating the outcomes of the inviting relationship is an important part of counselor accountability. Some counselors comment that they are so busy *doing* that they do not have time to evaluate what they *do*. But counselors are responsible not only for what they do, but also for demonstrating that what they do makes a positive difference. To do this, counselors require both informal and formal means of assessing their counselor-client relationships.

Informally, counselors and their clients can evaluate the outcome of counseling by analyzing their progress on particular goals during their counseling sessions. During this evaluation process the counselor should be as encouraging as possible. An important quality of counselors is not only to be optimistic themselves, but also to invite optimism in their clients.

With the approval of the client, the counselor might also check with significant people in the client's life who could verify the client's progress or lack of it. Such persons could include spouses, parents, peers, employers, teachers, or friends. Conversations with these individuals can frequently provide valuable information about a client's progress.

Formally, the counselor can utilize standardized tests and interest inventories, behavior rating scales, biofeedback techniques, physical measurements, or other means to evaluate a client's progress. But whether informal or formal, it is essential that evaluation takes place.

Because the inviting relationship often involves a marriage of remedial relationships with developmental ones, evaluation is not the final step. The purpose of invitational counseling is to form an alliance that will achieve even more beneficial sequences of development. One successful sequence generally follows another as trust in the inviting relationship develops.

Developing trust. As Dorothy noted in *The Wizard of Oz,* the classic MGM film of 1939: "To get to a place you have never been you must go by a road you have never taken." In the inviting relationship, a single invitation is a small step in a long walk. As trust develops it provides the impetus for the client and counselor to continue their journey. Successful human relationships require countless inviting actions, each based on ever-growing trust.

The level of trust that exists between people within any interaction is related not only to each individual's past experiences but also to the intensity of the immediate relationship. This trust level is influenced by past experiences, the intensity of the relationship, the nature of the undertaking, and the dependability that each person brings to the relationship. Without a reasonable level of trust neither the client nor the counselor will self-disclose, explore new options, or take the risks necessary to find new ways of being.

The inviting process is cyclical; one inviting sequence leads to another. While the 12 steps outlined in this chapter have been highlighted for the sake of analysis, it is necessary to state again that the inviting relationship consists simultaneously of many separate activities, each created according to this overall process. In this sense, counseling can be viewed as an overarching invitation for people to see themselves as able, valuable, and responsible and to function accordingly.

An important aspect of invitational counseling apparent in each of the previous 12 steps is that decisions are continually made that affect the counseling process, positively or negatively. These decisions can be grouped under the four choices of the invitational model introduced in Chapter 1: (1) sending, (2) not sending, (3) accepting, and (4) not accepting. Each of these four choices has a role to play in all human interactions, but each has a special role in invitational counseling.

THE CHOICES

> I sometimes react to making a mistake as if I have betrayed myself. My fear of making a mistake seems to be based on the hidden assumption that I am potentially perfect and that if I can just be very careful I will not fall from heaven. When I have listened to my mistakes I have grown.
>
> H. Prather, *Notes to Myself: My Struggle*
> *to Become a Person,* 1970, p. 17

From an invitational perspective, every human interaction involves at least one of four basic choices, each with accompanying risks. The first two choices, sending or not sending, lie in the realm of the inviter. The second two, accepting or not accepting, are in the domain of the invited.

Sending

Sending any invitation inevitably contains certain risks. The one receiving the invitation is presented with options, including accepting, rejecting, postponing, or even ignoring the invitation. Thus the sender faces risks of rejection, misunderstanding, ignominy, or even acceptance! But risk taking is necessary if one is to live life well. As noted in an earlier book, "The greatest hazards in life are to risk nothing, send nothing, accept nothing, be nothing" (Purkey & Novak, 1984, p. 48). This concept was enriched by a graduate student in counseling at the University of North Carolina at Greensboro who wrote: "It is better to invite and be rejected, than not to invite and be dejected." Risks are inevitable in the inviting relationship for both the counselor and client.

Counselors take risks when they invite their clients to explore present options and future opportunities. They face the possibility that their efforts will be misunderstood, rejected, or ignored. They risk their professional reputations as they search for options, offer suggestions, and relate intimately with their clients. Clients take risks by self-disclosing aspects of their lives that leave them vulnerable. By sharing their feelings they put themselves in the hands of the counselor. As such, counseling is a most intimate human relationship.

Sending an invitation involves much more than the content of a message. It also involves *verbal behavior,* such as voice tone and rate of delivery; *nonverbal behavior,* such as facial expression, body stance, and eye contact; *personal appearance,* one's clothing, hair styling, and makeup; and even *physical space,* which includes physical contact (touching), and the *external environment,* temperature, appearance, and degree of privacy. To send an invitation that is most likely to be accepted requires a match between the counselor's signal system and the client's perception of what is inviting.

Human beings are sometimes indecisive about whether or not to invite others: "Should I or shouldn't I?" Invitational counseling has a partial answer to this age-old question. When the evidence for sending or not sending is about equally divided, it is probably better to send than not to send. Few things in life are as sad as a missed opportunity. When an invitation is extended, there is no guarantee that it will be accepted, but if it is not extended, there is the absolute assurance that it has no chance of being accepted no matter how potentially beneficial. Recently, one of the authors was chatting with a colleague who had joined the faculty three years before. In the course of the conversation the author expressed how glad he was that this colleague had become part of the faculty. The colleague responded by saying, "I have been here for three years and you are the first person to say that to me. I appreciate it more than you know."

Of course, there are times when it is inappropriate or uncaring to invite. As examples, if you know that a friend has a drinking problem, you don't encourage a happy hour, or if he is trying to lose weight, you don't send him candy. Paradoxically, the most inviting thing to do in such a situation is *not* to send those sorts of invitations.

Not Sending

In *Education and Ecstasy,* George Leonard noted, "Many a liberal educational reform has foundered on lack of specific tools for accomplishing its purposes —even if a tool may be something as simple as knowing precisely when to leave the learner entirely alone" (Leonard, 1968, p. 18). A similar statement is appropriate for counseling: Not sending an invitation may be the most caring and appropriate thing a counselor can do.

Uncaring or inappropriate invitations can be very disinviting. Examples of uncaring or inappropriate behaviors include offering a cigarette to a client who is trying to quit smoking, providing an answer for a struggling client who could have found it without help, or being overly friendly or overly protective. The skills used by counselors to make caring and appropriate choices regarding sending or not sending are related to the skills described earlier in this chapter. Because these skills are also important in accepting or not accepting invitations, it is helpful to understand the nature of these choices as well.

Accepting

To the degree that clients accept the opportunity to participate in the helping process, to that degree invitational counseling will be successful. But as with sending, accepting also involves risk. By accepting the counselor's invitations, the client is saying, "I trust you." As explained in Chapter 1, trust is a central ingredient of invitational counseling. When trust is demonstrated by accepting behaviors, the relationship is enriched. Accepting an invitation is a special way of sending one in return, beginning a chain reaction. But without some trusting acceptance of what life offers, living can be hollow. Perhaps the greatest tragedies happen during life: not inviting, not being invited, not accepting, not even having the opportunity to accept or reject what life offers.

When appropriate, and where care exists, accepting an invitation can be a most marvelous act of loving and giving. But having stated the importance of accepting, it is necessary at this point to recognize that not accepting can also be a most caring and appropriate process. It is folly to think that all invitations should be accepted, and it is irresponsible to do so. Knowing when *not* to accept is an essential part of the inviting relationship.

Not Accepting

There are times when the most appropriate and caring response is *not* to accept an invitation. For example, at the end of a party there comes a time to go home, even though the exhausted host is encouraging you to stay a while longer. Because of time, appropriateness, care, commitment, individual taste, and countless other factors, many invitations are not accepted.

When nonacceptance occurs in counseling, the sender should recognize the difference between rejection and nonacceptance. When a client declines a counselor's invitation, it does not necessarily mean that the counselor has been rejected or that all future invitations will be rejected. Sometimes clients need time to reflect on consequences before they take action. Moreover, at times people do not accept even the most attractive offers because they cannot accept the responsibilities of acceptance, cannot engage at the particular time or place, or simply do not know how to handle the situation in an appropriate and caring fashion.

A counseling student at the University of North Carolina at Greensboro pointed out that one of the major problems young people face is how to turn down an invitation without being disinviting. He noted: "When I was growing up I remember one girl in particular who I asked to a school dance, only to find myself in the embarrassing position of being tersely turned down. Being turned down to a school dance was certainly not a new experience for me, but the way it was done was particularly hurtful. It was not that she disliked me. I believe it was the only way she knew how to decline an invitation . . . or I'm an ugly ogre. I prefer the former explanation."

Sometimes people will not accept an invitation in order to verify its sincerity. But even then, their intention is not to reject. They may be seeking to determine if the invitation is sincere, or to see if the relation is strong enough to survive the initial rejection and to move toward a more lasting relationship.

As with the other three choices, nonacceptance involves risk, perhaps the greatest risk of all. People who continuously reject invitations risk the possibility of living lonely, isolated lives. When this begins to occur they often mask their loneliness by pretending they *prefer* isolation. They claim that they do not want to be invited. While this pretense is a temporary defense against further hurt, continued nonacceptance increases the likelihood of permanent loneliness and isolation. Such people can benefit from professional counseling even though they have great difficulty in seeking it. Unfortunately, those who could benefit most from professional help are often the last to seek it. Their isolation is their final protection against further hurt.

Most experienced counselors realize that people who seek counseling are often resistant to the very help they seek. Counselors who are sensitive to this phenomenon will be patient and consistent in inviting these clients to make adjustments, seek opportunities, and choose more beneficial directions in their lives. The world was not created in a day, and neither are people.

Sensitive awareness of how and when to invite—or not—or how and when to accept—or not—can be a vital learning process for clients. But it is even more important for counselors, for it determines their success or failure as professional helpers.

SUMMARY

This chapter presented a 3-stage, 12-step sequence of the inviting process and explained how it can be integrated into a counseling relationship where the various parts become a seamless whole. The stages and steps of invitational counseling are similar to other counseling models, particularly those that are based on optimism, respect, trust, and intentionality and that contain introduction, exploration, and action phases.

In invitational counseling the entire sequence is seen as both an expanded model for the counseling relationship and a dependable structure for interacting with clients. The sequence includes the desire to invite, the evaluation of available resources, the selection of appropriate and caring messages, the process of sending and receiving them, the interpretation of results, and using follow-up to build trust in the relationship.

Incorporated into the inviting process are many of the counseling skills required in most if not all professional helping relationships. These skills include reflecting, listening, attending, clarifying, questioning, structuring, and confronting, among others that will be presented in the next chapter. As with other counseling models, invitational counseling involves the use of skills that researchers have found to be effective in helping clients set goals, explore concerns, and take action.

This chapter concluded by analyzing four choices of interacting, each with its opportunities and risks. These were: sending, not sending, accepting, and not accepting. Counselors who adopt the invitational model work to understand the dynamics and effects of these four choices on the inviting relationship.

OPPORTUNITIES FOR FURTHER READING

Well, all those damned books you read . . .
What good are they?
Why do you read them?

Zorba, *Zorba the Greek,*
Mikos Kazantzakis, 1953, p. 269

BENJAMIN, A. (1981). *The helping interview,* 3rd ed. Boston: Houghton Mifflin. In this book Benjamin described the helping interview as a conversation between two people, a conversation that is serious and purposeful. Whether the interviewee comes willingly or comes against his or her will, the ultimate question for the interviewer is always: "How can I best help this person?"

CARKHUFF, R.R. (1985). *The art of helping,* 5th ed. Amherst, Mass.: Human Resource Development Press. Carkhuff provides a practical guide for developing and improving listening and communication skills while encouraging human development. Carkhuff's presentation of empirically based helping skills is clear and succinct.

EGAN, G. (1982). *The skilled helper: A model for systematic helping and interpersonal relating,* 2nd ed. Monterey: Calif.: Brooks/Cole. This text stresses the importance of method, technique, and skill in professional counseling. It presents an expanded and clarified three-stage model of helping. Stage I explores and clarifies the problem situation. Stage II sets goals based on an understanding of the situation. Stage III designs ways to accomplish goals.

FROMM, E. (1956). *The art of loving: An inquiry into the nature of love.* New York: Harper & Row. In this book Erich Fromm considered love in all its richness; not only erotic love or romantic love, but also love of self and love of God. According to Fromm, "Love is the only sane and satisfactory answer to the problem of human existence."

GAZDA, G.M., ASBURY, F.R., BALZER, F.J., CHILDERS, W.C., & WALTERS, R.P. (1977). *Human relations development: A manual for educators,* 2nd ed. Boston: Allyn & Bacon. This text presents an overview of the helping process and the communication skills required to help others. It is a particularly useful training manual for both classroom teachers and counselors.

HACKNEY, H., & CORMIER, L. (1979). *Counseling strategies and objectives,* 2nd ed. Englewood Cliffs, N.J.: Prentice-Hall. Hackney and Cormier have presented a clear explanation of counseling skills that are needed in the inviting relationship. Of special value are exercises that help the reader to practice helping skills.

IVEY, A.E., & AUTHIER, J. (1978). *Microcounseling: Innovations in interviewing, counseling, psychotherapy, and psychoeducation,* 2nd ed. Springfield, Ill.: Charles C Thomas. Ivey and Authier introduce microtraining, which is the process of identifying effective counselor behaviors and systematically training persons to use these behaviors during interviews.

PATTERSON, L.E., & EISENBERG, S. (1983). *The counseling process,* 3rd ed. Boston: Houghton Mifflin. In this third revision, Patterson and Eisenberg outlined basic tenets and skills inherent in the process of professional counseling.

PIETROFESA, J.J., HOFFMAN, A., & SPLETE, H.H. (1984). *Counseling: An introduction,* 2nd ed. Boston: Houghton Mifflin. This book is one of the most up-to-date presentations on the theory and practice of counseling. The authors focused on the counselor, the counseling process, and some basic issues embedded in professional functioning.

PIRSIG, R.M. (1974). *Zen and the art of motorcycle maintenance: An inquiry into values.* New York: William Morrow & Co. Hidden beneath this story of a man's search for himself are rich insights into some of the most perplexing human dilemmas. This book deals with people and explores what living is all about. Perhaps most importantly, the book invites a special appreciation of Planet Earth.

5

THE FOUR CORNER PRESS

BEING PERSONALLY INVITING WITH ONESELF
    Emotionally
    Intellectually
    Physically
BEING PERSONALLY INVITING WITH OTHERS
    Developing Friendships
    Celebrating Life
BEING PROFESSIONALLY INVITING WITH ONESELF
    Continuing One's Education
    Exploring New Directions
BEING PROFESSIONALLY INVITING WITH OTHERS
    Communication Skills
        Attending
        Listening
        Clarifying
        Questioning
        Probing
        Structuring
        Summarizing
        Interpreting
        Compromising
        Confronting
    Evaluation Skills
        Assessment
        Follow-up

An Eclectic Orientation
    Remediation of problems
    Realization of potential
SUMMARY
OPPORTUNITIES FOR FURTHER READING

And as an amateur I am convinced that what this country needs is more bum music, provided it is hand-made rather than a product of the machine age. Perfect music may be had, in these days, so easily that attaining it is no achievement at all. Merely by putting a record on the talking machine and twitching a lever I can hear the *Ave Maria* played perfectly by a great artist. . . . Splendid music the American people have in greater abundance than any other people ever had it before. But bad music, made by a handful of amateurs gathered in a private home, grows rarer and rarer.

> G.W. Johnson, *A Little Night-music:*
> *Discoveries in the Exploitation*
> *of an Art,* 1934, pp. 7–8

This book has emphasized an expanded perspective for professional helping and has maintained that the inviting relationship requires the acceptance of four basic assumptions embedded in the invitational model: optimism, respect, trust, and intentionality. Also embedded in the model are four levels of professional practice, four factors that influence human behavior and development, four choices inherent in the inviting process, and four "corners" of functioning. The levels, factors, and choices have been described in earlier chapters. This chapter elaborates on the four corners of functioning (nicknamed the "Four Corner Press" because intentional effort is required in each of the four) and explains their relationship to invitational counseling. These four corners are: (1) being personally inviting with onself, (2) being personally inviting with others, (3) being professionally inviting with oneself, and (4) being professionally inviting with others. The incorporation of these four corners of functioning into the total therapeutic stance of the helper is central to the inviting relationship.

The practice of invitational counseling requires a special way of being with oneself and others, both personally and professionally. Neglecting any one of the four corners detracts from the other three. It would be difficult, for example, to imagine an optimally successful counselor who is a failure in the social company of other people. All the success in the world in one area will not make up for lack of success in other areas. Thus the development and orchestration of each of the four corners of functioning contribute directly to the successful practice of invitational counseling.

BEING PERSONALLY INVITING WITH ONESELF

> One's own person becomes an instrument in the practice of the art, and must be kept fit, according to the specific functions it has to fulfill.
>
> Eric Fromm, *The Art of Loving,*
> 1956, p. 110

Counseling is a special sort of caring, and counselors are in a much better position to care for others when they properly care for themselves personally. Specifically, counselors who employ the invitational model work to be personally inviting with themselves emotionally, intellectually, and physically.

Emotionally

Being personally inviting with oneself emotionally requires a focus on two areas of personal development. First, it requires attention to the appropriateness of emotional control. Second, it recognizes the value of emotional expression. Both of these processes are important because they relate to the concept of therapeutic authenticity introduced in Chapter 1.

Effective counselors understand the need to have control of their emotions, particularly when assisting clients who face highly emotional issues. The counselor's ability to control one's own emotions in the face of extreme adversity increases the likelihood that he or she will be able to understand, accept, and reflect—at a deeper than surface level—the perceptions strongly defended by others. Emotional control is established by the process of understanding perceptual worlds, appreciating emotional response patterns, understanding the role of self-concept, and learning about body language and other physical responses to various emotional states.

Countless ways exist to be personally inviting with oneself emotionally. Monitoring one's feelings, practicing positive and realistic self-talk, learning meditation and relaxation techniques, using biofeedback, and following healthy diet and exercise patterns are just a few of the ways. Counseling is an emotionally demanding profession, and so it is important that counselors establish emotional control within themselves. Emotional control, however, does not imply emotional denial. On the contrary, where appropriate and caring, counseling is based on full and unabashed emotional expression.

Psychologically healthy people allow themselves avenues for emotional release. Being personally inviting with oneself emotionally may mean "whooping it up" at a football game, cheering at a political rally, behaving silly at a party, crying at a sad play, engaging in happy, childlike play, or encouraging "hoopla" at an annual convention. However, not all emotional expressions need be public. Too often people overlook simple and private means of emotional expression such as a private laugh at one's own follies, feeling angry at injustice, or fully experiencing the lump in the throat when the national anthem is played.

It is a sad commentary on North American values that emotions are so often discouraged. For instance, the "boys don't cry" syndrome was witnessed by one of the authors while attending the movie *E.T.* with a combined group of adults and children. Upon leaving the theater a young boy asked, "Why were you all crying?" To which one man replied, "It was a joyous movie and so I cried." The boy said emphatically, "I didn't cry!" The man responded, "That's O.K. We each express our joy in different ways." After a moment the boy confessed, "Well, I felt one tear . . . but I held it back." It is ironic that little boys are first taught *not* to cry, then later, in therapy, big men are taught *how* to cry.

Inviting oneself emotionally means caring for one's mental health and learning ways to make appropriate and caring choices in life. This is particularly important for professional helpers. Counselors who know how to handle stress and reduce anxiety in their own lives, who are able to function in psychologically healthy ways, and who are confident about their personal concerns will be in a strategic position to help others in these same areas.

Counselors can be personally inviting with themselves emotionally by enjoying activities away from the stress of professional responsibilities. By taking up a new hobby, relaxing with a good novel, spending time alone, or experiencing spiritual renewal, a person can rejuvenate his or her psychological energy level. A list of ways to be personally inviting with oneself is provided in Appendix A.

One additional way that counselors can be personally inviting with themselves emotionally is by using counseling services. Counselors who are able to accept help are in a much better position to give it. Moreover, they can benefit from counseling by exploring emotional concerns and setting goals for continued intellectual development. Just as they can be personally inviting with themselves emotionally, counselors can also be inviting with themselves intellectually.

Intellectually

For human beings to develop optimally they need intellectual stimulation. Being personally inviting with oneself intellectually requires participation in a wide variety of activities that increase knowledge, sharpen thought processes, and improve the overall power of the mind. Inviting oneself to read extensively on a variety of subjects removed from one's professional interests, to visit zoos, museums, and science exhibits, and to join organizations such as nature clubs, discussion groups, and historical societies are only a few of the countless ways counselors can be personally inviting with themselves intellectually.

Counselors who are well-read, curious, and intellectually alive are in favorable positions to create similar opportunities for their clients. A broad knowledge base and diverse experience contribute to the ability of helpers to offer appropriate suggestions and encourage the exploration of choices. Counselors who expand their intellectual horizons recognize the important relationship between mind and body. In addition to inviting themselves personally in both emotional and intellectual areas, they are inviting with themselves physically.

Physically

The ways people function are directly related to their physical health. It is difficult for people to be personally inviting with themselves emotionally or intellectually if their physical selves are in poor condition. When their physical selves are neglected or in disrepair, it is unlikely that counselors will be able to maintain appropriate emotional health or expand intellectually. Invitational counseling requires a commitment to care for the physical self. The attitude of taking good physical health for granted is replaced by intentionally encouraging physical vitality.

The importance of good health was underscored by Knowles (1977) who observed: "Most individuals do not worry about their health until they lose it. . . . I believe the idea of a 'right' to health (guaranteed by government) should be replaced by the idea of individual moral obligation to preserve one's own health—a public duty if you will" (Knowles, 1977, p. 59). Governmental programs designed to encourage good physical health are unlikely to succeed until people make commitments to be inviting with themselves physically. Such commitments include restricting high cholesterol foods and moderating consumption of sugar, salt, alcohol, and other substances that reduce wellness. It also includes exercising regularly, eliminating smoking or other drugs that contribute to physical problems, and drinking water in preference to other kinds of liquids. Although specific ideas are too numerous to mention here, some suggestions are provided in the Appendix. In the inviting relationship a good health "stance" is of great importance.

Counseling is a profession that is as demanding physically as it is emotionally. It is imperative that counselors maintain proper physical health to cope with these demands. A counselor's physical self adds to, or detracts from, the counseling process. A counselor who encourages clients to eat moderately, exercise regularly, and drink reasonably will be a more credible model if he or she is being personally inviting with oneself in these and other physical areas.

There are many specific ways to be personally inviting with oneself intellectually, emotionally, and physically. The ones presented here are only representative. But being personally inviting with oneself, while necessary, is not sufficient. People are social beings and require the company of others. Thus, it is necessary that counselors in the inviting relationship develop and maintain their own "life support systems": to involve themselves intimately with those they love and who love them.

BEING PERSONALLY INVITING WITH OTHERS

Love has really been ignored by the scientists. It's amazing. My students and I did a study. We went through books in psychology. We went through books in sociology. We went through books in anthropology, and we were hard-pressed to find even a reference to the word "love." This is shocking because it is something we all know we need, something we're all continually looking for, and yet there's no class in it. It's just assumed that it comes to us by and through some mysterious life force.

Leo Buscaglia, *Love,* 1972, pp. 16–17

People are social beings. To develop fully they require the nurturing of fellow human beings and the giving of nurturing in return. A major source of nurturing is to love and be loved, which is needed throughout life. Without love people cannot develop intellectually, emotionally, physically—in fact, they are unlikely to develop at all. It is through loving relationships that people develop friendships and celebrate life.

Developing Friendships

Through sharing the company of others and through countless inviting acts, given and received, people establish close friendships. A student of one of the authors explained the creation of friendships by using the analogy of a cup being gradually filled with respectful and caring acts. When the cup finally overflows, a friendship is formed.

It is difficult to overestimate the importance of invitations sent to and received from fellow human beings. Personal invitations extended to others more than equal the power of invitations sent to oneself because they affirm both parties. They create opportunities for people to create one another. It is through friendships that people celebrate their kinship with all humanity.

Celebrating Life

Life can be a continuous celebration. This celebration is not simply the clamor, activity, and hoopla of a Mardi Gras. It is a more meaningful celebration of the deeper significance and richness of life. More specifically, celebrating life is a particular stance that one takes that, although not usually conspicuous or extravagant, contributes to a variety of developmental processes. The perceptual tradition and self-concept theory assume that human existence is greatly influenced and guided by events and relationships experienced and incorporated into the self-structure. Building on this foundation, the invitational model maintains that those who consistently are inviting with themselves and others are most likely to receive numerous invitations from others to develop friendships and celebrate life.

Personal satisfaction is a prerequisite for professional satisfaction. Counselors who are personally inviting with others become involved with community life, expand their social experiences, and develop an accurate and enthusiastic appreciation of the people, places, policies, and programs surrounding them. This accuracy and enthusiasm are helpful later in professional life in broadening counseling services beyond the confines of the office and into community service. Thus being *personally* inviting with oneself and others facilitates the process of becoming *professionally* inviting as well.

BEING PROFESSIONALLY INVITING WITH ONESELF

Counseling is an emerging profession that requires counselors to constantly keep pace with world changes that influence the course of human welfare and development. This fast-paced emergence of the counseling profession is highlighted in Chapter 7 of this book. Counselors as well as other professional helpers are held responsible for being informed of social forces, technological advances, medical discoveries, vocational patterns, and other trends that have an impact on their performance. This responsibility is met partly by the counselor's practice of being professionally inviting with oneself: a process that includes accepting the need for continual education, a willingness to explore new counseling practices and research, and a commitment to stay alive professionally throughout one's career.

Continuing One's Education

As with other professionals, counselors pursue years of academic training to acquire their skills. These years of formal study usually conclude with a graduate degree in counseling or some allied field. However, observant counselors recognize that their education must be ongoing. They realize the importance of continuing their studies, updating their skills, mastering new techniques, learning new research findings, finding fresh ways to improve their professional functioning, and generally rekindling the fires of professionalism.

Continuing one's education takes many forms. It may mean reading current textbooks on counseling, enrolling in a refresher course at a university, attending professional conferences and summer workshops, entering the world of computer technology, or taking a sabbatical leave. It may also mean conducting research, either quantitative or qualitative, and presenting one's work at local, state, provincial, national, or international professional meetings. The research and preparation of programs are excellent ways of being professionally inviting with oneself while at the same time sharing one's work with colleagues.

It is especially important to continuously educate oneself professionally to avoid stagnant, outdated, or obsolete approaches to professional helping—to avoid living a counseling half-life. In the fast-moving field of counseling, those who do not invite themselves professionally will be obsolete in a very short time. The sad part is they may not even know it! To keep abreast it is vital to continue one's education and expore new directions.

Exploring New Directions

Many counselor educators have written about future trends that will have an effect on the counseling profession and how counseling will be practiced in the years to come (Schmidt, 1984a; Wilson & Rotter, 1982; Wrenn, 1973). Some of these trends are presented in Chapter 7 of this book. Counselors who are professionally inviting with themselves are willing to explore new ways of being. This exploration is an ongoing process that incorporates a wide variety of professional activities. It may include participating in counseling associations, attending innovative training institutes, sharing informal "what works for me" sessions with colleagues and visiting and observing creative counseling programs.

Participation in professional organizations offers excellent opportunities to explore new trends in counseling. Attending meetings and workshops, corresponding and networking with colleagues, reading professional journals, and assuming leadership roles in organizations are only a few of the many ways that counselors can keep abreast of professional issues.

As with all of human development, professional development consists of various activities and experiences that allow individuals to progress through successively higher levels of functioning. Learning is a lifelong process, and for invitational counseling, this is fundamental. Counselors who realize this continue to be professionally inviting with themselves throughout their careers and even beyond! They make a lifelong commitment to be professionally inviting with themselves and this, in turn, strengthens their capability to be professionally inviting with others.

BEING PROFESSIONALLY INVITING WITH OTHERS

By being *personally* inviting with oneself and others, and *professionally* inviting with oneself, a counselor is in an excellent position to complete the four corner press by being professionally inviting with others. Being professionally inviting with others includes the communication skills employed by counselors, the evaluation processes they use to assess counseling outcomes, and the adoption of a "wide lens" approach to helping.

Communication Skills

Invitational counseling consists of the qualities enumerated in earlier chapters and a systematic application of counseling skills. As explained in Chapter 4, many authors have identified and described counseling skills in detail (Brammer, 1985; Carkhuff, 1985; Egan, 1975; Hackney & Cormier, 1979; Ivey, 1983). Several of these skills will now be reviewed. Readers who desire detailed explanations of these skills are referred to sources referenced throughout this section.

Attending. In the initial phases of the counseling relationship, as well as throughout the helping process, attending behaviors greatly facilitate client–counselor interactions. Attending behaviors include eye contact, vocal patterns, posture, and body movements. How well a counselor "attends" to what a client is saying often determines, early on, the degree of success their relationship will achieve in the future. While cultural differences should be considered when discussing attending skills, it is generally accepted in North American society that friendly eye contact, a warm and steady gaze, congruent voice patterns, forward leaning posture, squaring shoulders with the client (forming an intimate "box"), and selected body movements are important ways of expressing interest in what the client is saying. Attending skills contribute to a counselor's ability to listen carefully to what clients are saying as well as to what they are *not* saying. Seeking to understand what is happening, what is not happening, what is being felt, and what has ceased being felt, requires careful listening.

Listening. One of the greatest gifts a person can give another is to truly listen to what the other is saying. Counselors need two big ears, one small mouth, a little privacy, and the desire to understand the perceptual world of the client.

In counseling, listening skills are manifested by *paraphrasing* and *reflecting* client messages. Paraphrasing is the restatement of the essence of a client's message by using similar, but usually fewer, words and phrases. Paraphrasing demonstrates reception of the content of client statements. It has three purposes: (1) to help crystallize the client's comment by bringing it into clearer focus, (2) to let the client know he or she is being heard, and (3) to check the accuracy of the counselor's perceptions. When paraphrasing is on target, the counselor is likely to see a lot of client head-nodding.

Reflecting, a skill closely related to paraphrasing, is a process that shows an understanding of the underlying feelings of the client. The primary purpose of reflecting feelings is to help the client attain a clearer understanding of his or her emotions. At the same time, reflecting feelings can help counselors check the accuracy with which they are interpreting client statements. For example, if the counselor says, "I sense that you are very angry with your father," and the client responds, "Not really angry, more like annoyed," the reflecting skill and feedback from the client help to facilitate the counseling process.

The accuracy of paraphrasing and reflecting skills is usually measured by clients' acceptance and acknowledgment of counselor statements. For example, when counselors accurately reflect feelings, by paraphrasing or reflecting, clients usually show feelings of appreciation for being understood in ways such as nodding and saying, "Yes, that's *exactly* how I feel!" In contrast, when counselors paraphrase or reflect client messages inaccurately, nonacceptance or nonrecognition usually results: "No, that's not it at all." Through paraphrasing and reflecting the counselor can check the accuracy of his or her perceptions, and let the client know that he or she is being heard.

Frequently, counselors in training comment that paraphrasing and reflecting skills appear to be simple when they read about them. In practice, however, budding counselors soon develop an appreciation of the complexity of these processes. As Brammer (1985) and others have cautioned, inaccurate or inappropriate use of listening skills can destroy rather than facilitate counseling relationships. Their accurate and appropriate use will greatly assist in the clarification of clients' concerns.

Clarifying. Sometimes paraphrased and reflected statements by counselors are not accepted by clients. At these times it is necessary for counselors and clients to work together to review information so that there is some agreement on the issues and concerns expressed. This clarification process is sometimes neglected by counselors (Schmidt & Medl, 1983) which causes a loss of agreement, communication, and understanding. Counselors who do not clarify issues may end counseling sessions believing the client is going to manage the situation or concern successfully. The client, however, leaves the session thinking the counselor is going to handle things. When they meet for their next session both the çounselor and client will be disappointed.

In addition to paraphrasing and reflecting of feelings and content, clarification also calls upon a counselor's questioning skills. These skills can either be inquiries or statements that directly or indirectly seek additional information or opinions from clients.

Questioning. As with previously mentioned skills, questioning can either encourage or discourage the inviting relationship. Basically, there are two types of questions—"open" and "closed"—and both are useful in the counseling process.

Open questions are nonjudgmental inquiries that invite clients to freely explain or expand upon a particular issue or point. These types of questions are useful in clarifying client perceptions, values, and understanding their situations. An example of a *direct* open question in marriage counseling is: "Could you describe the leadership roles you and your spouse assume in your marriage?" In contrast, a direct, but closed, question would be: "Who's the leader in this marriage?" An example of asking these questions *indirectly* is: "In most relationships, such as your marriage, partners assume different leadership roles. Describe how it is in your marriage relationship."

Closed questions are more limiting than open questions, but they are also useful in counseling. Generally these questions are used to seek specific information, bring the session back into focus, or regain direction in the relationship. For example: "What are some ways you and your spouse enjoy leisure time together?" Either closed or open questioning can facilitate the inviting relationship. Sometimes, however, it is necessary to probe at a deeper level.

Probing. Occasionally counselors find it necessary to ask questions beneath the present level of verbal interaction. These questions tend to be open and aimed at subjective information a client appears reluctant to disclose. It may be that feelings are at a level of sensitivity that prevents the client from dealing with them, even privately. Yet these feelings are so powerful that they cannot be ignored if the client is to benefit from the counseling relationship. Encouraging clients to express deeper feelings can help them to bring ill-defined or suppressed emotions into clear focus.

An example of probing is illustrated by a session one of the authors had with a graduate student who was experiencing great difficulty relating to one of her professors. At one point in the session the counselor said, "I sense that feelings you have toward your professor are very strong, even painful, and perhaps are related to past experiences you have had with others in your life who were very close to you." The woman then began crying and self-disclosing many deep emotions about her relationship with her father. During this self-disclosure she became aware of how much the professor reminded her of her father, even his physical appearance.

By becoming aware of how past experiences and emotions influence present functioning, and by bringing them into clearer focus, clients are in a better position to make adjustments and choose constructive ways of behaving. Counselors who accurately and appropriately probe beneath the more superficial levels of verbal interaction can assist their clients in gaining and strengthening their abilities to make adjustments and direct their own lives.

Structuring. The decisions counselors make in choosing the types of questions or levels of interacting influence the direction of the counseling relationship. By analogy, the counselor does not try to drive the client's car, but he or she can arrange the traffic signs, direction signals, and speed limit. This ability to direct "traffic" is demonstrated by the effectiveness with which counselors structure the sessions with their clients.

Communication skills not only facilitate counseling relationships but also help to structure these relationships. Structuring skills are used by counselors to set the course of the relationship, identify goals for change, and keep the counseling sessions on task. In addition to the proper use of communication skills, structure is accomplished through such factors as the physical arrangement of furniture, seating positions, lighting, temperature, privacy, time allocation, introductory remarks, physical contacts, and the agenda established for each counseling session. By structuring, counselors set the tone of the helping relationship and influence its direction and speed.

Summarizing. A skill that helps counselors maintain consistency in direction is summarizing. This skill is used to synthesize information, ideas, and feelings so that a common focus can be achieved and maintained by both the client and counselor. Summarizing can be done at any point in the counseling process: during the introductory phase, throughout the interactive process, and in the concluding stage.

In the beginning of a counseling session it is useful for counselors to summarize the interactions and decisions that occurred in previous meetings. Communicating this information helps the client understand where the present session will begin and what initial direction it will take. The counselor also summarizes at various points during the session to tie together statements of content and feeling in order to give the session a reasonably clear focus. At the conclusion of a session, summarizing is useful in highlighting what was discussed and decided upon. It is also useful in setting the stage for outlining what is to be done through homework and in future counseling sessions.

Summarization depends on the counselor's attending, listening, and clarifying skills. Without these, a counselor's summaries of content, ideas, or feelings would be less than accurate. Accuracy is important in all communication, but it is essential in professional counseling, particularly when counselors interpret what clients are expressing verbally and nonverbally.

Interpreting. Beyond paraphrasing, reflecting, clarifying, and summarizing, a further communication skill is the ability to interpret statements, behaviors, and events to a client. Unlike earlier skills, which are designed to help counselors understand, accept, and reflect their clients' perceptual worlds, interpretation is a means of offering clients alternative ways of perceiving the events around them.

As Ivey (1983) and others have noted, the use of this skill is closely related to a counselor's theoretical orientation. As we have seen, the inviting relationship embraces the perceptual tradition and self-concept theory. Counselors who employ the invitational model tend to base their interpretations on the present experiences of their clients, the basic assumptions of perceptual psychology, and the foundations of self-concept theory.

The process of suggesting alternative perspectives, providing new insights, and exploring new meanings are facilitative in two ways. First, interpretation in counseling allows clients to explore, consider, and accept new possibilities in a secure, nonthreatening setting. As explained in Chapter 2, an assumption of self-concept theory is that individuals cling to their perceptions as a drowning person clings to a straw. It is no easy matter for people to let go of perceptions that have guided their behavior over the years. Exploration and acceptance of new possibilities help people to expand their own frames of reference, which in turn enables them to become more fully functioning human beings. Second, by considering different interpretations of events and imagining future activities, clients prepare themselves to explore and accept new alternative actions. Assisting the client in recognizing new and appropriate ways of behaving is a fundamental goal of invitational counseling. Often this goal is achieved through the process of compromising.

Compromising. Sometimes even the most beneficial invitations are not accepted. When they are not accepted, it is helpful to negotiate particulars so that new and more appropriate invitations can be sent and acted upon. The skill of compromising is particularly useful in invitational counseling. For example, when using behavioral contracts with clients, counselors sometimes find it necessary to renegotiate parts of original agreements that may have required too much too soon. Counselors who negotiate effectively and compromise appropriately demonstrate that they respect the perceptions and integrity of their clients.

Compromising calls upon the abilities, insights, and knowledge of *both* counselor and client. It requires a collaborative, cooperative posture with both parties and exemplifies the "being with" stance so essential to the inviting relationship. On occasion, however, compromise is not achieved and the counselor and client find themselves locked in an uncompromising, uncooperative position. If this situation persists, the counseling skill of gentle but firm confrontation may be in order.

Confronting. Changing one's perception about oneself, others, and the world is difficult. People cling to their perceptions for these create their reality. As explained in earlier chapters, the only reality a person can know is that which he or she has experienced.

Clients often resist the counselor's invitations to make alternative interpretations of events, to accept new perceptions, alter habitual behaviors, or make fresh decisions that will improve their lives. When this resistance continues and progress is not being made in the relationship, the most inviting thing counselors can do is gently but firmly confront clients regarding the situation. A useful and simple technique is to ask the client to replace his or her "I can't" statements with "I won't." This change in wording can help a client to reconsider the situation and recognize his or her own self-directing powers. Such confrontation, when done appropriately, caringly, and empathetically, communicates the inconsistencies between what clients are doing and what they say they are doing, or what clients say they want to happen and what they are willing to do to make it happen.

Confronting is useful to point out inconsistencies between a client's verbal and nonverbal behavior. This is illustrated by the client who says she is happy but whose eyes show that she is on the verge of tears, or the client who states he does not need anyone, but whose hands unwittingly reach out in an imploring manner. Trying to smile when one is unhappy often results in a lopsided smile, with one corner up, and the other down. Some clients wear so much psychological body armor (clenched jaw, hunched shoulders, furrowed brow, crossed arms, and so forth) that it is almost possible to hear them clanking as they enter the room. What clients express with their bodies is often more revealing than what they say with their words. Confronting clients with their contradictory signals can often help them to face themselves fairly and resolve painful contradictions.

Finally, confronting can be used to encourage clients to negotiate and compromise particular invitations so that more acceptable ones can be agreed upon. "You don't want to practice this homework activity in assertive behavior? Okay, what homework activity are you willing to do?" This process of confronting, compromising, seeking, and finally reaching agreement enables the inviting relationship to proceed toward a successful conclusion.

Invitational counseling is predicated on the appropriate and caring use of all the communication skills presented in this chapter as well as other counseling techniques not covered in this brief review. By employing these various communication skills, counselors are able to establish and maintain a dependable stance in being professionally inviting with others.

Evaluation Skills

The focus of this book does not permit a full treatment of the many research and measurement skills that counselors employ to evaluate themselves, their clients, and their counseling relationships. Yet it is important to emphasize that the inviting relationship is far more than "good" feelings or "nice" interactions. It is a professional human service activity where evaluation is an essential component. Evaluation skills are as necessary in invitational counseling as they are for other approaches to counseling.

The evaluation of people, places, policies, and programs has been a difficult philosophical and methodological issue for the counseling profession. But regardless of difficulties, demands by consumers as well as concerned professionals have made it imperative that counselors be concerned with the evaluation of their professional performance. In meeting these needs for evaluation, counselors should become familiar with accountability models such as those outlined by Pietrofesa, Hoffman, and Splete (1984), Vacc and Bardon (1982), and others. Vacc and Bardon (1982) compiled and edited a wide spectrum of articles pertaining to assessment and appraisal issues in counseling. In a special edition of the journal *Measurement and Evaluation in Guidance,* Vacc and Bardon presented an excellent resource guide for program evaluation, test utilization, and other areas of evaluation.

Evaluation consists of research and measurement skills that enable counselors and their clients to determine their degree of success or failure in bringing about altered perceptions, new directions, or behavior changes that ameliorate concerns and improve human functioning. These research and measurement skills include standardized assessment techniques, self-monitoring and self-reporting procedures, structured interviews, biofeedback analysis, and behavior-management methods.

Assessment.   Assessment techniques, such as personality profiles, achievement testing, interest inventories, or attitude surveys, provide data by which counselors and clients can determine if any traits, attitudes, or interests have been influenced during the course of the counseling process. Self-report instruments, self-concept measures, and self-monitoring procedures, such as behavioral frequency counts, can also assess perceptual or behavioral changes. Survey information gathered by behavior rating scales or other questionnaires is useful in verifying behavioral changes identified as goals in the counseling process.

Biofeedback assessment helps people monitor their physical responses to behavioral events, while behavioral-management charts the occurrence of specific behaviors to determine increases and decreases in their frequency. For example, a client who wishes to lose weight might set a goal to eat only three meals a day and allow a predetermined maximum number of calories at each meal. By charting calorie intake at mealtimes, in addition to keeping a daily weight chart, the client can evaluate his or her progress in managing eating behaviors.

Follow-up.   In addition to emphasizing evaluation processes, the inviting relationship also depends on follow-up activities. In the inviting relationship successful remediation of concerns does not automatically signal the end of a counselor-client relationship. Invitational counseling encourages follow-up activities in which counselors seek to help clients recognize opportunities and explore new goals that will move them to higher levels of personal and professional functioning. It is through these follow-up activities that counselors demonstrate their continued desire to be professionally inviting.

An Eclectic Orientation

The skills presented in this chapter are common to most counseling theories and approaches to professional helping. As mentioned earlier, the inviting relationship embraces a number of approaches and techniques formulated and researched over the years in the helping professions. The incorporation of these approaches and techniques into the inviting relationship exemplifies the expanded perspective of invitational counseling, which has sometimes been associated with an eclectic orientation.

The eclectic orientation in professional counseling has been presented, condemned, and praised for many years. Recently, the debate has been rejuvenated in the counseling literature (Brabeck & Welfel, 1985; Patterson, 1985a; Rychlak, 1985) as numerous integrative models of counseling have been introduced (Beutler, 1983; Hutchins, 1979; L'Abate, 1981; Lazarus, 1981; Ward, 1983). The expanded perspective of the inviting relationship is close to the view of C.H. Patterson (1985a), who encouraged an integrated practice that "takes as its basic foundation the common elements of all the major theories. These common elements constitute the therapeutic relationship" (Patterson, 1985a, p. 350). Chapter 6 of this book explores some of the common elements found in counseling theories that are compatible with the inviting relationship and that can be integrated into invitational counseling.

The inviting relationship presents an encompassing perspective for delivering human services. It applauds the importance of the "core conditions" as outlined and researched by client-centered therapists (Carkhuff, 1969a, 1969b; Patterson, 1959, 1985a; Rogers, 1957). It also accepts the empirical contributions of the various behavioral and cognitive approaches that have formulated effective techniques useful with specific disorders (Mahoney, 1977; Martin & Pollard, 1980; Rimm & Masters, 1974). Moreover, the assumptions and beliefs of perceptual psychology (Combs & Snygg, 1959), self-concept theory (Combs, Avila, & Purkey, 1978; Purkey, 1970), the influence of the individual psychology of Alfred Adler (Ansbacher & Ansbacher, 1956; Dinkmeyer, Pew, & Dinkmeyer, Jr., 1978; Dreikurs, 1967; Sweeney, 1981), and the personal construct theory of George Kelly (1963) all provide important tools for invitational counseling.

While respecting the contributions of various theories and models to the counseling process, the inviting relationship also recognizes the philosophic and theoretical differences in these approaches. In seeking an expanded perspective for professional practice, the inviting relationship respects each theory's own beliefs and assumptions. Methods and approaches exist that are *not* congruent with invitational counseling and should not be considered as such. Any approach to counseling that employs fear, coercion, aggression, duplicity, seduction, embarrassment, ridicule, subversion, or physical punishment, *regardless* of good intentions or successful outcomes, should not be viewed as an inviting relationship.

A major feature of invitational counseling is that it provides an expanded structure in which compatible theories and approaches can be organized into a consistent pattern of personal and professional functioning. This structure is based on a set of principles applicable to countless, seemingly unrelated, situations in counseling. A case of mild agoraphobia demonstrates how the inviting relationship incorporates seemingly unrelated theories and approaches.

An older adult client is experiencing anxiety about being in a large sheltered workshop. If the client can identify a specific environmental reason for the anxiety, the counselor may be able to employ techniques that systematically alter the physical setting, resulting in an environment that is less threatening to the client. In reducing anxiety, a knowledge of learning theory is useful to the counselor. If the most anxiety-producing stimulus is found to be the noisy work area with loud machines and clanging locker doors slammed by other workers, the counselor could initiate a behavioral program with the client and begin a gradual process of helping her become accustomed to the physical surroundings of the sheltered workshop. At the same time, the counselor could consult with the sheltered workshop director to explore the creation of noise-abatement systems aimed at reducing noise levels.

If a dominant factor is not specific places or policies, but rather a "people" problem, such as the client worrying about what others may think about her, or her concern about succeeding with assignments, the counselor might choose a rational-emotive or other cognitive model to help the client confront and alter irrational thoughts. This could be combined with small-group counseling for sheltered workshop participants to form a support group. The group counseling process would focus on how belief systems contribute to anxieties. It would also seek to develop client self-confidence and strengthen peer relationships. Whatever approaches to helping are involved, the counselor views the handling of the anxiety as only the first step of a developmental process designed consistently to invite each person to thrive in a healthy environment. This "wide angle" approach to helping is likely to benefit others in the sheltered workshop as well as the single anxious adult. The inviting relationship provides a structure through which counselors may combine various approaches to professional helping into an orchestrated means of improving places, enhancing policies, managing programs, and assisting people to resolve problems and realize potential.

One additional quality of the invitational approach that is related to its expanded perspective is *balance*. The inviting relationship emphasizes an orchestrated dual purpose of professional counseling: to remediate problems and develop potential.

Remediation of problems. To view counseling as a remedy for conflict, anxiety, or personal misfortune seems an unnecessarily narrow definition of the professional helping relationship. At the same time, defining counseling in terms of self-fulfillment without considering barriers to development seems unrealistic. The inviting relationship seeks a balance between remediation and enrichment. The following illustration demonstrates the importance of maintaining this balance.

Marriage counselors who seek to reduce marital conflicts without guiding those involved toward the enrichment of their relationship may be providing superficial "band-aid" solutions that prolong or even increase the pain of an unhealthy marriage. Reducing tensions or removing problems, while helpful, will not necessarily enrich the partnership. It is important to move beyond remediation and toward enrichment. By teaching couples the communication skills to reach out toward each other, and by assisting them to improve their lives, the counselor can assist couples in resolving immediate concerns and gnawing frustrations, at the same time strengthening their marriage and enriching their lives.

Conflict resolution is not enough. When counseling children, for example, it is important to help youngsters discover alternative and socially acceptable ways of handling situations, rather than to simply eliminate problem behaviors in the most assertive manner. As Herbert (1981) pointed out, problem behaviors have the potential to help the child discover better ways to deal with difficult situations and to help focus on the child's assets that can be marshaled toward personal development. The removal of negative forces does not ensure a therapeutic relationship, just as the absence of hate does not ensure love, or the removal of harmful insects ensure a good harvest. The inviting relationship seeks to go beyond remediation of problems and toward the realization of potential.

Realization of potential. People do not have to get sick to get better. The inviting relationship is designed to remediate those forces that are hindering a person's growth, but remediation is only the beginning of a developmental process that promises to have a longterm positive influence.

Beyond efforts to benefit people directly, practitioners of invitational counseling work to improve environments, systems, and institutions. By integrating professional knowledge, organizational techniques, consulting processes, administrative methods, and human relations skills into a broad spectrum of professional helping, counselors can be a beneficial presence in the lives of those they seek to serve.

It is important to pause at this point and specify for whom invitational counseling is intended. Many people who are coping successfully and contributing adequately can still benefit from invitational counseling. Highly successful people can seek further enrichment opportunities through the services of professional counselors. For example, countless individuals make mid-career changes in already profitable occupations, or seek enrichment opportunities upon retirement from successful careers. The inviting relationship is designed to highlight the opportunities existing in each person's life, and to invite clients to take advantage of these opportunities.

In the process of helping people to realize their potential, the inviting relationship requires that counselors be able to identify and evaluate social, psychological, and physical human needs. At the same time it requires that counselors realize and accept the boundaries of their own expertise. In instances when client problems are severe, appropriate medical, psychiatric, or other clinical interventions and referrals should be obtained for the client. Acting in a professionally appropriate and caring manner is an integral part of the inviting relationship as it is for other approaches to professional helping.

SUMMARY

This chapter has described in detail the four areas of invitational counseling introduced in Chapter 1: (1) being personally inviting with oneself, (2) being personally inviting with others, (3) being professionally inviting with oneself, and (4) being professionally inviting with others. The inviting relationship integrates these areas of functioning with other assumptions and components of the invitational model presented throughout this book.

Being personally inviting with oneself is a prerequisite to being personally inviting with others. Counselors who care for their "person" by being personally inviting with themselves emotionally, intellectually, and physically are in an excellent position to expand their horizons and reach out personally to others in these same areas.

Being personally inviting with others provides a "life support" system for the counselor. This system is made up of people who cherish the counselor and who are cherished in return. The point was emphasized that not all the professional success one could imagine would make up for a lack of success with those whom one loves and who love in return.

Being professionally inviting with oneself incorporates a desire to change and a willingness to take risks. This desire and willingness are exemplified in the efforts counselors make to experience educational rebirth, explore professional change, and continue lifelong professional development.

Being professionally inviting with others in the most beneficial ways is the ultimate goal of invitational counseling. To accomplish this goal counselors are encouraged to use a rich assortment of communication skills and evaluation techniques reviewed in this chapter. They are summoned cordially to evaluate their professional work through an array of assessment techniques and follow-up activities.

Invitational counseling is an expanded perspective of professional practice. This expanded perspective is reflected in its emphasis on the need for balance between remedial services that assist people with immediate concerns and problems, and enrichment activities that focus on human potential. The next chapter explores this expanded perspective and describes a structure by which counselors can examine characteristics of many counseling approaches to determine their compatibility with invitational counseling. Four counseling approaches, each compatible to some degree with the inviting relationship, will be presented.

OPPORTUNITIES FOR FURTHER READING

Every writer, by the way he uses the language, reveals something of his spirit, his habits, his capacities, his bias. This is inevitable, as well as enjoyable.

W.J. Strunk and E.B. White,
The Elements of Style, 1959, p. 53

ANGELOU, M. (1970). *I know why the caged bird sings.* New York: Bantam Books. This autobiographical narrative is a story of childhood suffering, of powerfully inviting and disinviting messages sent, received, and acted upon. Some of the incidents Angelou depicted are wonderfully funny, but it is an unconditionally involving memoir of the "Black experience."

DERLEGA, V.J., & CHAIKIN, A.L. (1975). *Sharing intimacy: What we reveal to others and why.* Englewood Cliffs, N.J.: Prentice-Hall. This book describes the process by which people allow themselves to be known by others. Of particular value is the way the authors emphasized appropriateness, and demonstrated that nondisclosure of one's self, or too much disclosure too soon, are related to symptoms of mental disorder.

EGAN, G. (1982). *The skilled helper: A model for systematic helping and interpersonal relating,* 2nd ed. Monterey, Calif.: Brooks/Cole. Egan's text stresses the importance of method, techniques, and skill in professional counseling. His emphasis on strategies has helped to create sharp debate among professionals as to the basic nature of counseling.

EMERY, S. (1978). *Actualizations: You don't have to rehearse to be yourself.* Garden City, N.Y.: Doubleday. Emery's book seeks to enable the reader to recognize the conditions that add to, or detract from, human relationships. Particular attention is given to the creation of inviting environments in which relationships become "joyful, nurturing, satisfying" adventures in mutual growth.

GAZDA, G.M., ASBURY, F.R., BALZER, F.J., CHILDERS, W.C., & WALTERS, R.P. (1977). *Human relations development: A manual for educators,* 2nd ed. Boston: Allyn & Bacon. This text provides an overview of the helping process and a description of the communication skills needed to help others effectively. It is a useful manual for classroom teachers and counselors. Training exercises are included.

IVEY, A.E. (1983). *Intentional interviewing and counseling.* Monterey, Calif.: Brooks/Cole. Using the premise that intentionality is an essential characteristic in effective counseling, Ivey has outlined several communication, observation, and other skills that enable counselors to become more intentional in their professional functioning.

JOHNSON, G.W. (1934). *A little night-music: Discoveries in the exploitation of an art.* New York: Harper & Row. This little book presents a defense of amateurism and the importance of taking risks to live life more abundantly. Counselors will find many invitations, and a few disinviting comments in this witty presentation.

JOHNSON, S.M. (1977). *First person singular: Living the good life alone.* Philadelphia: Lippincott. In this book Johnson gave unusual emphasis to the value of friendship and saw it as perhaps even more important than the passion of love. The book contains some beautifully written passages on loneliness and the need for friendships.

JUNG. C.G. (1974). *The undiscovered self.* New York: Mentor Books. In this classic book, Jung explained the predicament of the human being in an uncertain and restless world. He offered a solution to pressures through understanding the inner self.

KELLEY, H.H. (1979). *Personal relationships: Their structures and processes.* Hillsdale, N.J.: Erlbaum. Kelley demonstrated that the outcomes (benefits and costs) that participants in a relationship experience depend on the joint activities they undertake. Moreover, Kelley emphasized responsiveness, which is the degree to which a person takes into account, in making choices, the consequences of those choices for the partner.

MAYEROFF, M. (1971). *On caring.* New York: Harper & Row. This small book deals with two related themes: a generalized description of caring, and an account of how caring can give comprehensive meaning and order to one's life.

McGINNIS, A.L. (1979). *The friendship factor.* Minneapolis: Augsburg Publishing House. This work presents many ideas for inviting others personally. At the heart of each personal relationship is the friendship factor—the essential ingredient is caring.

COMPATIBLE SYSTEMS OF COUNSELING

Another great challenge of our time . . . is to develop an approach that is focused on constructing the new, not repairing the old; that is, designing a society in which problems will be less frequent, rather than putting poultices on those who have been crippled by social factors. The question is whether our group can develop a future-oriented preventive approach or whether it will forever be identified with past-oriented remedial functions.

                                            Carl R. Rogers, *A Way of Being,*
                                                            1980, p. 240

The Inviting Relationship was written to provide an expanded perspective of professional counseling in which many compatible approaches can be woven into an integrative framework. Therefore, this chapter considers four elements of compatibility that may be considered when integrating various approaches to professional helping.

Many theories and practices in counseling are compatible with the views and practices presented in this book. Invitational counseling relies on a variety of approaches to professional helping, and counselors can select from a wide range of activities and techniques. Fortunately, in the counseling profession a rich array of approaches, activities, and techniques exist from which to choose. Selecting those that have harmonious theoretical and philosophical views and which demonstrate remedial and developmental value is both a challenge and an opportunity.

To facilitate the selection of activities and techniques, invitational counseling offers several identifying elements that reflect the views and expectations of the invitational model presented in Chapter 1. Although the following list of elements of compatibility is not inclusive of those that counselors might consider, it is a starting point for counselors who wish to practice invitational counseling.

ELEMENTS OF COMPATIBILITY

The following four questions should be asked when considering counseling theories and techniques for inclusion in the inviting relationship. Answers to these questions can also assist counselors in answering the "why" of their activities as well as helping them to maintain a dependable and consistent stance in their professional practice.

Is There a Perceptual Orientation?

Approaches to professional helping that are compatible with invitational counseling emphasize the importance of individual perceptions, particularly perceptions of self-identity, self-regard, and self-efficacy. Counseling theories that neglect these individual perceptions tend to view human development from an external perspective. Such a viewpoint is incongruent with invitational counseling because it can result in a manipulative "I-it" posture rather than a cooperative "I-thou" one. An orientation based on the perceptual tradition described in Chapter 2 encourages the counselor to focus on the ability and responsibility that people have in choosing the course of their own development.

Human beings are unique in that they have the ability to reflect on and reinterpret their past as well as to envision and direct their future. Individuals are not only aware, but they are aware of their awareness. Through this awareness they can reassess their experiences and influence the pattern of their lives. Recognizing the power and responsibility of the human spirit to assert self-control over developmental processes is fundamental to invitational counseling.

Is There an Emphasis on the Self?

Acceptance of a perceptual orientation goes hand in hand with the assumption that self-concept is a dynamic force in human development. Counselors who see self-concept as a mediating variable in individual behavior seek to observe, analyze, and understand human development from an internal point of view. This process is also significant as counselors seek to understand their own feelings. Self-understanding is the basis for a consistent stance in helping. It is also a hallmark of invitational counseling.

Self-concept theory places primary emphasis on the individual's active role in determining a direction for his or her development. Approaches to professional helping that bypass the self-concept tend either to interpret human development as an external process rather than an internal one or to view behavior as determined by unconscious forces rather than conscious ones. By contrast, invitational counseling is based on the assumption that the active, guiding self-concept offers clients and counselors countless opportunities for ameliorating present difficulties while seeking positive enrichment.

Is the Approach Humanely Effective?

While respect for individuals and their perceptions is a vital measure of acceptability into invitational counseling, the short- and long-term effectiveness of counseling methods also requires consideration. Clients deserve helping relationships that are likely to achieve expected beneficial results. By definition, any invitation has purpose and direction, and invitational counseling is a goal-directed helping process. Counselors who employ the invitational approach are aware of the intended beneficial effects of both remedial and developmental relationships, and they stand ready to evaluate the effectiveness of their work.

But effectiveness, while necessary, is not of itself a sufficient part of the inviting relationship. Thus the term *humanely* is needed to modify the concept of effectiveness. There may be counseling methods in existence that, while measurably effective, tend to belittle, denounce, seduce, punish, or dehumanize in ways that violate important elements of the inviting relationship. Such methods are counter to the very nature of the approach presented in this book, and they should not be considered as invitational counseling regardless of how effective they may be.

Does the Approach Encourage Applicability?

Because invitational counseling advocates a balance between the resolution of present concerns and the realization of future aspirations, it can be employed in a variety of settings with many types of clients. This applicability should be of special interest to counselors who wish to apply their skills across a broad spectrum of developmental, preventative, and remediational activities. Counselors who include individual and group counseling, preventive educational interventions, and consulting activities in their programs are in a stronger position to maintain a balance of services for a broad spectrum of human concerns and needs.

It is fairly easy to list available counseling theories and therapies that contain elements of the invitational model. They have a perceptual orientation, an emphasis on self-concept; they are humanely effective; they encourage applicability. This chapter presents four of these compatible theories along with a cameo portrait of their creators. The purpose of presenting these four representative theories is to illustrate how various counseling approaches can be integrated into the inviting relationship. The four theories, which have developed from a variety of orientations by widely divergent individuals, offer theoretical bases and practical applications that are in essential agreement with invitational counseling and can be incorporated into an expanded inviting relationship.

ADLERIAN COUNSELING

> If today so many theoretical trends in psychology seem to take the direction which Adler originally took, this has, in our opinion, not come about fortuitously, but because their formulations fitted better the more carefully observed subjective and objective data and the practices which proved most effective. Inasmuch as Adler stands at the beginning of this trend, his work can serve as a synthesis in retrospect, while it is indeed in the nature of a remarkable original creation and anticipation.
>
> Heinz and Rowena Ansbacher, *The Individual Psychology of Alfred Adler: A Systematic Presentation in Selections from His Writings,* 1956, p. 18

Alfred Adler was born in 1870 in Vienna, Austria, second-born in a family of six children. He attended the University of Vienna where he first studied ophthalmology and later psychiatry. In 1895 Adler graduated with a degree in medicine and soon afterwards married Raisa Timofeyewna Epstein, an acquaintance of Sigmund Freud. His interest in psychology and philosophy led Adler to join Freud's group of psychoanalytic thinkers. A nine-year association with Freud ended in 1911 over Adler's rejection of Freud's psychosexual theory. Upon leaving Freud's group, Adler founded the Society for Free Psychoanalysis. A year later, in 1912, he changed its name to the Society for Individual Psychology.

His use of the term *individual* was designed to emphasize the wholeness and uniqueness of the person. He wrote: "By starting with the assumption of the unity of the individual, an attempt is made to obtain a picture of the unified personality regarded as a variant of individual life-manifestations and forms of expression. The individual traits are then compared with one another, brought into a common place, and finally fused together to form a composite portrait that is, in turn, individualized" (Adler, 1929/1969, p. 2).

From the early 1900s until his death in 1937, Adler's theory did not receive general acceptance. It was not until many years later that the writings of Rudolph Dreikurs, Heinz and Rowena Ansbacher, Manford Sonstegard, Don Dinkmeyer, Tom Sweeney, and others helped to translate Adler's often complex ideas into more fluid and understandable language. Thanks to the interpretations of these writers, Adlerian counseling is receiving considerable attention from professional counselors.

Among Adler's assumptions is the contention that, rather than sexual influences, the primary motivation for human development is a person's desire to be successful. Adler proposed that people, being basically social beings, consistently strive to find their positions in life. This striving for success demonstrated to Adler's satisfaction that all behavior has purpose and is goal-directed. This purposefulness and goal-directedness are indicative of an individual's "style of life," which is each person's private interpretation of the world and his or her function in it.

As people strive for success, it is important for their own welfare and for the welfare of their social group that they maintain a high degree of "social interest." This social interest, Adler believed, is a quality of caring for and cooperating with other human beings. A lack of social interest is an indication of psychological difficulties.

Today, Adlerian counseling is a popular therapeutic approach found in schools, family centers, mental health facilities, and numerous other settings. The ideas of Alfred Adler, modified to some degree by others, are taught in many college and university counselor training programs, by numerous national and international organizations, and in two American institutes for study—the Alfred Adler Institutes in New York and Chicago. The popular appeal of Adlerian theory can be partially explained because it can be combined with many other approaches to counseling. In particular, it is compatible with invitational counseling in its view of human nature.

Human Nature

Adler believed that individual behavior and human development are influenced by several common factors. These include people's feelings of inferiority, their need to compensate, their fundamental desire to seek superiority, and the belief that all behavior is purposeful and goal-directed. Each of these factors interacts with all others in formulating a developmental path for each individual. Adler's focus on these factors placed strong emphasis on the person's perceptions of events and experiences as well as the environmental events and experiences themselves.

Inferiority. In his early writings, Adler concentrated on the physical, organic inferiorities of people. He proposed that biological deficiencies and weaknesses (such as blindness, hearing loss, speech impediments, amputations, damaged organs, or other handicaps) were largely responsible for difficulties in people's lives. Because the human body functions as an integrated whole, Adler believed that people have the potential to *compensate* for these organic deficiencies by either developing ways to overcome the weakness or by focusing on activities in which the specific defect is less of a factor. He pointed to accounts of people who overcame physical adversities to accomplish great things. In many cases they turned an apparent handicap into a distinct advantage. Biological inferiority, according to Adler, could be deemphasized by the development of skills that either replace or compensate for a handicap.

In his later writings, Adler shifted his focus from the physical self to the psychological self. Human inferiority was no longer restricted to biological weaknesses and deficiencies but was expanded to include feelings of inadequacy. Adler believed that all people early in life exhibit feelings of inferiority, perhaps caused by their total dependence on adults during infancy and into early childhood. As children grow and develop, Adler theorized that they become more aggressive to overcome their feelings of dependency and weakness.

For Adler, feelings of inferiority are quite normal and often provide the motivational stimulus to encourage an individual to strive for higher achievements in life. In this way, feelings of inferiority can be a positive force. However, when carried to extremes these feelings can burden a person to such a degree that nothing can be accomplished. These extreme feelings of inadequacy, according to Adler, create a neurotic personality. The difference between a person who is overwhelmed with feelings of inferiority and a person who capitalizes on his or her weaknesses lies in differences between their perceptual worlds.

Adler's belief in the importance of perception, which may have been influenced by his early ophthalmological studies, is congruent with and complementary to the inviting relationship. The assumption of invitational counseling regarding the uniqueness of the human spirit allows for an ever-deepening appreciation that individuals can perceive the same situation in sharply different ways. This variability in perceptions, according to Adler, is at the heart of individual differences for it influences the goal-directed behavior of each person.

Goal-directed behavior. Goals are important aspects of Adlerian counseling as they are for the inviting relationship. Past experiences and early relationships are vital influences in development, but Adler believed that an even more powerful influence may be found in the goals chosen by individuals in their daily existence. Adler was inspired by the writings of philosopher Hans Vaihinger who maintained that people are directed by the fictions they construct to bring meaning to their lives. Vaihinger contended that fictional goals enabled people to plan and organize their lives so that there would be purpose to their existence. These are fictitious notions that have no basis in reality, but they enable people to cope with reality better than they could without such goals. As Heinz and Rowena Ansbacher (1956) noted, "the statement 'All men are created equal' would be an example of a fiction. The statement is in contradiction to reality; yet, as an ideal, it is of great practical value in everyday life" (Ansbacher & Ansbacher, 1956, p. 77).

By incorporating Vaihinger's theory of fictionalism, Adler gave his own theory a futuristic tone and moved it further away from the deterministic posture of both the Freudian and behavioral psychologies of the time. For Adler, all behavior is purposeful and goal-directed. While past events are important in gaining understanding of a person's development, what is vital in developing a helping relationship is assisting the client in identifying the purposes and goals of his or her behavior.

Adler's emphasis on purposeful, goal-directed behavior correlates highly with invitational counseling's emphasis on intentionality. Just as the invitational model proposes that the intentionally inviting person consistently acts with beneficial intent toward oneself and others, personally and professionally, Adlerian theory holds that healthy people are able to adjust their goals as their life situations change. As Hergenhahn (1980) explained, "For healthy individuals, such goals, ideas, or plans are means of living a more effective, constructive life. For the neurotic, the idea that these things are only tools is lost. The goals, ideas, or plans become ends in themselves, rather than means to an end. As such, they are retained even when they have become ineffective in dealing with reality" (Hergenhahn, 1980, pp. 83–84). Some individuals are so trapped in habitual behaviors that they lose sight of realistic alternatives and options. For example, the corporate executive whose fictional goal is to be the most successful businessman in town may become so obsessed with his business that he unintentionally destroys his family and peer relationships. He is unable to distinguish between a goal as a means to an end and a goal as an end in and of itself.

According to Adler, the healthy person uses appropriate fictional goals to compensate for his or her feelings of inferiority and to strive for feelings of superiority. An unhealthy person uses inappropriate fictions and becomes either consumed by feelings of inadequacy or obsessed with desires of superiority, to the degree that the welfare of others is neglected or even abused. The striving for superiority is fundamental in human nature and, as with feelings of inferiority, can result in either gains or losses depending upon the overall direction a person chooses in life, which Adler called the individual's "style of life."

Style of life.   Adler believed that children accumulate and integrate early experiences and perceptions into a conclusion about life and their position in it. This conclusion helps formulate their choices in approaching life situations. Dreikurs (1968) described this formation of the "life style" as the key to the personality of each person: "It encompasses the unity of his personality; all acts and attitudes are only facets of this general life style, based on his central evaluation of himself and his abilities" (Dreikurs, 1968, p. 18). This description is comparable to the various descriptions of the "self" as provided by self-concept theory and which serve as a basis for the invitational model. Adler believed that the construction or formulation of a style of life was a product of the individual's "creative self."

Creative self.   The concept of creative self, as used by Adler, maintains that each person actively participates in his or her own development by incorporating and integrating perceptions and experiences into a general world view containing specific attitudes toward self and others. These attitudes are uniquely created by each individual. As such, the creative self emphasizes the power of each person to determine one's own style of life and ultimate destiny. This view is congruent with the perceptual tradition, self-concept theory, and invitational counseling.

Adler believed in the value of people actively combining their abilities with their environments to develop successful directions in their lives. His "Psychology of Use" (Ansbacher & Ansbacher, 1956) emphasized more than the existence of human capabilities; it celebrated their potential contribution to total human development. This philosophy is compatible with the expanded perspective of invitational counseling, which advocates the value of people, places, policies, and programs in encouraging individuals to develop fully in all socially acceptable ways.

However, self-development is not, according to Adler, the single most important goal for a healthy life. He believed strongly that humans had the innate need to strive, not only for the superiority of self but also for a superior society. Human functioning without interest in others is not self-fulfilling. This belief is echoed in invitational counseling's emphasis on the development of mutual trust and respect and the employment of the "four corner press" presented in Chapter 5. Adler referred to the process as developing *social interest.*

Social interest. For Adler, a well-developed social interest, what he termed *Gemeinschaftsgefuhl,* is fundamental to becoming a healthy and fully functioning human being. Social interest is measured by a person's desire and ability to become a valuable and contributing member of society. Adler contended that a well-developed interest in others was necessary to successfully complete three main tasks of life: (1) vocational choice, (2) social development, and (3) love and marital relationships. Without social interest a person could never be fully successful at any of these important tasks. Regardless of an individual's own personal lifestyle or fictional goals, if he or she lacks a sense of belonging and consideration for others, that person will not become a productive member of society.

The concept of social interest, as defined by Adler, includes caring, empathy, and a desire to help others. These characteristics are also true of invitational counseling. The spirit of optimism, respect, trust, and intentionality advocated by invitational counseling is consistent with the concept of social interest advocated by Adler. Without this spirit of community, there is a danger of people becoming narcissistically locked into egocentric perspectives that neglect the well-being and common good of the group.

Components of Adlerian Counseling

The similarities between Adlerian and invitational counseling allow for a clear comparison of their therapeutic processes. The main components of Adlerian counseling are congruent with the inviting relationship, particularly in their emphasis on direction, a holistic perspective, equality, and positive involvement.

Direction. The Adlerian belief that all behavior is purposeful and goal-directed is also basic to invitational counseling and its foundations of the perceptual tradition and self-concept theory. Exploration of both perceived past events and present fictional goals is an Adlerian counseling technique useful in identifying more appropriate future goals. The emphasis, however, is not on the past events themselves, but on using the insights about those past events to help the client formulate future directions. In Adlerian counseling, helping is a cooperative relationship between the counselor and client in which goals are set and behaviors identified to reach those goals. The process of helping a client to examine current fictional goals, establish new goals, and choose appropriate alternative behaviors to reach those goals is similar to the steps of the inviting sequence presented in Chapter 4.

Holistic perspective.   The Adlerian belief that life is a holistic process conforms to the assumption embedded in invitational counseling that people, places, policies, and programs are influential variables in professional helping. Adler believed that the individual cannot be dissected into parts, such as behavior, feelings, and thoughts, but must be viewed as a total unit. In a similar way, invitational counseling believes that a wide-lens view is fundamental to fully understand and help people. This view includes the social, physical, and psychological worlds in which each person exists.

Equality.   Adler's basic notion that people constantly strive to overcome feelings of inferiority and to develop superior perceptions of self and others parallels the assumption of invitational counseling that people desire to be affirmed in their present worth while being invited to realize their potential. The views of Adlerian and invitational counseling both embrace a similar understanding of equality. Equality is interpreted not in the sense of "same as" or "identical to" but rather as an optimistic view of people being endowed with present value and future potential. As explained by Dreikurs and Soltz (1964), "Equality doesn't mean uniformity! Equality means that people, despite all their individual differences and abilities, have equal claim to dignity and respect" (Dreikurs & Soltz, 1964, p. 8). This definition of equality is endorsed by those counselors who are involved in the inviting relationship and who view their clients as respected and equal partners.

Positive involvement.   All the counseling techniques formulated and applied by practitioners of Adlerian counseling emphasize positive involvement. Democratic relationships in the family, marriage, classroom, clinic, and other settings are encouraged. Individual techniques, such as proper application of encouragement and the use of natural and logical consequences, rather than illogical rewards and punishments, are prominent in Adlerian approaches to counseling. As explained in Chapter 1, invitational counseling also stresses positive involvement and rejects any approach that devalues, degrades, demeans, or dehumanizes human beings.

Invitational counseling, with its levels of functioning, is consistent with the "encouragement process" of Adlerian counseling (Dinkmeyer & Dreikurs, 1963). Similarities between the process of becoming a more inviting person and the process of becoming a more encouraging person include the value placed on people's self-perceptions, self-directing capabilities, and goals in life. Both processes underscore the significance of perceptions and the importance of helping people to develop positive and realistic self-concepts.

The relationship between Adlerian "encouraging" and "discouraging" behaviors and environments is analogous to invitational counseling's "inviting" and "disinviting" people, places, policies, and programs. The encouraging and inviting processes are also similar in that they both emphasize the importance of goal-setting in helping people to develop their fullest potential.

Applications of Adlerian Counseling

Adler's theories of human development and behavior have been adopted by many theorists and practitioners and applied in numerous counseling programs. Adlerian theorists have developed counseling models for working with children, adolescents, parents, entire families, teacher groups, and other segments of society. Rudolf Dreikurs, for example, demonstrated how Adlerian principles could be applied to psychotherapy and counseling, parent education and child rearing, and classroom management and instruction (Dreikurs, 1967, 1968; Dreikurs & Soltz, 1964). More currently, Don Dinkmeyer has integrated Adlerian and self-concept theories into a number of child guidance activities, parent education programs, and teacher effectiveness training models (Dinkmeyer, 1982a, b; Dinkmeyer & McKay, 1976, 1983; Dinkmeyer, McKay, & Dinkmeyer, Jr., 1980). The application of Adlerian counseling to a wide range of helping relationships, from marriage counseling to classroom guidance, makes it particularly suitable for use in the inviting relationship.

REALITY THERAPY

> In *Reality Therapy,* the basic needs are described as the need for love and the need for self-worth. . . . If a person succeeds in giving and receiving love, and can do so with some consistency throughout his life, he is to some degree a success.
>
> William Glasser, *Schools Without Failure,* 1969, p. 12

Reality therapy was developed by William Glasser as a reaction to his dissatisfaction with traditional psychoanalytic approaches. He believed that Freudian psychology was too deterministic and pessimistic regarding the ability of people to take responsibility for their own lives. Since developing reality therapy, Glasser has continued to promote the belief that people have the power to be in control of their lives and accept the responsibility for their actions.

Born in Cleveland, Ohio, in 1925, Glasser was initially trained as a chemical engineer at the Case Institute of Technology. He later earned a master's degree in psychology. After completing his master's degree, Glasser entered medical school at Case Western Reserve University, graduated at age 28, and completed his residency at the Veterans' Administration Center and the UCLA School of Psychiatry. It was during his residency that Glasser began to openly question Freudian concepts, which at that time had a strong hold on the psychiatric profession.

From 1956 to 1968 Glasser was consulting psychiatrist to the Ventura School for Girls, a California institution for delinquent young women. From his experiences at Ventura, Glasser developed his theory, which he presented in his book *Reality Therapy* (1965). The concepts of reality therapy gained quick acceptance, particularly in schools. This led to Glasser's very popular book *Schools Without Failure,* published in 1969.

Since the late 1960s, Glasser has established several training centers that sponsor seminars in reality therapy. The Institute for Reality Therapy and the Education Training Center, both in Los Angeles, and the William Glasser LaVerne College Center, in Southern California, provide educational courses that train helping professionals from many fields in the concepts and approaches of reality therapy. In addition to *Reality Therapy* and *Schools Without Failure,* William Glasser has also written *The Identity Society* (1972), *Positive Addiction* (1976), *Stations of the Mind* (1981), and *Take Effective Control of Your Life* (1984).

Glasser's view of human behavior is generally a positive and optimistic statement about the ability of people to focus on their needs and to develop responsible strategies and actions for meeting them. According to Glasser, psychological, emotional, and social problems result from people's inability to meet their basic needs. In particular, the two most important psychological needs are the need to love and be loved, and the need to feel that one is worthwhile to oneself and to others (Glasser, 1965). Those who have chronically unfilled needs, or have lost the ability to fulfill needs, are likely to become mentally unhealthy or irresponsible. All of these needs center on the concept of identity.

Identity

Those who are capable of love and who have a high degree of self-worth are, according to Glasser, able to develop a successful *identity,* which he described as "the belief that we are someone in distinction to others, and that the someone is important and worthwhile" (Glasser, 1969, p. 14). This concept of *identity* is similar to positive self-regard emphasized in invitational counseling's first corner of the "four corner press" described in Chapter 5. Glasser's belief that people develop their identities from involvement with others is identical to invitational counseling's assumption, based on the perceptual tradition and self-concept theory, that the self-concept is organized and maintained as a result of countless significant interactions with people throughout one's life.

For Glasser, a person develops a successful identity through positive involvement with others and by behaving in responsible ways. Responsibility is a key concept of reality therapy and is defined as "the ability to meet one's needs without infringing on other people's rights" (Thompson & Rudolph, 1983, p. 37). By being responsible, individuals can avoid repeated failures that prevent them from becoming successful. On the other hand, irresponsibility leads to failure that subsequently leads to more irresponsible behaviors—resulting in a *failure identity.* A failure identity is reflected in self-critical, irrational, rigid, and ineffective behaviors. By contrast, a *success identity* is demonstrated by self-accepting, rational, and flexible behaviors. The role of the therapist is to accept and respect clients, but not to condone irresponsible actions. According to Glasser, responsibility consists of behaviors that show a degree of self-awareness, an understanding and acceptance of others, and are effectively flexible.

Glasser's description of responsibility is closely related to invitational counseling's concept of intentionality. Intentionality is the ability to be aware of one's behaviors and the feedback generated by those behaviors so that appropriate alternatives can be chosen. Self-awareness, acceptance of others, and flexible behaviors are components of both responsibility, as described in reality therapy, and intentionality, as defined in invitational counseling.

Behavior: Control of perception. In his book *Stations of the Mind* (1981), Glasser blended a biological understanding of the function of the human brain with perceptual processes and behavior development. He explained that people satisfy their basic needs by accepting or rejecting perceptions of their external worlds into their internal worlds. When incoming perceptions of the external world match the existing expectations of a person's internal world they are integrated smoothly with present behaviors. This is referred to by reality therapists as "controlled perception." When perceptions do not compare favorably with internal systems they are "uncontrolled perceptions" and result in *perceptual error*—the difference between the way a person wants things to be and the way things are perceived.

According to Glasser, people control for perceptual error by adjusting their behavior. He labeled the relationships among perception, brain functioning, and behavior as BCP, where *B* stands for behavior, *C* for control, and *P* for perceptions. The BCP system is used to explain how human behavior can control perceptions and compensate for perceptual error. Individual behavior is not simply a reaction to external stimulus but rather a response chosen to control perception.

The organization and explanation of BCP contain many similarities with the perceptual tradition and self-concept theory. Just as invitational counseling is based on the premise that human behavior is a means of validating existing self-perceptions, BCP maintains that behavior is a means of controlling perceptual error. What is important to both methods of viewing the relationship between behavior and perception is the idea that "it is only our world, or the world in our head, that counts for us" (Glasser, 1981, p. 91). External events have meaning only as they are perceived, interpreted, and accepted into the internal worlds of human beings. This concept is congruent with the perceptual tradition and self-concept theory presented in Chapter 2.

The orders of perception. Glasser outlined a hierarchy of perception that he referred to as "the orders of perception" (Glasser, 1981, p. 91). Every human experience is processed through this hierarchy as either simple perceptions, such as initial sensory contacts, or as more complex perceptions, such as moral decisions. Each experience begins at the lowest order of perception. This lowest order consists of simple energy signals, usually not consciously perceived, which enter through various sensory receptors. From that entry into the perceptual system, an experience can be processed through as many as ten orders. The higher the order of perception, the greater the value placed on the experience in controlling for basic needs.

The perceptual order described in Glasser's BCP model resembles in many ways the organized, dynamic, and modifiable self as described by self-concept theory. In particular, the self-concept spiral (Fig. 2-2) presented in Chapter 2 illustrates a hierarchical relationship among perceptions entering a person's internal world in much the same way that BCP depicts the order of perception from that of a lower sensory experience to a higher "personal state of perceptual control" (Glasser, 1981, p. 113). Both Glasser and invitational counseling recognize levels of awareness and a hierarchy of perceptions.

Process of Reality Therapy

Reality therapy identifies those internal and external factors that can be acted upon in bringing about healthy relationships. Not unlike invitational counseling, reality therapy relies heavily on educational processes that help people to identify their life goals, seek appropriate alternatives for reaching those goals, and accept responsibility for the alternatives and behaviors they choose.

Glasser (1965, 1981) outlined eight basic steps of the reality therapy process. These eight steps are congruent with invitational counseling's *optimism* in the client's ability to seek alternative solutions, its demonstration of *respect* for the client's capability to become successful, its *trust* in the relationship, and its *intentionality* on the part of the counselor or therapist. Brief descriptions of Glasser's eight steps follow.

Involvement. The first step in the reality therapy model is to be involved with the client. Glasser has stated that because "there is a basic need for belonging and that we almost always control for this need, it is important that the therapy relationship do as much as it can to satisfy this need in those who come for help" (Glasser, 1981, p. 267). During this phase of the counseling process, the reality therapist makes every attempt to develop a warm, caring relationship with the client, to learn as much as possible about the client's internal and external world, and to find out what it is that the client really wants.

Present behaviors. Upon the establishment of a genuine relationship, the reality therapist explores with the client the present pattern of client behaviors. This step often takes the form of the question, "What are you doing now?" Although reality therapy is concerned about people's emotions, counselors are discouraged from being misled by their clients' expressions of emotion. According to Glasser (1969), "People who fail fall back upon emotion to direct their behavior; people who succeed rely upon reason and logic" (Glasser, 1969, p. 20). For Glasser, emotion is the result of behavior, and only behavior can be changed directly. Positive emotional change will occur as a result of improved behavior.

Behavior assessment. Once the present behavior is identified it is necessary for the client to determine whether or not the behavior is beneficial to his or her success, and if not, to determine whether or not the behavior can be changed. This step is expressed by the question, "Is the behavior helping you?" Realization by the client that current behaviors are blocking the achievement of more personal or professional satisfaction leads to the fourth step: planning alternative behaviors.

Alternative behaviors. Step four in reality therapy is a process of exploring many possible alternative behaviors that will help the client find better ways to reach identified goals. This procedure of offering alternative behaviors and making direct suggestions to the client, while not acceptable in some totally nondirective approaches to counseling, is perfectly compatible with invitational counseling. By suggesting alternative behaviors, the reality therapist invites the client to explore numerous opportunities for self-actualization.

Commitment. Selecting appropriate behaviors and making a commitment to change is the fifth step of reality therapy. Both counselor and client during this phase of the relationship identify the most appropriate behaviors that provide direction and that offer the client a reasonable chance of being successful. Because the client makes a commitment to adopt these new behaviors, it is most important that a likelihood exists of achieving the intended goal. Reality therapists are careful not to set their clients up for failure by asking for commitments that are far beyond their clients' present abilities. This point is similar to an important question found in invitational counseling: "Is this the most appropriate and caring invitation to send to this person at this time?" An inappropriate invitation can be very disinviting.

Feedback. After the client has attempted the new behaviors the counselor and client assess the results. In this sixth step there are "no excuses." Glasser (1981) is explicit in this phase of the counseling relationship that if the initial commitment has not been kept, the therapist and client return to previous steps and make a new commitment. This approach demonstrates faith that the client has the power and capability to improve. This trust in human ability is also a hallmark of invitational counseling.

Consequences. Reality therapy endorses the belief that people learn best by experiencing the logical and natural consequences that follow their behaviors. Reasonable consequences, related to specific appropriate or inappropriate behaviors, are important learning strategies. While punishment, criticism, humiliation, and other punitive strategies are rejected by reality therapy, as they are by invitational counseling, removal of logical or natural consequences permissively protects people and is disrespectful of their ability to make decisions and solve problems. This concept is related to the idea featured in invitational counseling of "honoring the net" (Chapter 4).

Perseverance. The eighth step of reality therapy calls for both the counselor and client to maintain optimistic postures even in the face of the most frustrating difficulties. This is not always easy, but it is vital to the client's feelings of importance and belonging. According to Glasser, "A good therapist is stubborn and does not give up easily" (Glasser, 1981, p. 278). Sometimes a counselor's invitations are not accepted by the client. When that happens, counselors may renegotiate rejected invitations or offer new ones, but not give up readily. A student who was asked by one of the authors of this book, "How long does a counselor continue to invite?" offered a beautiful response: "As long as your heart can endure." The premise of "don't give up easily" holds for invitational counseling as it does for reality therapy.

Applications of Reality Therapy

Numerous articles have been written about applications of reality therapy in schools, particularly as applied to group counseling and classroom discipline. While educational settings continue to receive a major portion of the practice of reality therapy, many other clinical and preventive applications of Glasser's theory have been noted in the counseling literature. Naomi Glasser (1980) reported applications of reality therapy in nonschool settings in her book *What Are You Doing?* These included applications in marriage counseling, suicide prevention, adolescent counseling, counseling the handicapped, alcohol treatment, and caring for the elderly. The wide application of reality therapy has demonstrated its usefulness to counselors in many different professional settings. The same may be said of the invitational model, which has been applied to teaching (Novak, 1983), health care (Amos, 1985; Smith, 1985), nursing (Beeson, Bentley, & Dimeo, 1982; Ripley, 1985), physical education (Turner, 1983), college life (Murphey & Purkey, 1981; Parker & Scott, 1985), school counseling (Dougherty, 1981; Purkey, Schmidt, & McBrien, 1982), and special education (Russell, 1984), among others.

COGNITIVE BEHAVIOR MODIFICATION

> If operant training procedures could be improved by explicitly including in the treatment regimen a client's thoughts and images, then perhaps other behavior therapy techniques could similarly be improved.
>
> Donald Meichembaum, *Cognitive Behavior Modification: An Integrated Approach,* 1977, p. 107

A primary characteristic of behavioral psychology has been a strong emphasis on the roles environmental factors and external events play in human development. Coincidental with this emphasis has been a long-term debate within the behavioral school, as well as between behavioral and nonbehavioral theorists, about the importance of mental processes such as thoughts, feelings, and perceptions. Few differences among theoretical schools of counseling have been more passionately debated than has the dispute over the importance of internal thought processes. Yet from the cauldron of this issue has emerged some of the most popular and effective counseling approaches to be developed in the last two decades. These are the "semantic," or "cognitive," behavioral therapies.

Semantic Therapies

Semantic therapies (also called *cognitive therapies*) consist of a variety of counseling approaches whose main focus is to assist people in examining their present attitudes, beliefs, and assumptions about themselves and others to help them understand how these processes influence their mental functions and behavioral choices, and to alter self-defeating and counter-productive thought processes. Cognitive therapists attempt to educate clients about their faulty or irrational thought patterns that contribute to problems or inhibit development. Upon identification of these disabling internal thought patterns, the counselor proceeds to teach clients self-instruction techniques that will help clients to change specific misconceptions and alter their overall style of thought processing.

Perhaps the best-known cognitive theorist is Albert Ellis, developer of Rational Emotive Therapy (RET) (Ellis, 1962; Ellis & Harper, 1968; Ellis, 1984). According to RET, the emotional reactions people have to events in their lives result not so much from the events themselves but from their beliefs about the events. For example, it is not death itself but the ways people view death that determines their attitude toward it. When beliefs become irrational, people behave inappropriately, neurotically, and in ways that generally impede their development.

A recently developed cognitive therapy, "cognitive behavior modification" (Meichenbaum, 1977), seeks to identify and change people's specific negative self-statements rather than attempt a formal analysis of their irrational belief systems. The process of cognitive behavior modification involves instructing clients to learn and adopt specific problem-solving and coping skills that can be utilized in particular situations that contribute to behavioral difficulties. As an approach that attempts to bridge the gap between internal processes and behavioral techniques, cognitive behavior modification is congruent with invitational counseling.

Donald Meichenbaum, developer of cognitive behavior modification, earned his doctorate in clinical psychology in 1966 from the University of Illinois. A continuing interest in cognitive theory led him to formulate his doctoral dissertation research on the operant training of schizophrenic patients to learn and use relevant, understandable verbalizations. As a result of this study, Meichenbaum faced a most interesting issue. In his words, "An intriguing question thus arose: can schizophrenics (and perhaps other clinical populations) be explicitly trained to talk to themselves in such a self-guiding fashion and spontaneously to produce internally generated self-statements?" (Meichenbaum, 1977, p. 15). For the next ten years Meichenbaum pursued this question and culminated his search by publishing his first book, *Cognitive Behavior Modification: An Integrative Approach* (1977), which is now considered an influential sourcebook in the field of semantic and cognitive therapy. Meichenbaum has also authored other books, including *Stress Reduction and Prevention* (1983), and has written numerous articles and chapters of edited texts. He is currently professor of psychology at the University of Waterloo in Ontario, Canada, and a clinical psychologist in private practice.

Internal Dialogue

According to Meichenbaum (1977), a basic foundation for understanding behavioral development and behavioral change is the concept of internal dialogue, also known as *inner speech,* or simply *self-talk.* Meichenbaum pointed out three areas of research that have documented the importance of internal dialogue: (1) interpersonal actions and self-instructions, (2) cognition and stress, and (3) physiological effects. It will be useful to consider each of these in turn.

Interpersonal actions and self-instructions. Meichenbaum (1977) provided an overview of research findings related to the roles that interpersonal actions and self-instructions play in controlling behavior. Research on interpersonal instructions has demonstrated that these interactions consist of directional and motivational components that "provide the subject with a rule or principle by which he can mediate his own behavior" (Meichenbaum, 1977, p. 203). These self-instructions, or self-verbalizations, assist individuals in directing their attention, formulating hypotheses, and storing information in short-term memory. Similarities between interpersonal instructions and self-instructions indicate that both types can be monitored and altered by clients in attempting to change their behaviors.

The importance Meichenbaum gave to the self-directing aspect of intrapersonal instructions, or inner speech, is similar to the importance invitational counseling lends to the concept of "being inviting with oneself," which incorporates the qualities of optimism, respect, trust, and intentionality in one's own self-development. Self-monitoring and self-direction gained from increased intrapersonal skills described by cognitive behavior modification are necessary components for becoming more personally and professionally inviting with oneself.

Cognition and stress. According to Meichenbaum (1977), studies of stress factors support the role of self-instructions and self-verbalizations in controlling behavior. Research on high-anxiety subjects indicates that they tend to personalize stress situations more than low-anxiety people. For example, a young man who calls a girl friend for a date and is told she has too much school work and cannot go out may self-persecute by telling himself, "If I were only better-looking, she would go out with me. I'm too ugly to stand a chance with her. I might as well give up trying." A less self-deprecating instruction might be: "Too bad she can't go out; we would have had an enjoyable evening. Perhaps I'll try another time." Persons who self-verbalize in worrisome and self-defeating terms tend to handle stressful situations less appropriately than people who maintain more positive self-instructions.

The difference between self-enhancing and self-destructing inner speech can be related to the distinction made in invitational counseling between nonacceptance and rejection. An invitation not accepted is different from an invitation rejected. Nonacceptance simply means that the particular proposal is not acceptable at the moment. Moreover, it is important to recognize that even if the invitation is rejected, the rejection is no reason to assume that the invitation was worthless, or that the inviter is rejected. There are countless reasons why invitations are rejected that have little or nothing to do with the quality of the invitation or its source.

How a person assesses a given situation and self-instructs about it plays an important role in determining his or her respondent behaviors. When a person self-instructs that something he or she offered to another is not accepted because of the time or other logical reason, that person's responses are different from when he or she self-instructs that a nonacceptance is a rejection, or even worse, is a personal affront. A major function of changing thought and behavior through internal dialogue is to influence the individual's attentional and appraisal processes so that interactions can be more realistically and accurately assessed (Meichenbaum, 1977).

Physiological effects. Physiological effect is the third area of research related to internal dialogue. Meichenbaum (1977) reported that clients treated through the use of cognitive behavior modification were better able to identify physiological conditions as facilitative cues to assist them in choosing appropriate coping behaviors. "The physiological arousal that the client had previously labeled as totally debilitating anxiety and fear . . . was now relabeled as eagerness to demonstrate competence, as a desire to get on with a task, and as a sign to cope" (Meichenbaum, 1977, p. 207). What appeared to change in these cases were not the physiological responses, but rather clients' perceptions and self-verbalizations about those responses. This phenomenon echoes the belief central to the perceptual tradition that what is important is not so much the event itself as it is the person's interpretation of the event. The external event is not as important—for example, the fact that one is perspiring profusely—as it is the perception and interpretation of that event: how one translates the physical response of perspiring into self-instructed behaviors.

Meichenbaum (1977) illustrated the relationship among perceiving, interpreting, and self-instructing in his explanation of his choice of the word *dialogue* over the word *monologue*. He proposed that the process of *listening* to oneself is as important as *talking* to oneself. This process of speaking *and* listening to oneself creates a dialogue. In the cyclical relationship among perceiving, interpreting, and self-instructing, it is important to achieve closure within the sequence of events. It is through intrapersonal dialogue that healthy individuals are able to achieve closure by instructing themselves to alter cognitively the behavior patterns that may inhibit their development.

Cognitive Restructuring

Cognitive structure has been defined as the "organizing aspect of thinking that seems to monitor and direct the strategy, route, and choice of thoughts" (Meichenbaum, 1977, p. 212). Although Meichenbaum did not refer to self-concept, this definition of cognitive structure seems closely analogous to the self-concept construct. As defined in Chapter 2, the self-concept can be interpreted as a complex personal guidance system that is influential in behavioral development. Like the cognitive structure, the self-concept monitors events and influences choices. Just as invitational counseling concerns itself with self-concept development, cognitive behavior modification concerns itself with cognitive restructuring.

Cognitive restructuring is the therapeutic process of encouraging change not only in a client's thought patterns but also in the premises, assumptions, and attitudes underlying those patterns. The modification process in cognitive behavior therapy, like the inviting process in invitational counseling, is a cooperative partnership between the therapist and client. Throughout his description of cognitive behavior therapy, Meichenbaum has taken a strong position of shared responsibility that is in keeping with the "doing with" spirit so important to the inviting relationship. In this way, cognitive behavior modification is compatible with invitational counseling. Meichenbaum's (1977) three-phase process for behavior change illustrates the "doing with" spirit of invitational counseling and the therapists' teaching role in the helping relationship.

Mechanisms of Behavior Change

According to Meichenbaum's theory of cognitive behavior modification, three processes are to be considered when explaining behavior change. The first is the process of behavior itself. Before people can change behaviors they first must know which behaviors need their attention. Many people who are having difficulty are unaware how their own behaviors are contributing to their problems. These people tend to place blame on others, on bad luck, or on situations over which they claim to have no control. Cognitive behavior modification attempts to strengthen the client's awareness of his or her own behaviors by stressing self-observation techniques that encourage the client to monitor and attend to internal thoughts and physiological responses as well as external relationships and events.

A second process in cognitive behavior modification is identifying appropriate new behaviors. By observing and attending to specific behaviors, the client and counselor cooperate in reconceptualizing immediate concerns. In the reconceptualization, the counselor directly or indirectly assists the client in redefining the problem behavior. The recognition that a particular behavior is maladaptive leads the client to think and feel in ways that are in conflict with the old behavior pattern. Incompatible thoughts initiate a new internal dialogue, which in turn serves to guide new behaviors. Although the terms are different, the similarities between modifying cognitive behavior and changing self-concept, described in Chapter 2, are obvious. In both approaches the counselor assists the client in exploring alternative behaviors and creating more positive and constructive internal dialogue.

The third process is assisting the client in applying new behaviors outside the therapeutic setting. Simply focusing on appropriate behaviors in the counseling relationship does not bring about desired behavior change. It is necessary for clients to incorporate these new behaviors in their daily functioning. The evidence of how successful the counseling relationship has been, according to Meichenbaum (1977), is determined by the extent that clients change both their internal dialogue and their external behavior.

Applications of Cognitive Behavior Modification

Although cognitive behavior modification is still in its infancy it has attracted many researchers and practitioners who are applying its techniques in a variety of settings. For example, much work has been done using cognitive behavior modification methods with children (Abikoff, 1979; Harris, 1982; Mash & Dalby, 1978). Counseling areas such as self-management skills, parent education programs, and stress management techniques have also received the attention of cognitive therapists.

The potential contribution of cognitive behavior modification to the inviting relationship is readily apparent. Its applicability and effectiveness have been well documented in the counseling literature, and its implicit optimism, respect, trust, and intentionality are in harmony with invitational counseling. The contributions of cognitive behavior modification make it a therapeutic approach ideally suited for the inviting relationship.

PERSON-CENTERED COUNSELING

Individuals have within themselves vast resources for self-understanding and for altering their self-concepts, basic attitudes, and self-directed behavior; these resources can be tapped if a definable climate of facilitative psychological attitudes can be provided.

Carl R. Rogers, *A Way of Being,*
1980, p. 115

No single movement has had as significant an impact on the counseling profession as what has become known as *person-centered counseling.* The development of this theory of counseling emerged from the writings, research, and leadership of Carl Rogers. For almost half a century, from the 1940s into the 1980s, Rogers' contributions to counseling theory and practice have immeasurably enriched the emerging counseling profession and shaped its future direction. This emergence and future direction of counseling will be explored in the final chapter of this book. In particular, Rogerian counseling has helped counselors focus on the persons in the process. Even Rogers' own thinking (1980) has gradually moved away from a "client-centered" identity to a "person-centered" one. Rogers' major contributions to the perceptual tradition and self-concept theory have served as bedrock for invitational counseling.

Carl Rogers was born in Illinois in 1902 and raised in a family of six children. He attended the University of Wisconsin where he first studied agriculture but later majored in history. Upon graduation he enrolled in the Union Theological Seminary in New York. While in the seminary Rogers became interested in psychology and psychiatric work and began attending classes at nearby Columbia University.

Rogers' growing interest in psychology led him to apply for a graduate fellowship at the Institute of Child Guidance at Columbia University, where he received his Ph.D. In 1931, Rogers went to Rochester, New York, to work for the Society for the Prevention of Cruelty to Children. He spent 12 years in Rochester, the last four teaching at the University of Rochester. In 1939, the year before he left Rochester to teach at Ohio State University, Rogers' first book, *The Clinical Treatment of the Problem Child*, was published. This work introduced client-centered therapy.

Client-Centered Therapy

It was at Ohio State University where Rogers refined and further developed his theory of psychotherapy. In 1942 he published *Counseling and Psychotherapy*, which presented his ideas regarding the importance of creating a warm and responsive atmosphere in counseling relationships. His thoughts on nondirective counselor behaviors were a radical change from the traditional psychoanalytic views of psychotherapy then in vogue. Later he moved to the University of Chicago where he spent the next 12 years.

While at the University of Chicago, Rogers wrote *Client-Centered Therapy* (1951), which is the most comprehensive presentation of his theory and practice of counseling. His tenure at the University of Chicago was followed by a position at the University of Wisconsin. In 1966 he moved to LaJolla, California, to become a member of the Western Behavioral Science Institute. In 1968, Rogers and a group of colleagues founded the Center for Studies of the Person. It was during the 1970s and 1980s that Rogers' writings reflected a transformation of his personal views of psychotherapy by preferring the term *person-centered* over *client-centered* counseling.

Rogers has published at least ten books, hundreds of articles, and numerous book chapters. The theoretical position and supporting research he has contributed to the counseling literature are fundamental to the invitational model and are, of course, compatible with invitational counseling. Because Rogers' contributions to the practice of counseling have been so influential, and his theoretical beliefs are so basic to invitational counseling, this chapter concludes with an overview of person-centered counseling.

The following sections describe person-centered counseling according to the questions posed at the beginning of this chapter. It is by necessity a brief description. For an in-depth understanding of Rogerian counseling the reader is referred to the original works of Carl Rogers (1942, 1951, 1959, 1961, 1980). Students of person-centered counseling will particularly enjoy Rogers' *On Becoming a Person* (1961) and *A Way of Being* (1980).

Elements of Person-Centered Counseling

While the underlying theory of person-centered counseling encompasses a broad range of assumptions, it has some fundamental elements. These elements include Rogers' views of the importance of perception and self-concept, and his core conditions for successful counseling. An examination of these fundamental elements follows.

Perception. Person-centered counseling has as one of its theoretical foundations a strong commitment to the perceptual tradition. Rogers maintained that the individual exists as the center of his or her phenomenological or experiential field. However, only a portion of a person's perceived experiences are at a high level of awareness at any given moment. Other experiences are at some lower level. This phenomenon is observed, for example, when people ignore apparent dangers and risk their lives to save others. Often news reports give accounts of heroic acts in life-threatening situations that ordinarily would produce incapacitating fear, yet the dangers are largely overlooked by persons whose full attention is absorbed in a rescue operation.

Rogers held that people develop and behave according to their personal reality. This reality is formulated by a person's interpretations of his or her experiences. People react not to some external reality but to their perception of what is real. Because person-centered counseling emphasizes the importance of an internal or subjective reality, it places primary importance on counselor understanding of client perceptions within the helping relationship.

Even though no individual can ever fully understand the private perceptions of another, to overlook these perceptions would be to concentrate primarily on external factors. The counselor who overemphasizes objective reality while under-emphasizing subjective reality runs the risk of treating the client as an object rather than as a person. Balancing the objective and subjective frameworks is the key to successful helping. Objectivity and subjectivity have a combined importance in helping the client and counselor to test out new behaviors that may evolve from an altered perception of reality.

Rogerian counseling sees both internal "subjective" and external "objective" frames of reference as being important to the counseling process. The subjective view is vital to understanding an individual's development and behavior, while the objective view is needed to help clients and counselors select new alternative courses of action that are likely to meet with success. These views are identical with invitational counseling's emphasis on the importance of beliefs and behaviors working together.

Self-concept. Self-concept is a vital construct in person-centered counseling, and Rogers has written a great deal about the self and its influence on developmental processes. His beliefs about the self have also influenced his attitudes about his relationship with his own existence as it relates to professional helping. As Rogers (1980) stated, "I find that when I am closest to my inner intuitive self, when I am somehow in touch with the unknown me, when perhaps I am in a slightly altered state of consciousness, then whatever I do seems to be full of healing" (Rogers, 1980, p. 129). Recognition of the importance of the self in human existence influenced Rogers and other person-centered counselors to emphasize the role of self-concept in the helping process. As person-centered therapy emerged, and as practitioners observed and researched client behaviors and attitudes, the importance of self-perceptions in determining the direction of human behavior became apparent.

From a Rogerian vantage point, people are often confronted with incongruities between their self-perceptions and their experiences. When these incongruities interfere with their development, people seek assistance. The aim in person-centered counseling is to help the person's developing self become more congruent with existing experiences. In this way the self "becomes a fluid gestalt, always in the process of assimilating new experiences. The individual experiences . . . not as a static being, but as a process of becoming" (Grummon, 1972, p. 90).

The process of becoming, as characterized in person-centered counseling, is related to the "stance" of invitational counseling. Both underscore the potential of people to become more than what they presently are. The person-centered belief that humans have both the tendency and capacity for self-actualization, and that those qualities can be largely realized under optimally facilitative conditions, is consistent with the invitational counseling's thesis that human potential, while not always apparent, is always there, waiting to be discovered and invited forth.

Core conditions. Few theories of psychotherapy have been researched as intensively as person-centered counseling. Research reviewed by Grummon (1972), Thompson and Rudolph (1983), and others on both process and outcome variables has provided substantial support for its value. Studies have reported improved psychological adjustment, greater tolerance for frustrating situations, decreased defensiveness, accelerated learning, and other benefits of person-centered counseling (Axline, 1947; Grummon & John, 1954; Thetford, 1952).

Of particular interest to counselors has been the study of Rogers' therapist variables—empathy, respect, and genuineness. The works of Carkhuff and Berenson (1967) and Truax and Carkhuff (1967) have validated the important contributions these variables make to the counseling process. Empathy, respect, and genuineness have also been attributed to effective helping relationships in teaching (Aspy, 1972; Gazda and others, 1977).

It should be noted at this point that most research findings indicate that Rogers' condition variables of empathy, respect, and genuineness make up only a partial contribution to the total counseling process. Gendlin (1969), Carkhuff (1969a, b), and others have indicated that there are additional variables, including levels of interaction and counselor skills, which are needed beyond those initially presented in the person-centered approach. While additional variables are emerging,

Rogers' emphasis on client-centered interaction, empathetic understanding, and the egalitarian nature of counseling relationships, coupled with his focus on present "here and now" client concerns, are central to effective therapeutic processes and the inviting relationship.

Applications of Person-Centered Counseling

In its early development, client-centered therapy restricted its focus to individual therapeutic processes in nondirective relationships. However, its movement in recent years toward a person-centered perspective appears to have a much wider focus. By way of illustration, Rogers asked the question, "Do we dare be designers?" (Rogers, 1980, p. 240). In answering this question, he painted an optimistic vision of the person and the world of tomorrow, and he defined the proactive role that counselors can have if they summon the courage to become reconstructionists of society.

Rogers has encouraged professional helpers to become radicals "in the true sense of that word" (Rogers, 1980, p. 241). He suggested that counselors and psychologists leave their secure offices and actively counsel and consult with community workers, school administrators, teachers, parents, and others to help design and implement learning and living environments for future communities.

Describing the role of the future professional helper, Rogers suggested that "the task will no longer be to try to assuage the pain of the victims of the old system, for whom failure has become a daily experience; he will instead, have embarked on the broader task of building a flexible institution—if such is possible—with students as the core and all others as the servants of the learners" (Rogers, 1980, p. 241). The person-centered approach of Rogers has the potential to be applied in a variety of educational, psychological, political, industrial, managerial, recreational, medical, and other settings. This optimistic application of person-centered counseling to a broad spectrum of helping is congruent with the "people, places, policies, and programs" perspective of the inviting relationship.

SUMMARY

This chapter has presented four major approaches to professional helping that can be incorporated, either individually or in combination, into an expanded perspective for professional counseling. However, each of these four approaches has a distinctive orientation. Adlerian counseling has roots in psychodynamic theory. Reality therapy is often associated with behavioral approaches. Cognitive behavior modification combines, as its name implies, cognitive and behavioral theories. And person-centered counseling is closely associated with existential/humanistic schools of thought. In spite of their distinctive orientations, each approach values optimism, respect, trust, and intentionality, and each incorporates the belief that individuals have the power and responsibility to influence their own development.

These counseling approaches maintain a hopeful vision of people and their ability to make positive changes in their lives. The presence or absence of this vision is particularly significant in choosing approaches to be used in the inviting relationship.

Each of the approaches presented in this chapter is compatible with invitational counseling because of its optimistic viewpoint, its respect for people, its trust in the human organism, and its emphasis on intentional choice. Each provides part of an expanded perspective for professional counseling in a variety of settings.

There are other counseling approaches, many with qualities like the four presented here, that are compatible with invitational counseling and that can contribute to the inviting relationship. The ones described in this chapter are illustrative. They have been evaluated in light of the four questions regarding compatibility presented at the beginning of this chapter. A similar evaluation process can serve as a framework for practicing counselors to choose from a wider selection of counseling theories and to adopt appropriate and caring techniques that promise to enrich further the inviting relationship.

OPPORTUNITIES FOR FURTHER READING

ADLER, A. (1931). *What life should mean to you.* New York: Putnam. In this early book, Adler presented the fundamental assumptions of his theory of human nature and outlined the meaning and influence of a person's style of life.

ANSBACHER, H., & ANSBACHER, R. (1956). *The individual psychology of Alfred Adler: A systematic presentation in selections from his writings.* New York: Harper & Row. The Ansbachers provided a thorough examination and analysis of Adler's writings and his development of Individual Psychology. In particular, they offered useful comparisons and contrasts between Individual Psychology and other psychological and philosophical views.

COREY, G. (1982). *Theory and practice of counseling and psychotherapy,* 2nd ed. Monterey, Calif.: Brooks/Cole. This book is intended primarily for graduate students in counseling. It provides an insightful overview of the major theories of helping and explains how they apply to various human concerns.

DINKMEYER, D., PEW, L.W., & DINKMEYER, D., JR. (1978). *Adlerian counseling and psychotherapy.* Monterey, Calif.: Brooks/Cole. Dinkmeyer, Pew, and Dinkmeyer summarized the basic tenets of Adlerian counseling and psychotherapy. They described Adler's view of human development as well as processes and strategies used in Adlerian counseling. The book illustrates the applicability of Adlerian counseling in a number of professional settings.

DREIKURS, R. (1968). *Psychology in the classroom,* 2nd ed. New York: Harper & Row. This book presents some challenging case studies in which teachers face difficult questions related to child behavior and classroom management. Dreikurs commented on the cases from an Adlerian perspective. It is an excellent resource for teachers and counselors.

DREIKURS, R., & SOLTZ, V. (1964). *Children: The challenge.* New York: Duell, Sloan and Pearce. A popular book for parents that presents child rearing theory and strategies based on the Adlerian approach. Included are chapters on the goals of misbehavior, logical and natural consequences, and family council meetings.

GLASSER, W. (1965). *Reality therapy.* New York: Harper & Row. This is the basic text on Glasser's theory. In this book Glasser presented the fundamental assumptions of his theory and outlined the therapeutic processes used in the reality therapy model.

GLASSER, W. (1981). *Stations of the mind.* New York: Harper & Row. In this work Glasser integrated reality therapy with brain functioning, perceptual understanding, and behavioral development. It provides a view of how people can learn to be in control of their behavior.

HERGENHAHN, B.R. (1984). *An introduction to theories of personality,* 2nd ed. Englewood Cliffs, N.J.: Prentice-Hall. Hergenhahn presented an overview of the major theories of personality development. He included the Freudian, behavioral, Adlerian, and Rogerian, among others, in this comprehensive text.

MEICHENBAUM, D. (1977). *Cognitive behavior modification: An integrative approach.* New York: Plenum Press. In this book Meichenbaum described his model of cognitive behavior modification. He explained the role of internal dialogue in behavior choices and illustrated how cognitive behavior modification can be used to help people learn to control their internal dialogues while choosing more appropriate behaviors.

PATTERSON, C.H. (1985b). *The therapeutic relationship: Foundations for an eclectic psychotherapy.* Monterey, Calif.: Brooks/Cole. This book provides the reader with an understanding that the essence of successful psychotherapy depends on good human relationships. Patterson uses both philosophy and theory to propose an eclectic system of counseling and psychotherapy.

7

THE SETTING FOR INVITATIONAL COUNSELING
past, present, and future

There is, of course, a wide variation of what these thousands of counselors do.

C. Gilbert Wrenn, *The World of the Contemporary Counselor*, 1973, p. 251

133

Because the inviting relationship offers an expanded perspective for professional counseling, it is appropriate here to consider the need for an expanded perspective by placing invitational counseling in the context of the past development of the counseling profession, the evolution of present practices, and promises for the future of professional helping. The counseling profession, as with all professions, has been shaped by historical events that have influenced the roles and functions of practitioners and contributed to its present definition and future potential. An understanding of past and present events encourages an appreciation of the need for an expanded perspective for professional counseling.

This chapter highlights some prominent events in the history of the counseling movement, considers a number of theoretical and situational components that now shape various definitions of counseling, and presents several scenarios on the future of counseling. The reader who wishes to study historical events, the contemporary scene, or future predictions in detail is referred to works by Armor (1969), Aubrey (1977, 1982), Brewer (1942), Glanz (1964), Mathewson (1962), Shertzer and Stone (1966), Super (1955), Wilson and Rotter (1982), and Wrenn (1962, 1973) among others. These authors provide in-depth presentations of past, present, and future trends in professional counseling and offer evidence for the need of expanded perspectives for professional counseling.

A BRIEF HISTORY OF PROFESSIONAL COUNSELING

> We have not had time to learn inside ourselves the things that have happened to us.
>
> John Steinbeck, *America and Americans,*
> 1966, p. 141

The early roots of the counseling profession can be traced to the beginning of the twentieth century when the introduction of guidance programs to schools and other agencies came as a reaction to conditions in North American society at that time. Aubrey (1977) pointed out that the rapid shift in North America during the late 1800s and early 1900s from an independent, agricultural-based society of small farmers to that of an interdependent, industrial-based nation of employees resulted in tremendous social changes. These changes produced marvelous technological and industrial achievements, but they were accompanied by undesirable side effects and misery for many people. The creation of guidance programs in schools and other places was both an effort to ameliorate some of the undesirable aspects of those sweeping social events and to guide students and others into necessary job training and placement.

Vocational Guidance

Jesse B. Davis is credited by most counseling historians for developing the first curriculum-based guidance program in public schools. Davis, a Detroit, Michigan school principal from 1898 to 1907, recognized the social and vocational decision-making difficulties his students were experiencing. He therefore began to spend a significant portion of his time talking with young people about vocational choices. In 1907 Davis accepted the principal's position at Michigan High School in Grand Rapids. While there he introduced a "vocational and moral guidance" program through the English composition classes (Mathewson, 1962, p. 72). This action is considered to be a milestone in the history of counseling and guidance.

As Aubrey (1977) explained, guidance "was first viewed as something that could be taught by a teacher in a classroom to large numbers of males and females. Further, guidance was largely seen as a series of learning experiences complementing the existing curriculum by addressing important areas theretofore ignored and neglected" (Aubrey, 1977, p. 289). So it happened that guidance was initially incorporated into the school curriculum as an instructional component.

About the time that Jesse Davis was introducing guidance to English classes at Michigan High School, Frank Parsons, a Massachusetts social worker, was developing vocational guidance programs for out-of-school young people in Boston. In 1908 he founded the Boston Vocational Bureau to assist young men in securing employment. Often referred to as the "Father of Guidance," Parsons formulated a model of vocational choice that would greatly influence the early guidance movement.

While guidance services were being created in Michigan and Massachusetts, vocational guidance was beginning to make its mark in New York City; Cincinnati, Ohio; Des Moines, Iowa; Salt Lake City, Utah; Lincoln, Nebraska; Oakland, California, and other cities. The expansion of the vocational guidance movement led, in 1913, to the founding of the National Vocational Guidance Association (NVGA) and, in 1915, to the publication of the *Vocational Guidance Bulletin,* forerunner of the *National Vocational Guidance Association Journal.*

The social reform movement of the early 1900s, itself a response to the demand and pressures of an expanding industrial economy, provided additional support for the development of vocational guidance. As Roeber (1963) explained, "School dropout rates, exploitation of child labor, a restrictive school curricula, an expanding economy, advances in technology, and a constant surge in individualism are but a few examples of the conditions which contributed to a cultural readiness for vocational guidance, as well as educational guidance, and eventually the emergence of the school counselor" (Roeber, 1963, p. 2). The vocational guidance movement begun by Davis, Parsons, and others gradually developed into a broad concept of assisting young people through the total educational process.

During and after World War I, the development and utilization of an array of psychometric instruments designed to measure various mental abilities gave added credibility to the guidance movement. The use of mental ability tests to assign military personnel to appropriate responsibilities during World War I was employed after the war to assist people in matching their abilities and interests with appropriate vocational goals. This became known as "trait and factor" approaches to guidance.

Trait and factor models seemed to offer the precision hoped for in vocational guidance and they became very popular. They also, according to Aubrey (1977), reflected the somewhat static and authoritative attitude of society during the 1930s and early 1940s. In any case, the appearance of psychometric tests gave added impetus to the guidance movement.

Educational and Developmental Guidance

By the 1940s, guidance programs had gradually expanded their services from the narrow perspective of trait and factor models to a wider view of guidance for life adjustment. This era saw an emergence of guidance programs aimed at enhancing interpersonal relationships, developing social skills, and encouraging decision-making abilities in order to make responsible choices regarding future plans. These educational guidance programs incorporated vocational decision-making processes as one of many developmental areas with which students needed assistance. During this period the guidance worker was viewed as being able to assist students with varied educational, social, and career decisions.

Beginning in the 1940s and extending into the 1960s, the work of developmental theorists had a powerful influence on the guidance movement. For example, the identification of developmental tasks by Havighurst (1952), coupled with his explanations of the relationship of these tasks to various age groups, helped give birth to many innovative concepts and processes in guidance. Collectively, these concepts and processes came to be known as *developmental guidance.* Developmental guidance focused on the facilitation of young people's day-to-day development and played an important role in the establishment of guidance programs in North American schools during the 1960s and 1970s.

Although the first half of the twentieth century witnessed the creation and expansion of guidance, an identity for emerging professionals in the field of guidance was not clearly established. For several decades guidance personnel were given such titles as "guidance teacher," "guidance worker," "guidance officer," or "guidance counselor." As with professionals in other emerging fields, counselors faced an identity problem. But in spite of differences in titles and confusion with identities, the counseling profession continued to develop.

The expansion of guidance programs in the 1940s and 1950s was reflected by the founding of the American Personnel and Guidance Association (APGA) in 1952. At that time the National Vocational Guidance Association (NVGA) joined with the American College Personnel Association (ACPA) and the Association of Guidance Supervisors and Counselors (AGSC), later to become the Association for Counselor Education and Supervision (ACES). This established APGA as an umbrella organization for all guidance and counseling personnel.

Today the counseling profession continues to wrestle with the labels and descriptors that best characterize its purpose and membership. This is evidenced by the 1983 decision of the American Personnel and Guidance Association to change its name to the American Association for Counseling and Development (AACD). Further, growing numbers of state associations have changed their names by replacing the terms *guidance* and *personnel* with the terms *counseling* and *de-*

velopment. Although the gradual shift away from "guidance" and toward "counseling" is not uniformly popular, many professionals see the move as beneficial and long overdue.

Emergence of Counseling

During the early decades of the vocational and educational guidance movement, the term *counseling* was rarely used. However, as Aubrey (1977) noted, "Counseling as a psychological process is apparent in much of the legacy of the early mental health movement, the work of G. Stanley Hall and his disciples in the child-study movement, the introduction of psychoanalysis to this country in 1909 by Freud's lectures at Clark University, and the application of psychometrics following World War I" (Aubrey, 1977, p. 291). These events gave added momentum to a counseling interpretation of professional helping.

A highly significant influence in revolutionizing the guidance movement from a testing, instructional, and vocational placement emphasis to a person-oriented counseling focus was the monumental work of Carl Rogers (1942, 1951, 1961) and his concept of client-centered counseling, detailed in Chapter 6. This new focus moved the profession away from a data collection and dissemination service toward a person-oriented therapeutic process.

Rogers' client-centered counseling was soon followed by a proliferation of counseling theories, therapeutic techniques, and behavioral strategies. Simultaneously, helping professionals in a host of settings—mental health centers, school counseling offices, family clinics, private practices, pastoral counseling centers, correctional facilities, child guidance clinics, and rehabilitation institutions among others—began to create and adopt new theories, techniques, and strategies. These innovations helped to bring together counselors from many settings to form professional networks.

The gains made by Rogerian client-centered counselors were complemented by the contributions of others within the profession. These contributions included such valuable concepts as Alfred Adler's "life style disclosure technique," William Glasser's "reality therapy," Don Snygg and Art Combs' "perceptual psychology," Albert Ellis' "rational-emotive model," George Kelly's "personal constructs," Eric Berne's "transactional analysis," and Sidney Jourard's "self disclosure." Further contributions to the counseling movement were made by social workers, counseling psychologists, employment specialists, pastoral counselors, and others who used counseling in their work. All of these contributions called for ever-expanding perspectives for professional counseling.

Today's Counselor

Contemporary counselors function in a vast array of professional settings. Their differences are apparent not so much by their use of distinct counseling processes or techniques as by their varied work environments. For example, school counselors are primarily concerned with the educational progress and emotional health of students, while family therapists focus on the relationships that influence families and individual family members. There is, however, considerable overlap among the functions of these professional counselors. At times, observers will see school counselors counseling parents and families in conjunction with educational services, while family therapists will be seen counseling family members about educational or vocational concerns that are affecting family relationships. With such overlapping responsibilities and "territories," differences in viewpoints are inevitable, particularly when it comes to the question of the relative importance of the counseling process itself.

The counseling process, as opposed to other educational or vocational activities, has not received unanimous support within the profession, particularly in some school programs where other pressing needs such as testing, placement, advisement, and guidance are sometimes seen as more important than counseling. Consequently, practicing counselors continue to debate the merits of their various professional roles and functions. The debate is sometimes nurtured by the diversity of those in the counseling profession.

The diversity of today's professional counselors is demonstrated by the variety of divisions in the American Association for Counseling and Development (AACD). The present divisions of AACD include the Association for Humanistic Education and Development (AHEAD), the National Career Development Association (NCDA), the American Mental Health Counselors Association (AMHCA), the American Rehabilitation Counseling Association (ARCA), the American School Counselor Association (ASCA), the Association for Measurement and Evaluation in Counseling and Development (AMECD), the American College Personnel Association (ACPA), the National Employment Counselors Association (NECA), the Association for Multi-cultural Counseling and Development (AMCD), the Association for Specialists in Group Work (ASGW), the Public Offender Counselors Association (POCA), the Association for Counselor Education and Supervision (ACES), and the Association for Religious and Value Issues in Counseling (ARVIC). In addition to these groups, many professional counselors are members of organizations that are associated with specific professional practices, including the National Association of Social Workers (NASW), the National Association of School Psychologists (NASP), the American Psychological Association (APA), and the American Association of Marriage and Family Therapists (AAMFT). These organizations represent members from a wide spectrum of work settings.

Recently, AACD has helped to create a National Board of Certified Counselors (NBCC), which certifies qualified counselors based on documentation of appropriate professional training and completion of a comprehensive examination covering eight content areas of professional counseling. This national certification and identification process may help to draw counselors closer together than has traditionally been the case.

Beginning in the early 1900s, guidance and counseling literature and counselor education programs have offered many different approaches to assist children, adolescents, adults, and older adults in overcoming obstacles and enriching their lives while meeting the expectations of society. Most professional counselors have typically selected certain theories, strategies, and activities to direct their day-to-day functioning, but as responsibilities and roles continue to multiply, counselors have become increasingly aware of the need for a more expanded perspective for their professional functioning. This need has become increasingly more apparent as counselors face the challenges brought about by a growing technological world and emerging moral and social concerns. As Jantsch (1980) pointed out, every discipline is in the midst of a revolution. This seems particularly true of contemporary counseling.

CONTEMPORARY COUNSELING

Faced with rapid advances in technology, the counseling profession, like industry, is finding it difficult to keep up with human adaptations. For the most part, this technology has demonstrably altered and improved the quality of life. But these advancements have been accompanied by difficulties that complicate, impede, or even threaten human existence. In some cases, as with nuclear weaponry, chemical or biological warfare agents, or "star wars" destructive forces, advancements actually place at risk the existence of humans on this earth. Thus we have a scientific paradox.

A Modern Paradox

Scientific advancements, such as the discovery of nuclear power, the exploration of space, or the invention of the microchip, are coupled with the fears of nuclear holocaust, war in outer space, or the domination of machines over humans. The spectacular progress of computer technology, for example, while having a revolutionary impact on information processing, carries the corresponding risk of personal isolation, as illustrated by a counselor's complaint that her supervisor was "terminally" hunched over his microcomputer. The use of computers, data banks, and instant retrieval systems by governments, schools, and other institutions, coupled with advanced surveillance technology, also increases the possibility of invasion of privacy and threatens other civil rights as well.

As computers and robots are used to perform tasks formerly done by people, there may be less opportunity for men and women to work cooperatively—if they are able to find work at all. Instead, each employed person may be paired with a unit of electronic equipment or a robot that works round-the-clock without weariness or complaint. Lacking human contact, workers may feel a decreased sense of belonging and an increased sense of personal isolation. The same phenomenon may be found in the field of medicine.

In recent years medical achievements have significantly extended the average lifespan, and they promise to continue to do so in the future. By the end of this century it is likely that the basic causes of most diseases will be understood and preventative or curative measures developed. Scientists are already finding ways to use DNA markers to predict whether a person will develop particular diseases later in life. In the immediate future people who develop heart-lung difficulties will probably receive complete heart-lung transplants along with gene therapy to alter the immune system and prevent rejection of the transplant. Among the most active and exciting medical frontiers is the replacement of damaged body parts with various anatomical and mechanical substitutes. In sum, living well beyond four score and seven years of age will probably become common.

But medical miracles have also raised social and moral issues that evade clear-cut answers. Increasing lifespans will result in a growing population of older adults. People will live longer, but will they live better? What will be their role in future society? Science can now prolong life by extraordinary means almost indefinitely to the extent that the meaning of "life" eludes consistent definition. Life and death continually take on new meanings, forcing society to consider complex moral, legal, and ethical questions. When does life begin, when does it end, and who is qualified or responsible for making such determinations? What are the ethical, moral, and legal issues in transplanting major organs from humans to humans, or from other animals to humans? Certainly future counselors will play an important role by assisting people in these and other issues.

Social Transformations

Transformations in society have, for the most part, contributed greatly to an improved quality of life, but they too have created problems. Many of today's jobs and responsibilities will vanish, while worldwide industrial and manufacturing realignment will continue to uproot literally millions of North Americans from familiar geographic locations and vocational roles. Moreover, unemployment, particularly for the undereducated, mis-skilled, or unskilled, will remain a problem, resulting in increased stress, anxiety, and alienation.

A major new social transformation underway for the past several decades is the growing number of women in the North American work force. Women are presently being hired and being successful in many occupations once considered unsuitable or "off limits" for females. The result is that dual-career families are commonplace. Moreover, professions that have traditionally depended on female applicants to fill their ranks, such as teaching and nursing, are hurting as many women turn to other professions. As traditional sex roles are successfully challenged, both in the home and workplace, counselors are being called on as never before to help ease tensions and recognize opportunities brought about by changing perceptions and conditions regarding the roles of men and women in society.

One further illustration of the changes brought about by rapid social transformations is the increase of professional specialties. Social progress, educational opportunities, and the need for specialization have resulted in the training of highly skilled professionals to help with complex scientific, medical, educational, industrial, and human relations issues. Paradoxically, the growing trend toward specialization has sometimes resulted in an overprotection of professional boundaries. Rather than working together so that each can offer his or her expertise, professionals occasionally find themselves in competitive postures, protecting domains while hindering human service. For example, competition and resulting conflicts in the helping profession may sometimes be found among clinical psychologists, mental health counselors, social workers, counselors in private practice, school counselors, educational psychologists, and others. Such competition and conflicts seldom result in improved human services.

Other forces within the counseling profession sometimes run counter to its development. For example, the increasing need for highly skilled counselors, combined with the willingness of counselors to provide services in a variety of settings for an endless number of concerns, can result in counselor burnout. Burnout may be found in counselors who have stretched themselves too far or too fast and have neglected the first two corners of the "four corner press" described in Chapter 5: being personally inviting with oneself and being personally inviting with others. Their own personal well-being and the well-being of their family and friends have taken a back seat to pressing professional demands. The value of caring for oneself and others personally to ameliorate stress and burnout has been emphasized throughout this book.

Finally, the contemporary emphasis of the counseling profession on self-development requires that this emphasis be balanced with genuine social interest and a deep concern for the human community. What Alfred Adler referred to as a lack of social interest can emotionally paralyze individuals as well as groups (Papanek, 1973). The desire to self-discover, self-improve, self-enhance, and self-actualize can receive inordinate attention, as evidenced by the vast array of personal development and self-help books, such as *The Art of Selfishness* (Seabury, 1974), *Looking Out for Number One* (Ringer, 1977), and *Pulling Your Own Strings* (Dyer, 1978). In light of the continuing emphasis on the promotion of oneself, it is critical for counselors to develop all four corners of the "four corner press" and to strike a healthy balance between self-enhancement and a spirit of oneness with others. Self-realization can only be obtained when people develop and maintain profound respect and trust for others and an optimistic view of their value, abilities, and self-directing powers. This balance reduces alienation and fosters a spirit of community.

From this overview of contemporary counseling it is clear that counselors face a complex, ever-changing, ever more specialized technical world. Seldom if ever has society placed greater demands or held higher expectations on the professional counselor. Undoubtedly, these demands will continue to increase for future counselors.

Predicting the future of professional counseling is a risky business, for today's certainties may become tomorrow's fallacies. As Francis Bacon noted: "Dreams and predictions ought to serve but for winter talk by the fireside." Yet it seems self-evident that a need exists for an expanded perspective for counselors, whether it be called invitational counseling or something else. This will require a process of integrating compatible theories and philosophies with acceptable strategies and practices. A critical part of this process is defining what is meant by professional counseling.

Definitions of Professional Counseling

Professional counseling has been defined extensively in the literature. Extensively perhaps, but not consistently. Over the past half-century many authorities have attempted to define counseling. Their efforts have resulted in a wide variety of views, from Good's (1945) early definition of counseling as "individualized and personalized assistance with personal, educational, vocational problems" (Good, 1945, p. 104) to *Webster's Third New International Dictionary* (1976), which described counseling as a "practice of professional service designed to guide an individual to a better understanding of . . . problems and potentialities by utilizing modern psychological principles and methods" (*Webster's,* 1976, p. 518). Definitions of counseling offer a full spectrum of viewpoints regarding the nature of professional helping.

The variety of definitions can be attributed to three interrelated variables that influence the functioning of professional counselors. These variables are: (1) the theoretical beliefs of the counselor, (2) the focus and content of the counseling relationship, and (3) the professional setting. A brief consideration of each is in order.

Theoretical beliefs of counselors.   Reviews of counseling definitions and their origins by Arbuckle (1965), Shertzer and Stone (1974), and Stefflre and Grant (1972) demonstrate the influence that various theoretical orientations have had on the meanings given to counseling. From his client-centered perspective, Carl Rogers (1952) defined counseling as the process by which the basic nature of the self is relaxed in the safety of the relationship with the counselor, and where previously denied experiences are perceived, accepted, and integrated into an altered self.

In contrast to the definition offered by Rogers, Shaffer's (1947) behavioral view maintained that counseling should be defined as a learning process that enables the client to acquire skills to control his or her behavior. Shertzer and Stone (1974) combined self-concept and behavioral views in their definition: "Counseling is an interaction process which facilitates meaningful understanding of self and environment and/or clarification of goals and values for future behavior" (Shertzer & Stone, 1974, p. 20).

Counselors of a psychodynamic orientation have provided yet another definition of counseling. King and Bennington (1972) described an essential goal of counseling as one "to reduce the anxiety of the client to manageable limits in order for the ego to function in a more discriminating and effective manner" (King & Bennington, 1972, p. 187). A recent view of Adlerian psychology defined the primary goal of professional counseling as "behavior change within the existing lifestyle" and differentiated it from the goal of psychotherapy for which "a change in lifestyle is the desired outcome" (Sweeney, 1981, p. 144). Throughout the counseling literature, definitions of counseling are as varied as the beliefs of its practitioners. Each definition is a reflection of the basic assumptions held by the various authorities, and each emerges from the unique focus and content of the counseling relationship espoused by individual theorists.

Focus and content of the counseling relationship. The focus and content of the counseling relationship as reflected in the various counseling approaches have complicated the formulation of a precise or consistent definition of counseling. For example, trait-factor theory as outlined by Williamson (1972) describes the purpose of counseling as one that "emphasizes choice of school or work. This is not restricted to the initial choice of a career but to successive stages of development of the individual, including the intangible problem of value commitments" (Williamson, 1972, p. 137). Other definitions of counseling have focused on the counselee's needs, his or her development, and the importance of responsible decision making to bring about some desired change. Pepinsky and Pepinsky (1954) emphasized in their definition of the counseling process the goal of helping clients change their behaviors to resolve identified concerns and problems. Similarly, Belkin (1976) wrote about counseling as a problem-solving process. These and related definitions of counseling stress the resolution of problems.

Counseling has also been viewed as a goal-setting and planning process. Smith (1955) described counseling as a "process in which the counselor assists the counselee to make interpretations of facts related to choice, plan or adjustment which he needs to make" (Smith, 1955, p. 156). Likewise, Cottle and Downie (1970) stated: "Counseling is the process by which a counselor assists a client to face, understand, and accept information about himself and his interactions with others, so that he can make effective decisions about various life choices" (Cottle & Downie, 1970, p. 1). Bordin (1968) viewed counseling as "interactions where one person, referred to as the counselor or the therapist, has taken the responsibility for making his role in the interaction process contribute positively to the other person's personality development" (Bordin, 1968, p. 10). In these definitions the dominant theme is that counseling should help people achieve goals. Some of these may be remedial goals while others are developmental goals.

More recent definitions have reflected the counseling profession's movement toward a balance between remediation and development. Pietrofesa and others (1984) defined counseling "as a relationship between a professionally trained, competent counselor and an individual seeking help in gaining greater self-understanding and improved decision-making and behavior-change skills for problem resolution and/or developmental growth" (Pietrofesa and others, 1984, p. 6). This definition is perhaps the most comparable with the inviting relationship.

How the professional counselor perceives the purpose of the counseling relationship influences his or her definition of that process. The focus and content of counseling, while heavily influenced by the counselor's theoretical views, are also related to the professional setting where counseling occurs and to the specific counseling services being offered.

Settings and services. Counselors function in a variety of settings: family clinics, mental health centers, schools, industries, hospitals, retirement villages, court houses, child guidance clinics, military installations, religious institutions, recreational facilities, correctional centers, and private practice, among others.

These diverse locations contribute to the difficulty of achieving a consistent definition of counseling. Orr (1965) observed: "Counseling cannot be precisely defined. It is not a single activity nor is it the province of any one profession" (Orr, 1965, p. 3). Orr's statement seems understandable given the variety of responsibilities of professional counselors and the many settings in which these responsibilities are met.

In addition to working in a variety of settings, counselors confront such an array of human concerns that finding a common specific definition of their professional service is extremely difficult. Orr (1965) summarized the arduous task of defining professional counseling thus: "The breadth and diversity of counseling may be suggested by such characterizations as the following: It is the *art* of helping people to help themselves. It is the applied *science* of psycho-socio-biological pathology. It is the *process* of solving human problems in a professional setting. It is a *relationship* between a trained helping-person and other persons with problems from which the latter draw strength, confidence, and insight in the process of working out their own solutions to the difficulties" (Orr, 1965, p. 3). The helper who employs invitational counseling would add to Orr's description that it is also the *development* of programs, policies, and places that invite an improved quality of life for all people. Clearly, what counselors do, and with whom and where, are critical elements in how they define themselves and their work.

Though many definitions of counseling have been presented in the literature, each definition focuses on particular characteristics or aspects of the counseling relationship. Stefflre and Grant (1972) pointed out that the historical development of a definition of counseling has included educational, psychological, sociological, personal, vocational, and advice-giving components. Recent definitions incorporate developmental and preventive aspects of counseling as well.

Although there is a variety of perceptions about the definition of professional counseling, there is also common ground. Of all the descriptors used to characterize professional counseling, the one term that is most often used is the word *process*. From the many definitions of counseling quoted in this chapter *process* either appears or is implied in almost every one. Counseling is viewed by most theorists as a process of assisting others in making decisions and acting upon them. Because *process* is so central to the theory and practice of counseling, it is necessary to consider it more closely.

Counseling as a Process

A process can be defined as a systematic and continuous series of actions taking place in a definite manner and directed toward an identified goal or objective. By this definition, professional counseling is certainly a process. It can be viewed as a series of purposeful actions directed toward a goal or objective. Each action within the counseling relationship can be defined both as a process in and of itself as well as part of the total practice of counseling. Four common examples of processes used in counseling are: accepting, understanding, exploring, and evaluating.

Accepting behaviors, stressed at numerous points throughout this book, is vital to the establishment of the initial counseling relationship and to the facilitation of the counseling process. Counselors accept their clients for their unconditional worth. They also accept clients to increase the probability of opening and maintaining lines of communication and to understand the client's perceptions and feelings.

To relate to others effectively, counselors not only accept their clients but also seek to resonate with them; to empathize with their perceptions and respond to their feelings. An empathetic counselor actively seeks to understand clients' feelings and to demonstrate this understanding by reflecting it in his or her behavior.

Another example of process within the practice of counseling is exploration. Professional counselors seek to move beyond the accepting and understanding phases of their relationships to assist their clients with a deeper appreciation of themselves and the world. To do this, counselors encourage their clients to examine closely their feelings, experiences, and behaviors.

A third example of process is evaluation. Personal and professional development obtained through counseling culminates in the evaluation process. This occurs throughout the helping relationship but particularly during the action phase in which alternative behaviors are chosen and practiced by the client. Both the counselor and client evaluate the counseling process by their private thoughts, verbal agreements, and observable behavior changes. Evaluation is as important in counseling as it is in other professions.

To accept, understand, reflect, explore, and evaluate experiences and perceptions are vital in all counseling models. But without intentional movement to enrich experiences or alter perceptions, the inviting relationship does not exist. Counselors who employ the invitational approach work with their clients in identifying behaviors, environments, systems, policies, and programs that can be acted upon to bring about healthy changes in their lives. Identifying those factors and developing strategies to invite positive change are important for both the client and counselor. One unexpected product of sharing this action phase together is that, when successful, both the client and counselor move toward higher levels of personal and professional functioning described in Chapter 5.

Previously it was noted that of the many theories and models studied by counseling students and followed by practicing counselors, the majority emphasize a process to remediate deficiencies. Relatively few give equal importance to development. It will be useful, therefore, to again compare and contrast a remedial process with a developmental one.

Counseling as a remedial process.   The perspective that counseling is a remedial process begins with the premise that people have problems and come to counselors for help. As an illustration, Downing (1983) points out that the majority of counselors have accepted by default the classification system provided by psychiatry. This classification system is essentially negative and focuses on morbidity, psychopathology, neuroses, psychoses, and various mental illnesses. From this perspective the professional relationship focuses on specific problems and develops strategies that will eliminate them. From a remedial perspective, the counseling relationship ends successfully when problems are resolved.

Much of traditional behavior modification, for example, focuses on specific behaviors that are hindering a person from performing adequately or producing appropriately. Similarly, psychoanalysis explores inadequacies and developmental deficiencies that have influenced and continue to influence a person's personality development. Psychoanalysts spend many hours, months, and sometimes years helping clients confront past events and relationships that have hampered their ability to function satisfactorily.

Client-centered therapy, while viewing the client positively and maintaining an optimistic stance toward self actualization, also has tended to focus on client concerns, problems, and difficulties. In this sense, it too is a deficit model of counseling. However, the more recent transformation of client-centered therapy to person-centered counseling gives this approach a more developmental orientation.

Each of the approaches mentioned above, as well as many related counseling theories and therapies, can make valuable contributions to professional helping when used appropriately and caringly by skilled professionals. These approaches suggest ways to assist people with specific problems and to remove barriers to abundant living. Each makes an important contribution to professional counseling. Yet all are limited to the degree that they view the counseling relationship as initiated primarily to remediate concerns, remove barriers, and solve problems.

Professional counseling can be far more than the identification and remediation of problems. It can be a process for people who are functioning well in day-to-day living but who can benefit from assistance in recognizing and realizing their relatively boundless potential in all areas of human endeavor. The rapid growth of communtiy-career counseling, where successful individuals seek ways to expand their lives further, and the popularity of marriage-enrichment counseling programs are examples of developmental counseling.

Counseling as a developmental process.   When establishing helping relationships most counselors work to identify those areas that are hindering development and to assist clients in removing those roadblocks. However, an expanded perspective of professional counseling, advocated by invitational counseling, does more than assist people with problems. It seeks avenues that enable clients to recognize their potential, make proactive decisions, and develop more positive relations with themselves and others, personally and professionally.

Counselors who define the counseling process in terms of realizing of human potential encourage their clients to view counseling in the same way. Just as the skilled basketball player with excellent peripheral vision sees many scoring possibilities that others may miss, the person who is encouraged by a counselor to take a developmental view is more likely to recognize opportunities available to enrich one's own existence as well as that of others.

In addition to helping clients realize opportunities for potential growth, counselors who move from a remedial perspective toward a developmental one adopt a "wide-lens" view of helping. They use their skills not only to help clients cope with existing concerns but also to assist organizations, institutions, communities, and other groups in preventing problems and encouraging development. Invitational counseling manifests this relationship in its "people, places, policies, and programs" approach to professional helping.

Finally, counselors who adopt an invitational approach to helping recognize that successful counseling has the potential to enrich *their* lives as well as the lives of those they seek to help. In this sense, counseling can be an encompassing approach to human service. It can extend far beyond the remediation of immediate problems and transcend the walls of the counseling office. Counseling can be a special invitation to more abundant living.

THE FUTURE OF COUNSELING

I strongly suspect that we eventually will see the emergence of a new model of professional psychology which will not be like present clinical, school, counseling, organizational, or community psychologies of today. Instead, it will involve broad training intended to permit the professional psychologists to adapt to different settings and to offer interventions, programs, and services based on the needs of the client rather than on the predetermined biases and predilections of the specialty of psychology involved in offering the service. Training will emphasize understanding the importance of knowing a lot about *where* one works as well as *what* one does. The core program content will deal with a systematic approach to working with people as individuals, groups and systems.

Jack Bardon, "The State of the Art
(and Science) of School Psychology,"
American Psychologist, 1976, *31,* p. 785

As scientific discoveries and technological inventions continue to add to the complexity of everyday living, the corresponding needs of people to handle this complexity steadily increases. As professional specializations become the norm, counselors will become a more active force, influencing places, policies, and programs as well as working with people to facilitate human development. Counselors of the future will need a consistent stance from which to operate as they employ a wide selection of approaches and strategies that affirm people in their present value while inviting them to realize their potential.

Counseling and Technology

As counselors of the future examine the scope and emphasis of their services, vital decisions will be made about the impact of technological advances on the counseling profession itself. Future scientific discoveries that will have an impact on other professions will also influence counseling.

Technological influences on counseling are already apparent in the use of videotaping equipment to increase the effectiveness of counselor training programs. Audiovisual and microcomputer technology is already being used by counselors in clinical practice as well as in educational settings. Video playback is applied in counseling sessions to allow clients to see themselves as others see them. Clients often gain valuable insights by watching their own behaviors in a nonthreatening and nonjudgmental environment. Moreover, video and computer-assisted programs are being used to teach new coping behaviors, provide information about personal development, to demonstrate learning skills, or impart other useful knowledge. Soon, erasable videodiscs will make today's videotape recorders and microprocessors obsolete. These discs will be electronically encoded with sound and sight and played on machines the size of present portable tape recorders. Technological advances will strengthen the counselor's technical skill, but they may also add to the danger of neglecting the people in the process.

How counselors utilize new technology may be as important as the technology itself. Improved systems, places, programs, and policies can offer vital assistance to future counseling, but they cannot replace the human qualities that are essential to successful helping. Keeping the "human" in human development will be a challenge for tomorrow's counselors.

An example of how technology can be used to assist, rather than replace, the counselor may be seen in present computer-assisted counseling services. The key words are "computer-assisted" rather than "computerized." A computer-assisted program allows counselors and clients to maintain important human interactions while using technology as a tool to store information, present instruction, score inventories, and perform a number of other supplementary and supportive functions. On the other hand, a "computerized" counseling program implies a lack of human contact. According to the assumptions of invitational counseling, the phrase "computerized counseling" is a contradiction in terms. Invitational counseling depends on the human qualities and personal relationships of the "four corner press" presented in Chapter 5.

The challenge to future counselors will be how to accept "hi-tech" advances without neglecting "hi-touch" humanity. To become automated and computerized without primary regard for people in the counseling process would lead to a "doing to" rather than a "being with" profession. The inviting relationship requires that technological advances be constantly monitored and properly evaluated.

Social Change and the Human Condition

In earlier sections of this chapter, problems that result from social movements, scientific discoveries, and advanced technologies were identified. Additional descriptions of these three sources are presented here to explain how future counseling services might ameliorate these disinviting side-effects.

Scientific discoveries and technological inventions will continue to influence life expectancy as the nation's population ages. Future counseling services will help families and individuals to enjoy this additional life expectancy for the optimal benefit of the individual and society. As the average life span is extended, people will require a greater appreciation of developmental concerns in the aging process, including physical needs, medical services, availability of social activities, family and generational interactions, educational pursuits, and other areas related to the continued development of potential. Geriatric counselors who are prepared to meet the needs of expanding ranks of older adults should have little trouble finding positions. Meeting the needs of an aging population will offer many new service avenues and opportunities for professional counselors.

Simultaneously, the achievement of longer life spans may be accompanied by longer periods of dying. Medical advancements already can prolong an individual's life even in the most critical of situations. How the critically ill individual, his or her family members, and close friends cope with this side of medical progress will be a concern of future counselors.

When death finally comes, there is often a need for professional help on the part of those who have suffered the loss of a loved one. A growing number of hospitals, nursing homes, and funeral establishments are hiring counselors to provide bereavement counseling services. It is likely that many more will do so in the future.

Changing patterns in industry and business will also call for an increase in counseling and human services. As automation increases, more and more people will be working individually without the benefit of social groups. Increasingly, people are setting up work stations at home, using computers to do correspondence, accounting, bookkeeping, and catalogue sales for large businesses. Lack of social support in the work setting is likely to have negative effects. This will create a need for counselors who can facilitate people, design places, and encourage policies and programs that provide quality social interaction.

An unavoidable result of an ever-increasing life span, coupled with ever-growing automation, will be the time available for leisure activities. Workdays will be shorter, schedules more flexible, and vacations and sabbaticals longer. As Ferguson (1980) has indicated, the industrial transformation in future society will call for a change in attitude from "making a living" to "making a life." Future counseling services will be called upon to help people make this transformation. Leisure counseling, vocational planning, mid-career advising, and retirement counseling are only a few of the many services counselors will be asked to provide.

Finally, future counseling services will encourage a balance between personal feelings and social expectations. This balance will be needed in educational as well as in governmental, financial, corporate, business, and family settings. Counselors will require models that balance the remediational needs of people with their long-range developmental goals.

SUMMARY

Virtually every significant theory of counseling states that creating some kind of change toward growth in the client is the ultimate intended outcome of the counseling experience.

L.E. Patterson & S. Eisenberg, *The Counseling Process,* 3rd ed., 1983, p. 5

This chapter has presented an overview of the past, present, and future of professional counseling to establish a setting for the inviting relationship. Because of the rapid changes occurring, not only in the counseling profession but also in modern technological society, the argument was presented that a need exists for an expanded perspective of professional functioning.

The evolution of counseling has resulted in the many definitions of counseling now available. Most of the changes in the profession are related to the development of various counseling theories and techniques. The influence of these theories and techniques on the counseling profession parallel the influence of scientific, educational, and social forces on the larger North American community.

Counseling as a profession had its beginnings in the guidance movements of the 1900s. As guidance workers in those early years sought to help young people formulate goals and directions for their educational and vocational careers, they gradually became aware that more basic concerns of these young people needed to be addressed. In turn, this led to the realization that professional counselors could provide much more than guidance information to their clients.

More recently, scientific advancements, educational progress, and other social transformations have magnified the pressure and complexity of daily living and increased the demand for counseling services. Now more than ever, highly qualified counselors are needed to establish helping relationships with individuals, families, school populations, industrial workers, older adults, institutional residents, members of religious organizations, military personnel, and myriad other groups whose members wish to satisfy immediate concerns while seeking to develop optimally.

This chapter concluded with a theme echoed throughout this book: Future counselors will strive to integrate their belief systems and personal characteristics with their professional theories and counseling techniques into a developmental approach to human service. This integration requires a philosophy of professional helping that transcends specific approaches and techniques, extends far beyond the counseling center, and focuses on relatively boundless human potential. Thus an expanded structure for the ever-growing body of research findings that tie together seemingly unrelated aspects of professional helping seems essential. This book has proposed that the inviting relationship provides this structure for present and future counselors.

OPPORTUNITIES FOR FURTHER READING

Beware of the man of one book.

Isaac D'Isreali, *Curiosities of Literature,*
1791

ARBUCKLE, D.S. (1975). *Counseling and psychotherapy: An existential-humanistic view,* 3rd ed. Boston: Allyn & Bacon. A classic text that provides an existential perspective on the counseling profession and the counseling process from a deeply humanistic framework.

DEAL, T.E., & KENNEDY, A.A. (1982). *Corporate cultures: The rites and rituals of corporate life.* Reading, Mass.: Addison-Wesley. The major theme of this futuristic book is that strong organizations are those with a cohesion of values, myths, heroes, and symbols that "tie people together and give meaning and purpose to their day-to-day lives" (p. 5). The authors pointed out that we cannot return to the way it used to be because it no longer exists.

FERGUSON, M. (1980). *The Aquarian Conspiracy: Personal and social transformation in the 1980's.* Los Angeles: J.P. Tarcher. What is the Aquarian Conspiracy? Ferguson described it as a growing movement to create a society based on a vastly enlarged concept of human potential.

GOBLE, F.G. (1970). *The third force: The psychology of Abraham Maslow.* New York: Grossman. Goble presented a distillation of the ideas of Abraham Maslow. These ideas center on people: their goals, successes, and potential. Maslow maintained that we have been selling human nature short throughout history.

JANTSCH, E. (1980). *The self-organizing universe: Scientific and human implications of the emerging paradigm of evolution.* Oxford, England: Pergamon Press. Who among us ever thought of black holes, antimatter, genes jumping between chromosomes, inclusive fitness, or subatomic particles without mass? Jantsch described the information explosion and pointed out that every discipline is in the midst of a scientific revolution.

NAISBITT, J. (1982). *Megatrends: Ten new directions transforming our lives.* New York: Warner Books. Among the trends that Naisbitt identified are the growing importance of networks, the instantaneous distribution of information, and the increasing need for "hi-touch" cooperative human interaction.

REICH, C.A. (1970). *The greening of America.* New York: Random House. The question posed in this controversial best-seller is: How can we develop a new consciousness based on the value, ability, and self-directing powers of each person?

SHERTZER, B., & STONE, S.C. (1974). *Fundamentals of counseling,* 2nd ed. Boston: Houghton Mifflin. This popular text outlines the development of the counseling profession and presents basic concepts inherent in the process of counseling.

WRENN, C.G. (1973). *The world of the contemporary counselor.* Boston: Houghton Mifflin. Wrenn presented an excellent analysis of contemporary and future trends that require expanded visions of the roles of professional counselors.

VAILLANT, G.E. (1977). *Adaptation to life.* Boston: Little, Brown. This book presents a study of a small sample of male college graduates over a 35-year period following their graduation. Most manage life's problems with surprising strength and adequacy.

A

INVITING ONESELF PERSONALLY

Rehearse the future, not the past. So often when we make mistakes, we go over them again and again in our minds, in effect, *practicing* the mistakes. A better way is to ask: "How will I handle this problem the next time?" By concentrating on future response and/or behavior, we can rehearse the future, not the past.

Give yourself a celebration. Make a pledge to do something special for yourself, and only yourself, in the immediate future. Give yourself a hot bath, a window-shopping trip, a new outfit, a special hour for yourself, a good book, a special meal. At least once a week take yourself out to a movie, concert, dinner, or some other special event. When you celebrate yourself, it's easier to celebrate others.

Find a way to exercise. Professionals can be more inviting when they maintain their own physical health. Whether it is an organized sport (bowling, tennis, golf) or an individual effort (jogging, walking, weight lifting, swimming) find ways to maintain, protect, and enhance your physical body.

Talk with a friend. A good way to prevent professional burnout is to talk with a friend whose judgment you trust. Sometimes another perspective can help us avoid self-destructive behaviors and thought processes.

Plant a garden. Working in the soil can be a relaxing and rewarding experience, particularly when you watch a plant grow and produce. Even the smallest apartment has room for a window flower box, and a tiny garden can be rewarding with flowers and vegetables.

Form positive food habits. When planning your meals or eating out, try meats that are broiled, baked, or roasted rather than fried or sautéed. This way you will avoid excess calories and fat. And leave a little food on your plate. The childhood adage "clean your plate" has probably contributed to the weight problems of many professionals.

Live with a flourish. Avoid drabness, gain satisfaction from many sources, find ways to enrich your life; stand tall, dress well, eat less, and surround yourself with things you like.

Live a longer life. People live longer when they take responsibility for their physical health. Remove salt shakers from the table, eliminate smoking and other injurious substances, cut your alcohol intake, drink plenty of water, maintain dental hygiene, and fasten your seat belt!

Explore a library. For a relaxing experience, spend several hours browsing in a library. As you wander through the stacks, you'll have a world of knowledge at your fingertips—and it's all free!

Raise your drawbridge. While too much isolation is not good, some time alone to enjoy stillness, to contemplate and meditate on who you are, where you came from, and where you are going contribute to living and can be both personally and professionally rewarding. The goal is to be at one with the world and with the spirit.

Take a few risks. When chances of success are good, it usually pays to take a few chances. You have to risk life to live it well. Accept new people, ideas, and experiences that widen your perspective on life. One of the saddest things in life is a golden opportunity—missed.

Laugh. Subscribe to a happy little magazine titled *Laughing Matters*. It is published quarterly by Dr. Joel Goodman, Director, The Humor Project, 110 Spring St., Saratoga Springs, New York, 12866, and it will brighten almost any day.

B

INVITING OTHERS PERSONALLY

Name that tune. When planning a picnic, party, or other social event for friends or group members, give the occasion a lift with a special theme such as "Monte Carlo Night," "Octoberfest," "Roarin' Twenties," "Home on the Range," or "Hawaiian Luau." A theme costs little or nothing but will make planning easier, increase attendance, and build enthusiasm.

Promote "please" and "thank you." Do what you can to have all directional and other signs around your office, center, or workplaces begin with "Please" and end with "Thank You."

Celebrate birthdays and other special occasions. Birthdays or other special events of friends and colleagues can be marked on a private calendar in readiness for the special occasion. An unexpected happy note, greeting card, or delicious treat can add so much to a person's day.

Recognize the indispensable staff. Some time during the year, perhaps at a holiday season, it is important for counselors to express appreciation to the custodians, secretaries, cafeteria workers, and other staff people for their work. It is important to remember that all staff are part of the "family," and they add a great deal to the success—or failure—of counselors.

Send a "welcome back" note. We often think to send "get well" cards to friends, colleagues, employees, and others when they are ill. It is doubly appreciated when our thoughtfulness is extended to "welcome back" those who return after an illness, death in the family, or long business trip.

Plan comfortable meetings.   A careful check of facilities before an activity begins helps ensure that personal needs are considered. This includes seating, lighting, temperature, materials, restrooms, and related items of comfort. People participate best when they feel personally cared for.

Listen for the name.   When you are introduced to people, listen carefully to their name. Repeat it to yourself three times and use their name as you speak with them; they will appreciate the recognition!

Treat guests cordially.   If you have an office in your counseling center, arrange it so you have an informal area to talk with visitors. The informal area could include comfortable chairs, a coffee table, and an area rug.

Send double-strength invitations.   As nice as it is to receive complimentary words directly, it is even nicer to hear that kind words about you have been expressed to others. Rather than praising someone directly, praise the person to someone else. The original praise will probably reach the person with double the impact.

Offer refreshments to visitors.   Breaking bread together is an ancient sign of peace and friendship. By offering each visitor a beverage or light refreshment, the stage is set for the solution of concerns and facilitation of good feelings.

Keep a "mug" file.   Start and maintain a card file on those individuals with whom you have contact, both personal friends and professional colleagues. A single index card can hold a wealth of information about people you know. Each card can contain such personal items as the name of spouse, number and names of children, hobbies, interests. This card system can help to strengthen your memory and is one additional way to operate at the invisibly appropriate level.

Personalize some pencils.   For a few dollars it is possible to order pencils with some special greeting, such as "Season's Greetings to you from Mr. Smith." The pencils can be given before a holiday or other significant day. For example, school counselors can use the idea just before school ends for the summer: "Ms. Reynolds wishes you a great summer vacation!"

INVITING ONESELF PROFESSIONALLY

Carpool and adventure. Is a noted lecturer, important conference, counseling workshop, or other activity appearing or taking place in some other part of the country? Join with other counselors, "pool" your gas money, and attend as a group. At the conference, pick up brochures, handouts, and catalogues to share with colleagues who were unable to go.

Venture an invitation. Is there someone in your professional world that you admire and would like to know better? If so, be brave! Invite that person to lunch one day. The result may be exciting and bring future professional exchanges. After all, your dearest friend in all the world was once a total stranger.

Keep on schedule. Punctuality is a sign of intentionality. Being on time demonstrates professional caring for yourself and those who depend on your professional involvement. Place a small clock somewhere in your office so that a quick glance will keep you on schedule without distracting you from present conversations or tasks.

Visit another world. Take time to look at another vocational area. For example, visit a business, an industry, a hospital, a school, or other work setting different from your own and see how professionals in these areas do things. You'll collect many good ideas that will work in your own location.

Begin a museum. Start a special file of letters, awards, or memorable treasures that you have received over the years. When you feel a little blue and begin to doubt your own worth, take a tour through your own museum. It will help to lift your spirits and renew your faith in your own value, ability, and autonomy.

Cool down first. The professionally inviting counselor avoids responding while angry or upset. It is important to let tempers cool down a little before answering, particularly when you are responding in writing. Inappropriate comments exchanged in the heat of battle are often difficult to take back.

Manage your time. Develop a system (a checklist of "things to do" or a schedule of important events to attend) and manage your time accordingly. Budgeting your time helps you expend your energy evenly so that no one area or task consumes all your attention.

Be visible. For a helping professional, visibility is an important part of accessibility. You may benefit by being out of the counseling center as much as you are in it. Whether you counsel in an agency, hospital, school, or other institution, it would be good to eat in the cafeteria occasionally, walk the halls, greet passersby, and visit a colleague at the "far end of the hall."

Monitor college offerings. Keep up to date on classes taught at neighboring colleges and universities, particularly in your professional field. Also, by posting these offerings, you invite your fellow professionals to take advantage of them as well.

Obey the "rule of four." If you spend much of your time doing paperwork and other chores that could be done by a volunteer with only four hours of training, then you are violating the "rule of four." Training and using volunteers is an excellent way to cut down on heavy workloads.

Visit an exemplary program. Spend some time with a colleague whose work you have heard about at a conference or through another source. Contact the counselor and ask if you can visit for a day to learn about his or her counseling program.

Feed the feeders. Take time to publicize your program. Write an article for your organization's newsletter or call the local newspaper and ask if their "lifestyle" or "education" editor is interested in a story. Informing the public about counseling services is important for your professional identity.

Nourish simple ideas. The next time you have an idea about how to improve your counseling program, write it down. Expand upon it. Write an article about your idea. Share your article with colleagues and incorporate their suggestions. When your idea has developed into a completed article, send it to a state or national journal for publication.

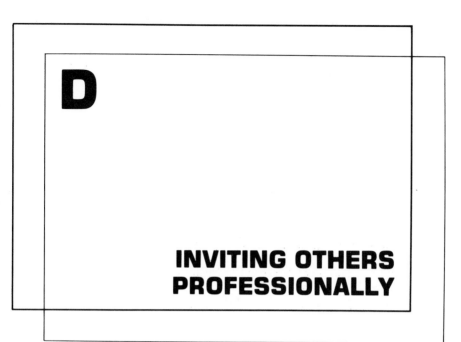

INVITING OTHERS PROFESSIONALLY

Share the consultant. When you schedule an in-service program, invite neighboring systems or related organizations to share the experience. Perhaps the cost of bringing the consultant can be shared as well. It makes good money sense, saves travel time for the consultant, and invites a feeling of professional cooperation.

Make the telephone your ally. Use the phone with professional courtesy. For example, identify yourself when calling others: "Good morning, this is Bob Smith. Is Mrs. Jones available?" By the same token, answer the phone in a friendly, open manner. A counselor who answers, "Counseling Center" could as easily say, "Good afternoon, Counseling Center, Bob Smith speaking."

Brighten up the center. Just because they stuck you in a closet is no reason it has to look like one! Hang posters, get some living plants, and make your office a place where people want to come. A fresh coat of paint does miracles. Moreover, be sure to consider the hallways, lounges, restrooms, lobby, and other public areas of your facility. They also add to, or subtract from, your counseling center.

Follow through promptly. One of the most significant characteristics of the professionally inviting counselor is that he or she follows through promptly. The most positive action, when long delayed, loses much of its value. In addition, when someone shares a problem, be sure to ask about it later. It is important to follow up your initial involvement with continued concern and interest.

Know your stuff.   An organized counselor is better able to share professional information readily. Being able to locate materials easily to share ideas with staff, administration, and clients is a sign of professionalism. Careful record keeping, filing, and organization benefits everyone.

Strangle the paper monster.   Unfortunately, counselors are sometimes among those who create forms for others to fill out. Try to keep the methods of communication between you and your clients and fellow professionals as easy and simple as possible. Time is precious. It should be valued highly and not spent on relatively unimportant activities.

Be positive.   Counseling is a very demanding and sometimes frustrating profession. It is important to remain positive amidst difficult times. Constant criticism is destructive. Counselors are in ideal positions to listen to criticisms, frustrations, and complaints with an understanding and sympathetic ear, and at the same time help the staff, administration, and clients find constructive alternatives. A counselor who joins the chronic complainers and feeds the fires of discontent often violates the spirit of the inviting relationship.

Send a professional gift.   Need to obtain a special gift for a colleague? Enter a subscription to a professional magazine or journal in that person's name. It is a gift that lasts all year, and perhaps even longer.

Hold a "happy hour."   Open your center after hours so that folks can drop by to enjoy refreshments and conversation. This time can be an excellent opportunity for the staff to develop a feeling of community as well as to present a mini-session for new ideas. These gatherings may be relaxing, with no business, or they may combine business with pleasure.

Give "expert" advice sparingly.   One of the basic tenets of the inviting relationship is recognition that every person has the potential to become more capable and self-supportive. For this reason, it is wise for counselors to be reluctant to provide the "ready" answer. Counseling is a way of helping people find alternatives and solutions and guiding them through decision-making processes to choose suitable courses of action. One of the best ways to help people is to invite them to do what they can and should do for themselves.

Maintain a giveaway library.   Keep a fresh stock of books on hand by visiting garage sales, library book sales, or flea markets. It is worth the small cost to watch a client's eyes when you say: "Here's a gift; it was written just for you."

Say "no" slowly.   When you must give a negative response to a request, let it come after you have listened carefully and considered the request fully. Failure to hear the person out can hurt more than the negative answer. The secret is to encourage the expression of the request fully before it is decided upon.

Check your timing.   Timing is very important in counseling. Too much, too soon, too little, or too late can weaken the best inviting relationship. When sending invitations, counselors should ask: *What* invitation, by *whom,* is most likely to be accepted by *this* person at *this* time?

Invite explicitly.   The more explicit an invitation, the more it lends itself to acceptance. Vagueness creates misunderstanding, and others wonder: "What was meant by that?" Precision and clarity are signs of the inviting relationship.

Float the staff meeting.   Move the staff meeting around the building and meet in different environments. This gives a freshness to meetings and a new outlook on problems. It also helps to get everyone involved. And no matter where you meet, remember to arrange for something to eat and drink. The "care and feeding" of staff members is most important. Even such simple fare as coffee or tea and cookies primes the pump for a successful meeting.

Encourage participation.   If you would like more participation in staff meetings, you can encourage discussion of important issues by dividing and subdividing the group. Start with pairs, then groups of four, and later larger groups if possible. It's difficult to remain silent and unresponsive when you're 50 percent of the group!

Invite positive public relations.   It's never a matter of whether or not a counseling center has public relations; it's a matter of what kind. To invite positive public relations, make sure that the majority of messages sent to colleagues, clients, and community members are positive.

Be accessible.   As a professional person you provide important services. If you set up office hours that are an imposition to other people, or if visitors must ask permission of the receptionist to see you, then few people will feel welcome to use counseling services. Moreover, if you put the "Do Not Disturb" sign on your office door, expect people to become "disturbed." Reasonable availability is a hallmark of the professionally inviting counselor.

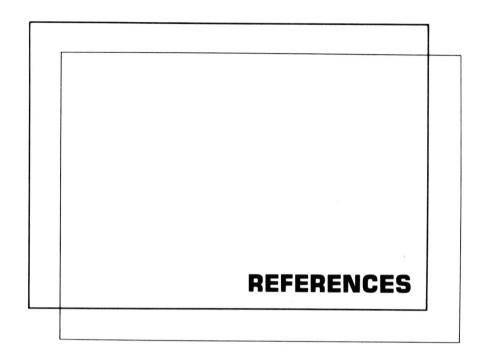

REFERENCES

ABIKOFF, H. (1979). Cognitive training interventions in children: Review of a new approach. *Journal of Learning Disabilities, 12,* 65-77.

ADLER, A. (1931). *What life should mean to you.* New York: Putnam.

ADLER, A. (1969). *The science of living.* New York: Doubleday. (Original work published in 1929.)

ADLER, M.J., & VAN DOREN, C. (1972). *How to read a book.* New York: Simon & Schuster.

ALLPORT, G.W. (1937). *Personality: A psychological interpretation.* New York: Holt, Rinehart & Winston.

ALLPORT, G.W. (1943). The ego in contemporary psychology. *Psychological Review, 50,* 451-478.

ALLPORT, G.W. (1955). *Becoming.* New Haven, Conn.: Yale University Press.

ALLPORT, G.W. (1961). *Pattern and growth in personality.* New York: Holt, Rinehart & Winston.

AMOS, L. (1985). *Professionally and personally inviting teacher practices as related to affective course outcomes reported by dental hygiene students.* Unpublished doctoral dissertation, School of Education, University of North Carolina at Greensboro.

AMOS, L., PURKEY, W., & TOBIAS, N. (March, 1985). *The invitational teaching survey.* Paper presented at the American Educational Research Association Convention, Chicago.

ANGELOU, M. (1970). *I know why the caged bird sings.* New York: Bantam Books.

ANSBACHER, H., & ANSBACHER, R. (1956). *The Individual Psychology of Alfred Adler: A systematic presentation in selections from his writings.* New York: Harper & Row.

ARBUCKLE, D.S. (1965). *Counseling: Philosophy, theory and practice.* Boston: Allyn & Bacon.

ARBUCKLE, D.S. (1975). *Counseling and psychotherapy: An existential humanistic view,* 3rd ed. Boston: Allyn & Bacon.

ARMOR, D.J. (1969). *The American school counselor.* New York: Russell Sage Foundation.

ARONSON, E., & CARLSMITH, J.M. (1962). Performance expectancy as a determinant of actual performance. *Journal of Abnormal and Social Psychology, 65,* 178-182.

ASPY, D.N. (1972). *Toward a technology for humanizing education.* Champaign, Ill.: Research Press.

AUBREY, R.F. (1977). Historical development of guidance and counseling and implications for the future. *Personnel and Guidance Journal, 55,* 288-295.

AUBREY, R.F. (1982). A house divided: Guidance and counseling in 20th century America. *Personnel and Guidance Journal, 16,* 198-204.

AVILA, D., COMBS, A., & PURKEY, W. (eds.). (1977). *The helping relationship sourcebook,* 2nd ed. Boston: Allyn & Bacon.

AVILA, D.L., & PURKEY, W.W. (1966). Intrinsic and extrinsic motivation: A regrettable distinction. *Psychology in the Schools, 3,* 206-208.

AXLINE, V.M. (1947). Nondirective therapy for poor readers. *Journal of Consulting Psychology, 11,* 61-69.

BARDON, J.I. (1976). The state of the art (and science) of school psychology. *American Psychologist, 31,* 785-791.

BASSO, K.H. (1979). *Portraits of "The Whiteman": Linguistic play and cultural symbols among the western Apache.* New York: Cambridge University Press.

BAUM, L.F. (Adapted by Horace J. Elias, 1939, renewed 1976). *The wizard of Oz.* Metro-Goldwyn-Mayer. Baltimore, Md.: Ottenheimer Publishers.

BEESON, S., BENTLEY, G., & DIMEO, E. (1982). Do you invite your patients to learn? *Nursing Life, 2*(6), 26.

BELKIN, G.S. (1976). *Counseling directions in theory and practice.* Dubuque, Ia.: Kendall/Hunt.

BENJAMIN, A. (1981). *The helping interview,* 3rd ed. Boston: Houghton Mifflin.

BEUTLER, L.E. (1983). *Eclectic psychotherapy: A systematic approach.* New York: Pergamon Press.

BLAILIFFE, B. (March, 1978). *The significance of the self-concept in the knowledge society.* Paper presented at the Self-concept Symposium, Boston.

BLOCK, D.A. (1952). The delinquent integration. *Psychiatry, 15*(2), 297-303.

BLOOM, B.S. (1976). *Human characteristics and school learning.* New York: McGraw-Hill.

BORDIN, E.S. (1968). *Psychological counseling,* 2nd ed. Englewood Cliffs, N.J.: Prentice-Hall.

BRABECK, M.M., & WELFEL, E.R. (1985). Counseling theory: Understanding the trend toward eclecticism from a developmental perspective. *Journal of Counseling and Development, 63,* 343-348.

BRAMMER, L.M. (1985). *The helping relationship: Process and skills,* 3rd ed. Englewood Cliffs, N.J.: Prentice-Hall.

BREWER, J.M. (1942). *History of vocational guidance.* New York: Harper & Brothers.

BUBER, M. (1958). *I and thou.* New York: Scribner.

BUBER, M. (1965). *The knowledge of man: Selected essays.* New York: Harper & Row.

BUGENTAL, J.F. (1965). *The search for authenticity.* New York: Holt, Rinehart & Winston.

BURNS, G. (1976). *Living it up, or, they still love me in Altoona.* New York: Berkley Publishing Corp.

BUSCAGLIA, L. (1972). *Love.* New York: Fawcett Crest Books.

CAMPBELL, D. (1974). *If you don't know where you're going, you'll probably end up somewhere else.* Niles, Ill.: Argus Communications.

CARKHUFF, R.R. (1969a). *Helping and human relations: A primer for lay and professional helpers: Vol. 1. Selection and training.* New York: Holt, Rinehart & Winston.

CARKHUFF, R.R. (1969b). *Helping and human relations: A primer for lay and professional helpers: Vol. 2. Practice and research.* New York: Holt, Rinehart & Winston.

CARKHUFF, R.R. (1985). *The art of helping V,* 5th ed. Amherst, Mass.: Human Resource Development Press.

CARKHUFF, R.R., & BERENSON, B.G. (1967). *Beyond counseling and psychotherapy.* New York: Holt, Rinehart & Winston.

CARKHUFF, R.R., PIERCE, R.M., & CANNON, J.R. (1977). *The art of helping III.* Amherst, Mass.: Human Resource Development.

CHAIKIN, A.L., DERLEGA, V.J., & MILLER, S.J. (1976). Effects of room environment on self disclosure in a counseling analogue. *Journal of Counseling Psychology, 23,* 479-481.

CHAMBERLIN, J.G. (1981). *The educating act: A phenomenological view.* Washington, D.C.: University Press of America.

COMBS, A.W. (ed.). (1962). *Perceiving, behaving, becoming.* Washington, D.C.: Yearbook of the Association for Supervision and Curriculum Development.

COMBS, A.W. (1965). *The professional education of teachers: A perceptual view of teacher preparation.* Boston: Allyn & Bacon.

COMBS, A.W. (1974). Why the humanist movement needs a perceptual psychology. *Journal of the Association for the Study of Perception, 9,* 1–13.

COMBS, A.W. (1982). *A personal approach to teaching: Beliefs that make a difference.* Boston: Allyn & Bacon.

COMBS, A.W., & AVILA, D. (1984). *The helping relationship,* 3rd ed. Boston: Allyn & Bacon.

COMBS, A.W., AVILA, D.L., & PURKEY, W.W. (1978). *Helping relationships: Basic concepts for the helping professions,* 2nd ed. Boston: Allyn & Bacon.

COMBS, A.W., BLUME, R.A., NEWMAN, A.J., & WASS, H.L. (1974). *The professional education of teachers: A humanistic approach to teacher preparation.* Boston: Allyn & Bacon.

COMBS, A.W., RICHARDS, A.C., & RICHARDS, F. (1976). *Perceptual psychology: A humanistic approach to the study of persons.* New York: Harper & Row.

COMBS, A.W., & SOPER, D.W. (1963). The perceptual organization of effective counselors. *Journal of Counseling Psychology, 10,* 222–227.

COMBS, A.W., SOPER, D.W., GOODING, C.T., BENTON, J.A., DICKMAN, J.F., & USHER, R.H. (1969). *Florida studies in the helping professions. Social Science Monograph No. 37.* Gainesville, Fla.: University of Florida Press.

COMBS, A.W., & SNYGG, D. (1959). *Individual behavior: A perceptual approach to behavior,* 2nd ed. New York: Harper & Row.

COOLEY, C.H. (1902). *Human nature and the social order.* New York: Charles Scribner's Sons.

COOPERSMITH, S. (1967). *The antecedents of self-esteem.* San Francisco: W.H. Freeman & Company Publishers.

COREY, G. (1982). *Theory and practice of counseling and psychotherapy,* 2nd ed. Monterey, Calif.: Brooks/Cole.

COREY, G., COREY, M., & CALLANAN, P. (1984). *Issues and ethics in the helping professions,* 2nd ed. Monterey, Calif.: Brooks/Cole.

COTTLE, W.C., & DOWNIE, N.M. (1970). *Preparation for counseling,* 2nd ed. Englewood Cliffs, N.J.: Prentice-Hall.

CURRAN, C.A. (1968). *Counseling and psychotherapy: The pursuit of values.* New York: Sheed and Ward.

CURTIS, R.C., ZANNA, M.P., & CAMPBELL, W.W. (1975). Sex, fear of success and the perceptions and performance of law students. *American Educational Research Journal, 12,* 287–297.

DEAL, T.E., & KENNEDY, A.A. (1982). *Corporate cultures: The rites and rituals of corporate life.* Reading, Mass.: Addison-Wesley.

DELL, D.M. (1973). Counselor power base, influence attempt, and behavior change in counseling. *Journal of Counseling Psychology, 20,* 399–405.

DERLEGA, V.J., & CHAIKIN, A.L. (1975). *Sharing intimacy: What we reveal to others and why.* Englewood Cliffs, N.J.: Prentice-Hall.

DESCARTES, R. (1912). *Principles of philosophy: A discourse on method.* New York: E.P. Dutton & Co. (Original work published in 1644.)

DEWEY, J. (1933). *How we think.* Lexington, Mass.: Heath.

DIGGORY, J.C. (1966). *Self-evaluation: Concepts and studies.* New York: Wiley.

DINKMEYER, D. (1982a). *Developing understanding of self and others,* (DUSO D-1). Circle Pines, Minn.: American Guidance Service.

DINKMEYER, D. (1982b). *Developing understanding of self and others,* (DUSO D-2). Circle Pines, Minn.: American Guidance Service.

DINKMEYER, D., & DINKMEYER, D., JR. (1977). Concise counseling assessment: The children's life-style guide. *Elementary School Guidance and Counseling, 12,* 117–124.

DINKMEYER, D., & DREIKURS, R. (1963). *Encouraging children to learn: The encouragement process.* Englewood Cliffs, N.J.: Prentice-Hall.

DINKMEYER, D., & McKAY, G.D. (1976). *Systematic training for effective parenting (STEP).* Circle Pines, Minn.: American Guidance Service.

DINKMEYER, D., & McKAY, G.D. (1983). *Systematic training for effecting parenting/Teen (STEP/Teen).* Circle Pines, Minn.: American Guidance Service.

DINKMEYER, D., McKAY, G.D., & DINKMEYER, D., JR. (1980). *Systematic training for effective teaching (STET)*. Circle Pines, Minn.: American Guidance Service.

DINKMEYER, D., PEW, L.W., & DINKMEYER, D., JR. (1978). *Adlerian counseling and psychotherapy*. Monterey, Calif.: Brooks/Cole.

D'ISREALI, I. (1791). *Curiosities of literature*. London: Printed for J. Murray, No. 32, Fleet Street. (Reprinted by Garland Publishing, Inc., New York, 1971.)

DOUGHERTY, A.M. (1981). The inviting middle school counselor. *The Humanist Educator, 20,* 50–57.

DOWNING, C.J. (1983). A behavior classification system for counselors: A new look at psychotherapy. *Humanistic Education and Development, 21,* 138–145.

DREIKURS, R. (1967). *Psychodynamics, psychotherapy, and counseling*. Chicago: Alfred Adler Institute.

DREIKURS, R. (1968). *Psychology in the classroom,* 2nd ed. New York: Harper & Row.

DREIKURS, R., & SOLTZ, V. (1964). *Children: The challenge*. New York: Duell, Sloan and Pearce.

DYER, W.W. (1978). *Pulling your own strings*. New York: Avon Books.

EGAN, G. (1982). *The skilled helper: A model for systematic helping and interpersonal relating,* 2nd ed. Monterey, Calif.: Brooks/Cole.

ELLIS, A. (1962). *Reason and emotion in psychotherapy*. New York: Lyle Stuart.

ELLIS, A. (1984). *Reason and emotion in psychotherapy*. Secaucus, N.J.: Citadel Press.

ELLIS, A., & HARPER, R.A. (1968). *Guide to rational living*. New York: Lyle Stuart.

EMERY, S. (1978). *Actualizations: You don't have to rehearse to be yourself.* Garden City, N.Y.: Doubleday.

FARBER, B. (1962). Marital integration as a factor in parent-child relations. *Child Development, 33,* 1–14.

FELKER, S.A. (1973). Intellectual ability and counseling effectiveness: Another view. *Counselor Education and Supervision, 13,* 146–150.

FERGUSON, M. (1980). *The Aquarian Conspiracy: Personal and social transformation in the 1980's.* Los Angeles, Calif.: J.P. Tarcher.

FESTINGER, L. (1962). *A theory of cognitive dissonance*. New York: Harper & Row.

FRANKL, V. (1963). *Man's search for meaning*. Boston: Beacon Press.

FRANKL, V. (1968). *The doctor and the soul: From psychotherapy to logotherapy*. New York: A.A. Knopf.

FROMM, E. (1956). *The art of loving: An inquiry into the nature of love*. New York: Harper & Row.

GAZDA, G.M., ASBURY, F.R., BALZER, F.J., CHILDERS, W.C., & WALTERS, R.P. (1977). *Human relations development: A manual for educators,* 2nd ed. Boston: Allyn & Bacon.

GENDLIN, E.T. (1969). Focusing. *Psychotherapy: Theory, Research and Practice, 6,* 4–15.

GLANZ, E.C. (1964). *Foundations and principles of guidance*. Boston: Allyn & Bacon.

GLASSER, N. (1980). *What are you doing?* New York: Harper & Row.

GLASSER, W. (1965). *Reality therapy*. New York: Harper & Row.

GLASSER, W. (1969). *Schools without failure*. New York: Harper & Row.

GLASSER, W. (1972). *The identity society*. New York: Harper & Row.

GLASSER, W. (1976). *Positive addiction*. New York: Harper & Row.

GLASSER, W. (1981). *Stations of the mind*. New York: Harper & Row.

GLASSER, W. (1984). *Take effective control of your life*. New York: Harper & Row.

GLOCK, M.D. (1972). Is there a Pygmalion in the classroom? *The Reading Teacher, 25,* 405–408.

GOBLE, F.G. (1970). *The third force: The psychology of Abraham Maslow*. New York: Grossman.

GOFFMAN, E. (1959). *The presentation of self in everyday life*. New York: Doubleday.

GOLDBERG, C. (1977). *Therapeutic partnership: Ethical concerns in psychotherapy*. New York: Springer-Verlag.

GOLDSTEIN, K. (1939). *The organism*. New York: American Book Company.

GOLDSTEIN, K. (1963). *Human nature in the light of psychopathology*. New York: Schocken Books.

GOOD, C.V. (ed.). (1945). *Dictionary of education*. New York: McGraw-Hill.

GRUMMON, D.L. (1972). Client-centered therapy. In B. Stefflre & W.H. Grant (eds.), *Theories of counseling,* 2nd ed. New York: McGraw-Hill.

GRUMMON, D.L., & JOHN, E.S. (1954). Changes over client-centered therapy evaluated on psychoanalytically based Thematic Apperception Test scales. In C.R. Rogers & R.F. Dymond (eds.), *Psychotherapy and personality change.* Chicago: University of Chicago Press.

HAAN, R. (1963). *Accelerated learning programs.* New York: The Center for Applied Research in Education, Inc.

HAASE, R.F., & DIMATTA, D.J. (1976). Special environments and verbal conditioning in a quasi-counseling interview. *Journal of Counseling Psychology, 23,* 414-421.

HACKNEY, H., & CORMIER, L. (1979). *Counseling strategies and objectives,* 2nd ed. Englewood Cliffs, N.J.: Prentice-Hall.

HALL, E.T. (1959). *The silent language.* New York: Doubleday.

HAMACHEK, D.E. (1978). *Encounters with the self,* 2nd ed. New York: Holt, Rinehart, & Winston.

HARRIS, K. (1982). Cognitive behavior modification: Application with exceptional children. *Focus on Exceptional Children, 15*(2), 1-16.

HAVIGHURST, R.J. (1952). *Developmental tasks and education,* 2nd ed. New York: Longmans, Green, & Co.

HERBERT, M. (1981). *Behavioral treatment of problem children: A practice manual.* London: Academic Press.

HERGENHAHN, B.R. (1980). *An introduction to theories of personality.* Englewood Cliffs, N.J.: Prentice-Hall.

HOBBS, N. (ed.). (1975). *The future of children: Categories, labels, and their consequences.* Nashville, Tenn.: Vanderbilt University Press.

HOBBS, N. (1982). *The troubled and troubling child.* San Francisco: Jossey-Bass.

HORNEY, K. (1939). *New ways in psychoanalysis.* New York: Norton.

HUNT, J. MC. (1961). *Intelligence and experience.* New York: Ronald Press.

HUTCHINS, D.E. (1979). Systematic counseling: The T-F-A model for counselor intervention. *Personnel and Guidance Journal, 57,* 529-531.

IVEY, A.E. (1969). The intentional individual: A process-outcome view of behavioral psychology. *The Counseling Psychologist, 1,* 56-59.

IVEY, A.E. (1983). *Intentional interviewing and counseling.* Monterey, Calif.: Brooks/Cole.

IVEY, A.E., & AUTHIER, J. (1978). *Microcounseling: Innovations in interviewing, counseling, psychotherapy, and psychoeducation,* 2nd ed. Springfield, Ill.: Charles C Thomas.

IVEY, A.E., & SIMEK-DOWNING, L. (1980). *Counseling and psychotherapy: Skills, theory and practice.* Englewood Cliffs, N.J.: Prentice-Hall.

JANTSCH, E. (1980). *The self-organizing universe: Scientific and human implications of the emerging paradigm of evolution.* Oxford, England: Pergamon Press.

JERSILD, A.T. (1952). *In search of self.* New York: Columbia University.

JOHNSON, D.W. (1981). *Reaching out: Interpersonal effectiveness and self-actualization,* 2nd ed. Englewood Cliffs, N.J.: Prentice-Hall.

JOHNSON, G.W. (1934). *A little night-music: Discoveries in the exploitation of an art.* New York: Harper & Row.

JOHNSON, S.M. (1977). *First person singular: Living the good life alone.* Philadelphia: Lippincott.

JOURARD, S.M. (1964). *The transparent self: Self-disclosure and well-being.* Princeton, N.J.: Van Nostrand.

JOURARD, S.M. (1968). *Disclosing man to himself,* 2nd ed. New York: Van Nostrand Reinhold Company.

JOURARD, S.M. (1971a). *Self-disclosure: An experimental analysis of the transparent self.* New York: Wiley-Interscience.

JOURARD, S.M. (1971b.) *The transparent self: Self-disclosure and well-being,* rev. ed. Princeton, N.J.: Van Nostrand.

JOURARD, S.M. (1974). *The undisclosed self.* New York: Mentor Books.

JUNG, C.G. (1974). *The undiscovered self.* New York: Mentor Books.

KAZANTZAKIS, M. (1953). *Zorba the Greek.* New York: Simon & Schuster.

KEGAN, R. (1982). *The evolving self: Problem and process in human development.* Cambridge, Mass.: Harvard University Press.

KEITH-LUCAS, A. (1972). *Giving and taking help.* Chapel Hill, N.C.: The University of North Carolina Press.

KELLEY, H.H. (1979). *Personal relationships: Their structures and processes.* Hillsdale, N.J.: Erlbaum.

KELLY, G.A. (1955). *The psychology of personal constructs.* New York: W.W. Norton & Co.

KELLY, G.A. (1963). *Theory of personality: The psychology of personal constructs.* New York: W.W. Norton & Co.

KING, P.T., & BENNINGTON, K.F. (1972). Psychoanalysis and counseling. In B. Stefflre & W.H. Grant (eds.), *Theories of counseling,* 2nd ed. New York: McGraw-Hill.

KNOWLES, J.H. (1977). The responsibility of the individual. In J.H. Knowles (ed.), *Doing better and feeling worse: Health in the United States.* New York: W.W. Norton & Co.

L'ABATE, L. (1981). Classification of counseling and therapy theorists, methods, processes, and goals: The E-R-A model. *Personnel and Guidance Journal, 59,* 263–265.

LAMBETH, C.R. (1980). *Teacher invitations and effectiveness as reported by secondary students in Virginia.* Unpublished doctoral dissertation, University of Virginia, Charlottesville, Va.

LAZARUS, A. (1981). *Multimodal therapy.* New York: McGraw-Hill.

LEONARD, G. (1968). *Education and ecstasy.* New York: Delacorte Press.

LINDBERGH, A.M. (1955). *Gift from the sea.* New York: Vintage Books.

LIPPITT, R., & WHITE, R. (1960). *Autocracy and democracy.* New York: Harper & Row.

LOWE, C.M. (1961). The self-concept: Fact or artifact? *Psychological Bulletin, 58,* 325–336.

LUDWIG, D.J., & MAEHR, M.L. (1967). Changes in self-concept and stated behavioral preferences. *Child Development, 38,* 453–467.

MAHONEY, M. (1977). Personal science: A cognitive learning therapy. In A. Ellis & R. Grieger (eds.), *Handbook of rational-emotive therapy.* Berlin and New York: Springer-Verlag.

MARTIN, R., & POLLARD, E. (1980). *Learning to change: A self-management approach to adjustment.* New York: McGraw-Hill.

MASH, E., & DALBY, J. (1978). Behavioral interventions for hyperactivity. In R. Trites (ed.), *Hyperactivity in children: Etiology, measurement and treatment implications.* Baltimore: University Park Press.

MASLOW, A.H. (1957). A philosophy of psychology: The need for a mature science of human nature. *Main Currents in Modern Thought, 13,* 27–32.

MASLOW, A.H. (1962). *Toward a psychology of being.* New York: Van Nostrand Reinhold Co.

MATHEWSON, R.H. (1962). *Guidance policy and practice.* New York: Harper & Row.

MAY, R. (1961). The context of psychotherapy. In M.I. Stein (ed.), *Contemporary psychotherapies.* New York: The Free Press.

MAY, R. (ed.). (1966). *Existential psychology.* New York: Random House.

MAY, R. (1969). *Love and will.* New York: W.W. Norton & Co.

MAYEROFF, M. (1971). *On caring.* New York: Harper & Row.

McGINNIS, A.L. (1979). *The friendship factor.* Minneapolis: Augsburg Publishing House.

MEAD, G.H. (1934). *Mind, self, and society.* Chicago: University of Chicago Press.

MEICHENBAUM, D. (1974). Cognitive behavior modification. *University Programs Modular Studies.* Morristown, N.J.: General Learning Press.

MEICHENBAUM, D. (1977). *Cognitive behavior modification: An integrative approach.* New York: Plenum Press.

MEICHENBAUM, D. (1983). *Stress reduction and prevention.* New York: Plenum Press.

METTEE, D.R. (1971). Rejection of unexpected success as a function of the negative consequences of accepting success. *Journal of Personality and Social Psychology, 17,* 332–341.

MORRIS, V.C. (1966). *Existentialism in education.* New York: Harper & Row.

MURPHEY, J., & PURKEY, W. (1981). Invitational engineering in the residence halls. *The Journal of College and University Student Housing, 11,* 13–16.

NAISBITT, J. (1982). *Megatrends: Ten new directions transforming our lives.* New York: Warner Books.

NOUWEN, H.J. (1975). *Reaching out: The three movements of spiritual life.* Garden City, N.Y.: Doubleday.

NOVAK, J. (April, 1983). *Revisioning invitational education.* Paper presented at the American Educational Research Association's Annual Convention, Montreal, Canada.

ORR, D.W. (1965). *Professional counseling on human behavior: Its principles and practices.* New York: Franklin Watts.

PAPANEK, H. (1973). Social interest and social conflict. In H.H. Mosak (ed.), *Alfred Adler: His influence on psychology today.* Park Ridge, N.J.: Noyes Data.

PARKER, W.M., & SCOTT, J. (1985). Creating an inviting atmosphere for college students from ethnic minority groups. *Journal of College Student Personnel,* January, 82–84.

PARLOFF, M.B. (1976). Shopping for the right therapy. *Saturday Review,* February 21, 14–16.

PATTERSON, C.H. (1959). *Counseling and psychotherapy: Theory and practice.* New York: Harper & Row.

PATTERSON, C.H. (1985a). New light for counseling theory. *Journal of Counseling and Development, 63,* 349–350.

PATTERSON, C.H. (1985b). *The therapeutic relationship: Foundations for an eclectic psychotherapy.* Monterey, Calif.: Brooks/Cole.

PATTERSON, L.E., & EISENBERG, S. (1983). *The counseling process,* 3rd ed. Boston: Houghton Mifflin.

PENTONY, P. (1981). *Models of influence in psychotherapy.* New York: Free Press.

PEPINSKY, H.B., & PEPINSKY, P. (1954). *Counseling: Theory and practice.* New York: Ronald Press.

PETERS, T.J., & WATERMAN, R.H., JR. (1982). *In search of excellence: Lessons from America's best-run companies.* New York: Harper & Row.

PIETROFESA, J.J., HOFFMAN, A., & SPLETE, H.H. (1984). *Counseling: An introduction,* 2nd ed. Boston: Houghton Mifflin.

PIETROFESA, J.J., LEONARD, G.E., & VAN HOOSE, W. (1978). *The authentic counselor,* 2nd ed. Chicago: Rand McNally.

PINES, A.M., & ARONSON, E. (with D. KAFRY). (1981). *Burnout: From tedium to personal growth.* New York: Free Press.

PIRSIG, R.M. (1974). *Zen and the art of motorcycle maintenance: An inquiry into values.* New York: William Morrow & Company.

POWERS, W.T. (1973). *Behavior: The control of perception.* Chicago: Aldine.

PRATHER, H. (1970). *Notes to myself: My struggle to become a person.* Moab, Utah: Real People Press.

PURKEY, W.W. (1970). *Self-concept and school achievement.* Englewood Cliffs, N.J.: Prentice-Hall.

PURKEY, W.W. (1978). *Inviting school success.* Belmont, Calif.: Wadsworth.

PURKEY, W.W. (in press). An invitational approach to classroom discipline. *Theory into Practice.*

PURKEY, W.W., & NOVAK, J. (1984). *Inviting school success,* 2nd ed. Belmont, Calif.: Wadsworth.

PURKEY, W.W., SCHMIDT, J.J., & McBRIEN, D. (1982). The professionally inviting school counselor. *The School Counselor, 30,* 84–88.

REICH, C.A. (1970). *The greening of America.* New York: Random House.

RIMM, D.C., & MASTERS, J.C. (1974). *Behavior therapy: Techniques and empirical findings.* New York: Academic Press.

RINGER, R.J. (1977). *Looking out for number one.* Beverly Hills, Calif.: Los Angeles Book Corp.

RIPLEY, D.M. (1985). *Invitational teaching behaviors in the associate degree clinical setting.* Unpublished master's thesis. School of Nursing, University of North Carolina at Greensboro.

ROEBER, E.C. (1963). *The school counselor.* Washington, D.C.: The Center for Applied Research in Education.

ROGERS, C.R. (1942). *Counseling and psychotherapy: Newer concepts in practice.* Boston: Houghton Mifflin.

ROGERS, C.R. (1947). Some observations on the organization of personality. *American Psychologist, 2,* 358–368.

ROGERS, C.R. (1951). *Client-centered therapy: Its current practice, implications, and theory.* Boston: Houghton Mifflin.

ROGERS, C.R. (1952). Client-centered psychotherapy. *Scientific American, 187*(5), 66–74.

ROGERS, C.R. (1957). The necessary and sufficient conditions of therapeutic personality change. *Journal of Consulting Psychology, 21,* 95–103.

ROGERS, C.R. (1958). The characteristics of a helping relationship. *Personnel and Guidance Journal, 37,* 6–16.

ROGERS, C.R. (1959). *Counseling and psychotherapy: Theory and practice.* New York: Harper & Row.

ROGERS, C.R. (1961). *On becoming a person: A therapist's view of psychotherapy.* Boston: Houghton Mifflin.

ROGERS, C.R. (1967). *Coming into existence.* New York: World Publishing.

ROGERS, C.R. (1969). *Freedom to learn.* Columbus, Ohio: Chas. E. Merrill.

ROGERS, C.R. (1974). In retrospect—forty-six years. *American Psychologist, 29,* 115.

ROGERS, C.R. (1980). *A way of being.* Boston: Houghton Mifflin.

ROSENTHAL, R., ARCHER, D., KOIVUMAKI, J., DIMATTEO, M., & ROGERS, P. (1974). Assessing sensitivity to nonverbal communication: The PONS Test. *Psychology Today, 8*(4), 64–68.

RUSSELL, D.W. (1984). Applying invitational theory by teachers of the gifted to regular classroom teachers. *Education, 104,* 354–358.

RUSSELL, D., PURKEY, W., & SIEGEL, B. (1982). The artfully inviting teacher: A hierarchy of strategies. *Education, 103,* 35–38.

RYCHLAK, J.F. (1985). Eclecticism in psychological theorizing: Good and bad. *Journal of Counseling and Development, 63,* 351–353.

SCHMIDT, J.J. (1982). Coordination and supervision of counseling services: An invitational approach. *Counselor Education and Supervision, 22,* 98–106.

SCHMIDT, J.J. (1984a). School counseling: Professional directions for the future. *The School Counselor, 31,* 385–392.

SCHMIDT, J.J. (1984b). Counselor intentionality: An emerging view of process and performance. *Journal of Counseling Psychology, 31,* 383–386.

SCHMIDT, J.J., & MEDL, W.A. (1983). Six magic steps of consulting. *The School Counselor, 30,* 212–216.

SEABURY, D. (1974). *The art of selfishness.* New York: Julian Mesner, Simon & Schuster.

SHAFFER, L.F. (1947). The problem of psychotherapy. *American Psychologist, 2,* 459–467.

SHAVELSON, R., HUBNER, J., & STANTON, G. (1976). Self-concept: Validation of construct interpretations. *Review of Educational Research, 46,* 407–441.

SHERTZER, B., & STONE, S.C. (1966). *Fundamentals of guidance.* Boston: Houghton Mifflin.

SHERTZER, B., & STONE, S.C. (1974). *Fundamentals of counseling,* 2nd ed. Boston: Houghton Mifflin.

SMITH, C.F. (1985). *The effect of selected teaching practices on affective outcomes of graduate nursing students: An extension and replication.* Unpublished master's thesis. School of Nursing, University of North Carolina at Greensboro.

SMITH, G.F. (1955). *Counseling in the secondary school.* New York: Macmillan.

SMITH, H.C. (1966). *Sensitivity to people.* New York: McGraw-Hill.

SNYGG, D., & COMBS, A.W. (1949). *Individual behavior.* New York: Harper & Row.

SPEARS, W.D., & DEESE, M.E. (1973). Self-concept as cause. *Educational Theory, 23,* 144–153.

STEFFLRE, B., & GRANT, W.H. (1972). *Theories of counseling,* 2nd ed. New York: McGraw-Hill.

STEHLE, C.F. (1981). *Invitational learning: A case study of the implementation of the sustained silent reading (SSR) program within the junior high school classroom.* Unpublished doctoral dissertation, The University of Rochester, Rochester, N.Y.

STEINBECK, J. (1966). *America and Americans.* New York: Viking Press.

STEINER, C.M. (1974). *Scripts people live.* New York: Grove Press.

STILLION, J., & SIEGEL, B. (1985). The intentionally inviting hierarchy. *Journal of Humanistic Education, 9,* 33-39.

STRUNK, W.J., & WHITE, E.B. (1959). *The elements of style.* New York: Macmillan.

SULLIVAN, H.S. (1947). *Concepts of modern psychiatry.* Washington, D.C.: William Alanson White Psychiatric Foundation.

SUPER, D.E. (1955). Transition: From vocational guidance to counseling psychology. *Journal of Counseling Psychology, 2,* 3-9.

SWEENEY, T.J. (1981). *Adlerian counseling: Proven concepts and strategies.* Muncie, Ind.: Accelerated Development, Inc.

THETFORD, W.N. (1952). An objective measure of frustration tolerance in evaluating psychotherapy. In W. Wolff (ed.), *Success in psychotherapy.* New York: Grune & Stratton.

THOMPSON, C.L., & RUDOLPH, L.B. (1983). *Counseling children.* Monterey, Calif.: Brooks/Cole.

TRUAX, C.B., & CARKHUFF, R.R. (1967). *Towards effective counseling and psychotherapy.* Chicago: Aldine.

TURNER, R.B. (1983). *Teacher invitations and effectiveness as reported by physical education students, grades 9-12.* Unpublished doctoral dissertation, University of North Carolina at Greensboro.

VACC, N.A., & BARDON, J.I. (eds.). (1982). Assessment and appraisal: Issues, practices, and programs. (Special Issue) *Measurement and Evaluation in Guidance, 15,* (1).

VAILLANT, G.E. (1977). *Adaptation to life.* Boston: Little, Brown.

VARGAS, A.M., & BORKOWSKI, J.G. (1983). Physical attractiveness: Interactive effects of counselor and client on processes. *Journal of Counseling Psychology, 30,* 146-157.

WARD, D.E. (1983). The trend toward eclecticism and the development of comprehensive models to guidance counseling and psychotherapy. *The Personnel and Guidance Journal, 62,* 154-157.

Webster's third new international dictionary. (1976). Springfield, Mass.: G.C. Merriam Co.

WHEELIS, A. (1973). *How people change.* New York: Harper & Row.

WILLIAMSON, E.G. (1972). Trait-factor theory and individual differences. In B. Stefflre & W.H. Grant (eds.), *Theories of counseling,* 2nd ed. New York: McGraw-Hill.

WILSON, N.H., & ROTTER, J.C. (1982). School counseling: A look into the future. *Personnel and Guidance Journal, 60,* 353-357.

WRENN, C.G. (1962). *The counselor in a changing world.* Washington, D.C.: American Personnel and Guidance Association.

WRENN, C.G. (1973). *The world of the contemporary counselor.* Boston: Houghton Mifflin.

WYLIE, R.C. (1979). *The self-concept: Vol. 2. Theory and research on selected topics.* Lincoln, Neb.: University of Nebraska Press.

ZARSKI, J.J., SWEENEY, T.J., & BARCIKOWSKI, R.S. (1977). Counseling effectiveness as a function of counselor social interest. *Journal of Counseling Psychology, 24,* 1-5.

ZIMMERMAN, I.L., & ALLEBRAND, G.N. (1965). Personality characteristics and attitudes toward achievement of good and poor readers. *The Journal of Educational Research, 59,* 28-30.

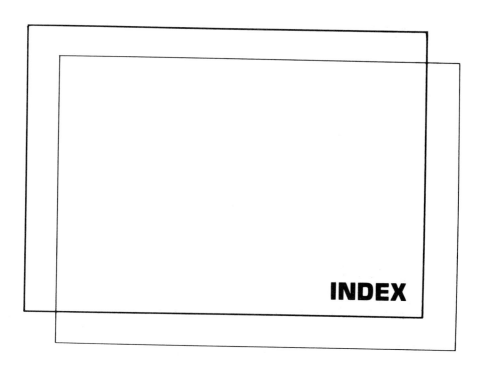

INDEX